Praise for *Mastering Magick*

"*Mastering Magick* encourages the reader to explore their boundaries to deepen and enrich their practice…Mat's views and exercises encourage even established practitioners to re-examine their techniques and existing relationships with spirits and allies. Posing questions to help us explore the energies we work with as witches, he asks us to look at them anew, considers how various traditions approach them, and suggests steps toward adjusting our thinking for more efficient attuning to—and use of—those energies." —**Arin Murphy-Hiscock, author of *The Green Witch***

"Mat Auryn provides both the backstory of his growth as a witch—at once heartrending and immediately relatable—and a wonderful bevy of spellwork that assists magickal seekers in becoming all that they can be. *Mastering Magick* reads beautifully as both literature and an advanced guide to spellcraft." —**Mitch Horowitz, PEN award-winning author of *Occult America***

"Vulnerable, raw, and unflinchingly real, *Mastering Magick* is as much a magickal memoir as a book of spells. Building on poignant moments from his difficult past, Mat Auryn demonstrates not only how to perform a wide variety of useful spells but also why such work can heal us. A perfect follow-up to the best-selling *Psychic Witch*." —**M. Belanger, author of *The Dictionary of Demons***

"If you would reach for the stars, you need your feet planted firmly on the earth. *Mastering Magick* will give you a solid foundation in the dynamics of practical magic and effective spellcasting." —**Phil Hine, author of *Condensed Chaos***

"A series of practical lessons and hands-on exercises, all designed to teach you how to get the magical results you want and need. *Mastering Magick* does for spellcasting what *Psychic Witch* did for psychic perception and energy work: present critical concepts and teach useful skills in an easy-to-follow format." —**John Beckett, druid and author of *The Path of Paganism***

"In *Psychic Witch*, Mat Auryn shifted the focus from rituals and spells to exercises that aid in developing actual psychic abilities. In *Mastering Magick*, he lays out a systematic training for the Witch to apply those powers to spells and rituals. This book shows how the inner actions of mind and energy are blended seamlessly with outer actions taken with candles, oils, and spoken charms." —**Jason Miller, author of** *Consorting with Spirits*

"It is a rare book that can teach you something new while being deeply vulnerable—*Mastering Magick* is such a book. Auryn has taken complex occult concepts that can seem opaque to even the most seasoned practitioner, and deftly rendered them accessible." —**Mortellus, author of** *The Bones Fall in a Spiral*

"Mat presents us with a rich and thoughtful tapestry of sources, ideas, encouragement, and, yes, practices aimed at one goal: your personal mastery of the Art…Whether you are new to pagan magick or a long-time practitioner, Mat's step-by-step course of study is certain to deepen your sense of spirit and inevitably guide you to empowerment." —**Timothy Roderick, author of** *Wicca: A Year and A Day*

"In straightforward language anyone can understand, Mat Auryn uses his experience to help the magical novice come into their own power. While in conversation with the elemental universe and honoring his own teachers and guides, Auryn offers us a book full of techniques, meditations, spells, and exercises that you'll want to return to again and again." —**Amanda Yates Garcia, author of** *Initiated* **and host of the** *Between the Worlds* **podcast**

"Mat breaks down the powers of the witch and magick in terms any practitioner can glean wisdom from, and he does so with the utmost love and reverence for the craft…Filled with inspiring musings, a cornucopia of potent spells and rituals for all occasions, and treatises that make even the most occulted concepts digestible, this book is sure to be a classic." —**Gabriela Herstik, author of** *Inner Witch*

"*Mastering Magick* inspires and empowers. No matter your experience level there are tips and tricks here to take your magickal practice to an even higher level…Superbly written and researched, *Mastering Magick* is a book you will return to again and again." —**Jason Mankey, author of** *The Horned God of the Witches*

"*Mastering Magick* guides readers deeper down the crooked path to becoming better magickal practitioners…Mat encourages readers to examine techniques perhaps taken for granted and to question the whys and ways of spellcraft, enacting magick, and communing with the spirit world. Beginners and experienced witches and practitioners alike have much to gain by reading and exploring this well-crafted course and guide."—**Danielle Dionne, author of** *Magickal Mediumship*

"Mat is one of those rare adept magickal practitioners who delights in sharing his considerable wealth of knowledge with others. His desire to help others grow into their full magickal selves and claim their rightful power is not only his strength as a writer and teacher, but also his spiritual calling. Mat has made the path of developing a personal magickal practice accessible, personal, powerful, and, dare I say, entertaining." —**Rachel True, actress and author of the** *True Heart Intuitive Tarot*

"*Mastering Magick* gives the reader clear direction on how to create the life you actually want…Here is a book that heals in a time we all need divine connection and wisdom."—**Damien Echols, author of** *Ritual and High Magick*

mastering
MAGICK

About the Author

Mat Auryn is the multiple-award-winning author of the internationally best-selling *Psychic Witch: A Metaphysical Guide to Meditation, Magick, and Manifestation*, translated in over ten languages. He is a witch, an occult teacher, a highly sought-after speaker, and a retired professional psychic based in the Bay Area of California. He has been drawn to the occult and metaphysical since an early age, reading books on witchcraft at eight years old. He is an initiate of Black Rose Witchcraft, the Cabot Tradition of Witchcraft, and the Temple of Witchcraft, as well as several other esoteric orders. He serves as a high priest in the Sacred Fires Tradition of Witchcraft. Mat has had the honor and privilege of studying under many prominent witchcraft teachers and elders.

He is an instructor at Modern Witch University and has been featured in various magazines, radio shows, podcasts, books, anthologies, blogs, and other periodicals, including his column in *Witches & Pagans Magazine* entitled "Extra-Sensory Witchcraft." Mat was the very first recipient of the "Most Supportive Witch Award" presented by *Witch Way* magazine for helping others in the witchcraft community and going above and beyond to make other witches feel like they are not alone.

Mat has had the honor of helping thousands of people throughout the world gain clarity through his skills of psychic ability and tarot reading over the last decade. Mat teaches various metaphysical and occult subjects such as psychic development, magickal empowerment, working with spirits, divination, energy healing, lucid dreaming, divination, and astral projection. To find out more about him and his work visit www.MatAuryn.com, www.Modern WitchUniversity.com, or on social media at @MatAuryn.

mastering
MAGICK

A Course in Spellcasting
for the Psychic Witch

MAT AURYN

Llewellyn Publications
Woodbury, Minnesota

FIRST EDITION
First Printing, 2022

Book design by Christine Ha
Cover art by Tim Foley
Cover design by Kevin R. Brown
Editing by Holly Vanderhaar
Interior Art
    Inner vision sigil (page 27) by Laura Tempest Zakroff
    Interior art (pages 19, 28, 30, 32, 120, 140, 143, 147, 178, 181, 190, 198, 207, 218, 219, 220, 223, 224, and 228) by the Llewellyn Art Department
    Seal of the Nine Heavens (pages 110–113) by Benebell Wen
Interior visual elements (eye, moth, stars) by Tim Foley

Llewellyn Publications is a registered trademark of Llewellyn Worldwide Ltd.

Library of Congress Cataloging-in-Publication Data (Pending)
ISBN: 978-0-7387-6604-1

Llewellyn Publications
A Division of Llewellyn Worldwide Ltd.
2143 Wooddale Drive
Woodbury, MN 55125-2989
www.llewellyn.com

Printed in the United States of America

Other Books by Mat Auryn

Psychic Witch:
A Metaphysical Guide to Meditation, Magick, and Manifestation

Forewords by Mat Auryn

Of Blood and Bones:
Working with Shadow Magick & the Dark Moon by Kate Freuler
(Llewellyn)

Seasons of Moon and Flame:
The Wild Dreamer's Epic Journey of Becoming by Danielle Dulsky
(New World Library)

Queering Your Craft:
Witchcraft from the Margins by Cassandra Snow (Weiser)

Mountain Conjure and Southern Root Work by Orion Foxwood (Weiser)

Pure Magic: A Complete Course in Spellcasting by Judika Iles (Weiser)

Consorting with Spirits:
Your Guide to Working with Invisible Allies by Jason Miller (Weiser)

In Memory of Scott Cunningham
(1956–1993)

Craft, then, is more than a manual art. It's a connection with ourselves; a valuable tool that we can utilize to alter our lives. The art of craft is one that can be mastered by anyone with a willingness to learn and a deep desire for self-transformation.

—Scott Cunningham
Spell Crafts: Creating Magical Objects

DEDICATION

This book is dedicated to these special individuals, without whom this book wouldn't exist—or at least would not exist as it is.

Jason Mankey, you were the first person to believe in my writing and give me an opportunity to blog on a major platform. You stuck by your decision even when other Pagan bloggers on other sites publicly wrote that no one cared what I had to say and that you must be desperate to pull me on. If it wasn't for that opportunity, I would not be writing books to begin with. I will never forget that.

Laura Tempest Zakroff, you are not only one of my favorite witches, artists, and occult authors, you're also one of my favorite human beings. Your friendship and assistance in the author life, from my very first book proposal to helping me navigate various elements of being a public writer, have been invaluable, including being an ear to vent to. May you manifest all the birches forever.

Elysia Gallo and Holly Vanderhaar, you aren't just editors, you are saints—in terms of your patience, your dedication, and your miraculous ability to take my writing and help me clarify it and make it comprehensible. I appreciate you both so much. Elysia, not only have you been incredibly helpful, but you've also always had my back, gone to bat for me, and helped represent my ideas and concerns in ways that assure me that Llewellyn is where I want to be.

Ivo Dominguez Jr., I often (half) jokingly say that when I "grow up" I want to be you. I have so much love, admiration, and respect for you on every level. You saw something in me from day one, and your belief in me has been a driving force of motivation for this work when I've felt overwhelmed. Without your books, your teachings, and your graciousness in taking my phone calls to discuss and help me clarify concepts, a large portion of this book wouldn't be what it is. Your guidance, informal mentoring, and most of all, your friendship, are priceless to me.

Mortellus, your sensitivity reading of this manuscript, your advice, patience, and guidance in navigating tricky language to ensure that this manuscript is welcoming to all has been such a blessing to me, as has your friendship. Thank you for helping me improve the inclusiveness and integrity of this book.

Chas Bogan, Devin Hunter, and Storm Faerywolf—the other three parts of House Fourlocks, I love you all so much. Thank you for your patience when I'm stressed about my manuscripts and isolating myself. I look forward to our future together and can't imagine it without any of you. A special thank you to Storm for your massive assistance in helping me polish the poetry in my spells and in helping to craft the elemental journey meditations.

Last but not least, to all of my readers. None of this would be possible without you. Even as an author, it's difficult to express in words the feeling I have when I read or hear you discuss how the previous book has changed your life and improved your craft and psychism. Your support, amazing reviews, and recommendations of my work to others mean the world to me. I am humbled, honored, and grateful for all of you. You are the reason I do this.

DISCLAIMER

The publisher and the author assume no liability for any injuries or damages caused to the reader that may result from the reader's use of content contained in this publication and recommend common sense when contemplating the practices described. The material in this book is not intended as a substitute for trained medical or psychological advice. Readers are advised to consult their personal healthcare professionals regarding treatment. Herbs, plants, and essential oils should be used with caution and thorough research of any plant mentioned in this book should be performed by the reader before working with it. Neither the publisher nor the author take any responsibility for any possible consequences from any treatment, action, or application of medicine, supplement, herb, essential oil, or preparation to any person reading or following the information in this book. Please be sure to practice fire safety precautions when working with fire and candles and never leave candles or other forms of fire unattended.

CONTENTS

SPELLS, FORMULAS, MEDITATIONS, AND EXERCISES

FIGURE LIST

Chapter 7: Synching with the Sun, Moon, and Seasons

Chapter 8: The Planetary Energies

CONSECRATION

This book is consecrated in the name of the moth-winged Soul who achieved apotheosis. She who is the resurrected wife of Love himself, who dwelt in the palace of darkness, collected the waters of the Under World, and ascended to the halls of Olympus.

This book is consecrated in the name of the rustic piper dancing in the grottos. He who is the prophecy-teaching faun of light and the shadowy satyr of mortal dread. He who incites ecstatic gnosis and whose body composes the entirety of all realms.

This book is consecrated in the name of the first of our kind, the Witch of Aeaea. The wand-wielding liminal child of Helios, who is the weaver of magick, the singer of spells, and the mistrex of transformation.

Hail to the soul of the human, the divinity of nature, and all that is betwixt and between.

OTHER ACKNOWLEDGMENTS

First and foremost, a special thank you to my sensitivity readers and my test group of folks with ADHD, aphantasia, and neurodivergency: Mortellus, Elizabeth Autumnalis, Rowan, Jade, Flora, Merc, Aaliyah, Imani, Josh, Mark, Sara, and those of you who asked not to be acknowledged or mentioned—you know who you are, and I appreciate you.

Another special thank you to all the amazing contributors to this book: Judika Illes, Madame Pamita, Juliet Diaz, Jake Richards, Durgadas Allon Duriel, Kate Freuler, Melanie Barnum, Lilith Dorsey, Devin Hunter, Storm Faerywolf, Benebell Wen, Christopher Penczak, Adam Sartwell, Theresa Reed, Astrea Taylor, Skye Alexander, and Laura Tempest Zakroff.

Thank you to Hannah Cartwright of Snow Ghosts, Chelsea Wolfe, the Boulet Brothers, Rachel True, Eliza Rickman, and Nika Danilova (Zola Jesus). To have the support of individuals I admire immensely is simultaneously humbling and a mind-blowing honor. Thank you for the art and entertainment that have deeply enriched my life.

Thank you to Modern Witch University, the Temple of Witchcraft, the Sacred Fires Tradition of Witchcraft, Black Rose Witchcraft, Assembly of the Sacred Wheel, the Cabot Tradition of Witchcraft, Coven of the Crown, the Black Flame Council, Nick Dickinson and the Circe Academy of Feral Witchcraft, Matthew Venus and Spiritus Arcanum, and, of course, Llewellyn Worldwide.

Most of all, thank you to Kai for sending your letters, your amazing artwork, and for the special rock. You remind me of myself when I was a kid writing letters to Silver RavenWolf after reading her books. You don't know how deeply it touched me and I wish you nothing but blessings in your life.

FOREWORD
By Silver RavenWolf

The journey of personal transformation begins with, "I choose." I choose to open my mind. I decide to explore the answers to mysteries—of life, of possibility, of myself. I seek fulfillment, change, success, freedom, knowledge, healing, peace…

I choose.

I decide to connect with others along my path. Mentors, authors, friends, craftspersons, artists, musicians, poets, visionaries, partners, business owners, ritualists, and those who offer kindness rather than discord.

I choose…to dance the web of our connection, to balance on the strands of light that lead me to the tools I can use to elevate my spirit.

And as I learn, those around me soar with my success and become successful as well, or they fly away.

They choose what they feel is right for them. And I honor that.

I embrace.

I embrace new experiences, new ideas, new ways of personal performance. I am giddy with gratitude for the miracles I have experienced.

The healing. The love. The joy. The success.

And I learn that the moment is the magick. That the breath is the power of connection. That the key…is me.

I discover that my true triumph lies in the accomplishment of those who I help. When I choose to open the door for someone else? That is a power that cannot be beaten.

And thanks to Mat's efforts, his love for his readers, and his respect for his path, you will find the tools to such unlimited power in this book.

His work will assist in forging you—your embodiment of the marvelous, glittering key that will move forward with confidence, joy, and success.

It is up to you how you will integrate his compelling information into your life and where you will ultimately take it. Not only has he provided valuable techniques that you will return to time and again, but he has also added contributions from some of today's top magickal minds—people who have generously provided exciting additions to this book in their fields of expertise. These folks include the delightful and knowledgeable Christopher Penczak, the dynamic Jake Richards, the talented Laura Tempest Zakroff, and the powerful Madame Pamita, as well as the wisdom of Storm Faerywolf, and more.

From embracing your own power to preparing your mind, from recognizing the science of intelligent energy to aligning your sacred space for optimum success, awakening your ritual tools, and strengthening your will, this book provides a well-constructed path with plenty of room for personal exploration.

Science! Timing! Shielding and warding and powerful protection magick—a compendium of relevant topics to enhance your practice and elevate the vibratory essence of your work. What a marvelous addition to your magickal library! I am sure this book will quickly become a prized go-to on your spiritual journey!

Don't wait! Dive in! This is a foreword, after all. So, let's move ahead with joy and embrace Mat's divine inspiration on the mastery of self! The next exciting chapter of your life awaits!

Peace with the gods

Peace with nature

Peace within

So be it.

—*Silver RavenWolf*

INTRODUCTION

A s a child living in a small town in Northern California, I devoured every book on witchcraft that I could get my hands on. I would save a tiny bit of my money from birthdays or holidays and go to the bookstore in the mall, and one by one, I slowly acquired a limited selection of books that seemed appealing to me. It was just enough to immerse myself into learning about the world of magick thoroughly, and still few enough to successfully hide from my strict religious grandparents, with whom I was living with at the time.

In middle school, I moved to Southern California to live with other family members, and sadly I had to leave my witchcraft books behind. However, I heard about a shop down by the beach referred to as a "witchcraft shop." In reality, it was a metaphysical store, but I soon found that they did indeed have a strong focus on Wicca, witchcraft, and other forms of magick. I eventually started taking bus trips there, and I remember vividly how magickal that shop seemed to me as a child.

With excitement, curiosity, and nervousness, I opened the door to the small shop. Bells jingled on the door handle, announcing my arrival. Immediately an exotic brew of scents greeted me. There was a smell of incense smoke and fragrant oils full of notes of frankincense, lavender, nag champa, sandalwood, and cedar, blending into an aromatic cornucopia that created the store's unique signature smell. The fragrance wove in the air with the music playing in the store—music unlike anything I had ever heard. It was exotic, soothing, and, most of all, created an aura of mysticism.

Greeting me from behind the counter was a friendly woman who welcomed me with a hint of reluctance and a bit of suspicion—which made sense, as I would soon find I was always the youngest customer to enter the store unattended. Nevertheless, I explored the store with awe and reverence, taking in its beautiful statues, ritual objects, and selection of crystals. I remember I carefully read each display sign, learning as much as possible with the limited amount of time I had while there.

Occasionally, the psychic tarot reader would exit her booth in the back and come and talk to the lady working at the register. I remember being so fascinated and terrified of the psychic reader. Could she read my mind? Did she know all my secrets? Best to try not to draw attention to myself and keep my head down low. The two women would chat for a bit before returning to her booth, which meant I could breathe a sigh of relief that she wasn't going to publicly announce whatever secrets my childhood brain thought were so important to safeguard.

As I became more of a regular at the store, despite being able only to afford the minor things like a few tumbled crystals or other small, inexpensive items, I began to feel more comfortable there. Slowly the shop became a haven for all my interests that seemed so weird to every other person I knew at that time. But here, these interests weren't considered strange at all—they were embraced. I slowly became more comfortable and would constantly ask the woman behind the counter as many questions as possible, while simultaneously trying to impress her with my limited knowledge of the occult and trying to learn anything and everything that I could from her.

It's been many years since I was that curious child seeker in a bookstore. I would go on to learn both magick and psychic development from every reputable teacher I could find and any book I could get my hands on; I still do to this day. If there's one thing I know about the magickal arts or psychic ability, it's that when you think you have it all figured out, you end up realizing that the rabbit hole of experience and knowledge keeps going deeper and deeper. These subjects relate to the mechanics and mysteries of the Universe itself. As such, there's always terrain to explore, including revisiting and reexamining the things we view as fundamental and foundational.

The focus of my first book, *Psychic Witch: A Metaphysical Guide to Meditation, Magick, and Manifestation*, was on awakening all of your inner senses and reverse-engineering that process to create magick that affects and influences change with just your mind, body, and spirit. The goal was to develop a strong foundation for energy perception and energy manipulation so that your inner world could make substantial changes in your outer world. The opposite is equally true, though; we can perform external spells and magick that assist in awakening, stirring, and enhancing our psychic abilities. The development of psychic faculties will make you more adept at performing magick and increasing psychic sensitivity. As Christopher Penczak writes in *Magick of Reiki*, "To the magickal practitioner, there is little difference between the inner reality and the outer reality. They are simply different viewpoints. To make a change in one, you must make a change in the other."[1]

I've written this book as a follow-up to *Psychic Witch*; as such, I will revisit a few key themes and practices from that book with a different perspective. First, that book focused on building a solid foundation of psychism and magick, so as to use as few external tools as possible aside from your mind, body, and spirit. Second, I had omitted traditional spells altogether so that the reader wouldn't be distracted from the inner work at hand within the book. But that isn't meant to suggest that conventional spells can't also be a powerful tool for psychic awakening.

Witches love to cast spells, myself included. If you're reading this book, there's a big chance that you love spells as well. There's nothing like lighting those candles in the dark and watching your incense smoke interplay with the flickering flame as you begin your work. There's something truly enchanting about casting spells that engage the primary physical senses and create an otherworldly atmosphere. My intention with this book is to share the mechanics and theory of magick and include many of my spells, magickal workings, prayers, and formulas directly aimed at psychic empowerment. I was also curious about what other witches and magickal practitioners do regarding spellcasting for psychism. So, I've sought out and asked a wide variety of magickal friends whom I respect to share some of their very own secrets, spells, and recipes for this book.

It is my firm belief that magick (paired with action) can heal and save our world. I believe that this is greatly needed. But, to do so, we need to re-enchant it. By re-enchantment, I don't mean using magick as a form of escapism or fantasy. By re-enchantment, I mean that we need to reconnect to

---

1. Penczak, *Magick of Reiki*, 5.

the world and truly see it for what it is before moving forward to healing it. Seeing the world for what it is doesn't just mean seeing people for who they are. It means to truly see nature for what it is, to genuinely connect with its spirit, with the spiritual ecology of where we live, and with all the inhabitants that exist here. It means creating bonds with these forces and spirits. Most of all, it means remembering who we are.

The path of the witch has always been one of sovereignty. By sovereignty, I mean taking personal responsibility for yourself, your life, and your impact on the world. One of my favorite quotes, which gets to the heart of this, is by Devin Hunter from his book *The Witch's Book of Power*; he writes, "We believe that if you have the ability and means to change your life for the better, then you have the spiritual obligation to do so. Because of this, our practices are centralized around obtaining personal power and influence and using them to better the world."[2]

Sovereignty is also about rising in your personal power and using it to help others come into their power as well. As a people, we have a horrible relationship with the concept of power. We often see the abuse of it by those in authority to try to dominate others with devastating and horrendous effects on people, animals, and nature. True personal power doesn't seek to dominate others because the empowerment of others is not viewed as a threat to one's own.

To change the world, we need to become spiritually empowered and cast magick for the betterment of the world, starting with ourselves and our lives. For these reasons, my first book is so heavily focused on strengthening psychic ability and meditation. Not only because magickal acts are greatly strengthened when you can be aware of the energy you are working with, but because psychic ability allows us to see things for what they are, little by little: ourselves, each other, and the world as a whole. It allows us to take the first steps in performing the Great Work of transformation, of becoming whole and empowered and balanced. The journey will take us to the darkest pits of our psyches and our souls' most transcendent and divine experiences. But first, we learn to confront ourselves to heal ourselves. It's not easy work, but it's essential work, the Great Work.

---

2. Hunter, *The Witch's Book of Power*, 4.

Many folks rush to magick thinking that spells can immediately fix all their problems. On the surface, that's somewhat true. Spells can remedy problems in our lives and make them easier to manage. However, most spells are often focused on addressing situations in our lives, be it money or dealing with difficult people and circumstances. The most potent, most effective magick you can indeed cast is upon yourself to awaken yourself, heal, and grow in wisdom. When you awaken your psychic senses, you open yourself up to having a direct experience with divinity. That divinity may be in the form of other spirits and gods and goddesses. However, it's also growing awareness of the divinity within all people and all things, and perhaps most importantly, within yourself. To do this, we must take our blinders off. Re-enchanting the world is about enchanting ourselves first to truly wake up so that we can respond to the world instead of reacting to it. Re-enchanting the world is about truly seeing, dreaming anew, and taking control of the narrative through magick paired with action.

Magick has completely transformed me and my life in unrecognizable ways, and I've witnessed the same effect on many others as well. It has helped me find a more profound sense of myself, as well as a deeper sense of connection to the world around me. I have found myself more open to new and different ideas and ways of thinking. I am more confident, and I have found my voice, which has helped me be more assertive where I was once a pushover. It has opened me up to new and exciting opportunities that I would not have been able to get to without it. I have found I am more compassionate toward others, and I am more aware of my power. It has helped me overcome my fears and insecurities, and it has removed me from volatile relationships and situations. It has helped me to heal myself and others, internally and externally. It has also altered the course of situations in my life in a way that has bordered on miraculous.

Some say magick has nothing to do with self-help, self-improvement, psychology, or self-transformation. I strongly disagree. Are these things the entirety of what magick is? No. But almost every magickal path I can think of focuses on improving and healing the individual to prepare them for greater and greater magickal works and experiences. In occultism, all of this is the Magnum Opus, the Great Work, which is the only true work worth doing. I wrote in *Psychic Witch* that "magick changes everything it touches." A good reflection and barometer of your path is to frequently stop and evaluate who you've been, who you are, and who you're becoming, and see if you're growing or not. Change must start inwardly in order for your life and world to change outwardly. "As within, so without." This isn't about being perfect, or neurotypical, or anything like that. It's about striving to become a better person, a better human being. I don't care how long you've been studying or practicing. Kind, loving, and empathic human beings are the most radically magickal things in the world. These types of people are as rare as witches were centuries ago. We need more. Focusing on improving the self assists you to be better equipped in improving the world and that is extremely impressive. That impresses me way more than any sort of occult knowledge or experience one might have. By self-transformation, I don't mean spiritually bypassing yourself or others. I mean actual, genuine growth and transformation, which is often ugly, messy, uncomfortable, and at times painful.

Mastery

The term "mastery" in magick means a lot of different things to a lot of different people. To me, mastery means a gradual and continual accumulation of knowledge, wisdom, and experience in a specific field that is often difficult to understand or convey in words, due to its subjective nature. Mastering magick isn't about learning everything there is to know and having nothing further to learn or experience. I will tell you right now that this is impossible while existing in this life. The dead end of stagnation comes when we stop seeking wisdom and experiences to grow in knowledge and spirit. The point of mastering magick is to continue to grow and expand; as we do, we begin to transform into the force of magick itself through recognition.

The point of mastery is not to do the most flashy or impressive spells and rituals or have the most extensive occult book collection or the most expensive assortment of witchcraft tools. While those things aren't inherently wrong in themselves, they aren't the point of pursuing this path. Mastering magick is not simply something you do. It's a state of being, of knowing yourself, others, and your reality as magick. It is something you slowly begin to realize through a magickal practice. You begin to see magick in everything and everyone, just as much as you begin to see it within yourself.

Yet, I still don't consider myself a master in the sense that most people understand the word, namely, someone who has reached the end of learning. But I would consider myself the master of the magick of my own life. I'm a master when it comes to understanding how magick has changed my life, how I've come to understand how it works, and how I've integrated this knowledge into my life so far. But mastery isn't a destination; rather, it is a lifetime pursuit in the never-ending path of personal evolution. Books, teachers, and traditions are all helpful on this path, but they can only take you so far in your experience and growth. A common complaint is that there aren't enough "advanced" witchcraft books available. That's because books can only take you so far. There comes the point where we must pursue connection to the force of magick, and it begins to guide and teach us. Scott Cunningham brilliantly writes, "Seek wisdom in books, rare manuscripts, and cryptic poems if you will, but seek it out also in simple stones, and fragile herbs, and in the cries of wild birds. Listen to the whisperings of the wind and the roar of water if you would discover magic, for it is here that the old secrets are preserved."[3]

While I do actively encourage people to learn from as many sources as they can, through formal training and informal study of books and other media, the path of mastering magick will always be the path of the solitary witch, and it always has been. The path of witchcraft is one that you travel by forging it for yourself. Upon this path, the witch is always alone and yet never truly alone either. That's because mastering magick is about how you personally connect to the force of magick, and how you choose to incorporate it into your own life. It's about how you relate to the spirits, the divine, others, and yourself, and how you experience the Mysteries of witchcraft.

In this sense, there is no one-size-fits-all answer, as we are all unique spiritual entities and expressions of the life force.

You will see throughout this book that a key concept for me is that of connection being at the core of witchcraft. This is the reason I placed such a strong emphasis on psychic ability and meditation in the previous book, and try here to focus on teaching magick through that viewpoint. Many people have compared prayers to speaking and meditation to listening. I liken

---

3. Cunningham, *Wicca*.

magick and psychic ability in the same manner. The four come together to create a genuine conversation with the Universe, one in which we are co-creating in sovereignty and service.

In the Witches' Rede, the advice is given "soft of eye and light of touch, speak ye little, listen much." This passage seems to be saying to try not to be judgmental of or harsh toward others, to be gentle in your actions, and listen more than you speak. Perhaps that is precisely what it means and all it means. Upon meditating on this passage, though, I've gained other insights on it. For me, this passage is also about a balanced approach to psychic ability (the soft gaze used when looking at energy or scrying) and magick (the touching and manipulating of subtle energy) for the witch's path of mastery. It's about consciously listening more than speaking in our conversation with the Universe. Of course, this is only my interpretation, and "Rede" simply means advice. However, I find merit in this interpretation. That is why most of the spells and magick within this book are aimed at the psychic arts in one way or another, to deepen our connection to the Universe around us, seen and unseen, and to come to know our True Will and our role we play in the intricate web of existence.

As a follow-up to *Psychic Witch*, I will continue to share my understanding, knowledge, experience, insights, practices, meditations, and spells. Know that these are my personal approaches and understandings, not necessarily those of every witch or magickal practitioner. Find what resonates with you and incorporate it into your practices; modify and adjust them; make them reflect your spiritual path, your relationship with magick, and your connection to the world of spirit. Find which key practices really speak to you and discern whether these are to be integrated as daily, weekly, monthly, or seasonal practices for you. It is my hope that through sharing how I approach magick, I will inspire you to begin formulating your own magickal practice or to incorporate new approaches to your already existing practice, and, of course, to become more proficient at casting spells that work.

In some ways, I am not so very different today from that little boy who wandered into that metaphysical shop all those years ago. I hungered for knowledge about the occult and the powers of the Universe. I devoured books, practiced spells, and experimented with my powers whenever I had the opportunity. I am constantly learning and growing, and I am hopeful that I always will be. When I look back on my life, I can see that my ravenous appetite for knowledge has been the guiding force; it has brought me to where I am today, and I have no doubts it will continue to do so. This pull toward magick is a familiar feeling among most witches in their lives, whether they acted upon it early or late in life. If you're reading this book, then you most likely have this pull toward it as well.

I often compare the path of mastering magick to that of a hungry caterpillar. Eventually, there comes a time when the simple accumulation of knowledge and training isn't sufficient on its own. You must begin applying all that knowledge you've gained into practice, spinning and weaving it like a silk cocoon around yourself and focusing inward. In doing so, your view of yourself, others, and the world begins to completely flip, like the Hanged Man card in the tarot, suspended like a moth cocoon that dangles as an ornament on the World Tree. Witchcraft is an inherently transformative practice, but just like the caterpillar within the cocoon, it is a process that is an entirely solitary experience and unique for each person. I hope to provide a solid enough foundation to help you weave your own practice of spellcrafting and spellcasting in hopes that you will embark on the transformational process to unlock the mastery of magick within your own life, guided by the subtle and sacred moonlight of your intuition.

HOW TO USE
THIS BOOK

T eaching magick and spellcrafting in a way that will set you up for proficient results while also touching the Mysteries is an overwhelming task, particularly because a lot of the concepts that we learn can't be taught in a linear manner. In the way our secular education is set up, we learn in a progressive manner: we start with a simple concept and build from there. Occultism is a field where you're continually returning to previous concepts and ideas and finding new layers of depth and understanding as you progress, experience, and learn more on the path. While occult understanding definitely does build on itself as you progress, there's a constant return to the foundational concepts and practices, which take on new meaning when revisited; this changes one's understanding of ideas that may have once seemed basic.

This was also my biggest obstacle with *Psychic Witch*: how to teach these things in a linear manner as much as possible, without going back and forth. With this book, it's a bit more difficult than it was with *Psychic Witch*. I've decided to stick with the primary process that I teach in *Psychic Witch*, and which I employ in my personal practice. This uses the seven planes of reality, and the Three Souls, Three Worlds, and Three Cauldrons. As we rise through the planes of reality throughout this book, I'll be teaching aspects of spellcrafting and spellcasting through that framework. That means that the first time you go through this book you may be casting a spell, but after going through it a second time you will be equipped with even more tools and knowledge to re-cast the same spell with even more proficiency. Since my magick and the contents of this book rely heavily on my spiritual cosmology of the self and universe, as well as previous concepts and techniques explored as a foundation in *Psychic Witch*, I thought it would be helpful to review some of the primary concepts and to bring a bit more information and understanding to those concepts. You will find that the concepts begin weaving in and out of each other and start forming a tapestry of a more intricate and proficient understanding in regard to how magick works. If you are a beginner witch, some of the information in this book may feel a bit advanced at times, or it may refer to something you're unfamiliar with. If that happens, just keep reading along as everything will be explained. For example, a spell might refer to a zodiac sign or planetary sign before that topic is explored in depth. I've tried my best to try to explain everything in a beginner-friendly manner, in as plain and accessible language as possible without patronizing or infantilizing you by dumbing anything down. No matter your level of experience, it's my hope that you will read this book more than once and pick up new insights with each read.

Chapter 1
EMBRACING THE POWER OF THE WITCH

I f there's one thing I want to impart to you it's that you are powerful beyond measure, even at your seemingly weakest points of your life. Sometimes magick comes to us when we need it the most, when we are at the darkest points in our lives. At least, it did for me. When I was a tiny child around the age of six, I finally settled into living with my new guardians. Over the three years before this, I had lived with several different relatives, foster care facilities, and foster families. After years of caretakers changing as often as Mr. Rogers changed shoes on television, I had begun to feel unwanted, as if I were a burden to others. Now, finally, I had a place I could call home. Yet, despite finally having a bit of stability, I was at the most disempowered time of my life. My grandfather and his new wife had gained custody of my older brother and me after quite the legal fight. I would quickly learn, though, that despite all the ways my life was enhanced, my grandfather was a controlling and abusive man, physically, mentally, and emotionally.

Being a very muscular and intimidating man despite his age, my grandfather quickly trained me to silence my voice; his motto was "children are to be seen and not heard." Every time we addressed an adult, we had to address them as sir or ma'am—to break any of these rules led to severe consequences. My older brother got less of the severity as he was more traditionally masculine. In contrast, I was a more traditionally femme-acting child, more interested in playing with Treasure Trolls and My Little Ponies than toy guns and trucks. I even used to introduce myself as a "sensitive boy" to people as a child. He would often tell me (with disdain in his voice) that I reminded him of my mother. So, I learned to be invisible and silent, to shrink myself in the presence of others.

One memory still sticks with me to this day as if it was yesterday, and it would change my life and create the setting for who I would become. I don't remember the exact circumstances, but my teacher had called my grandfather about my behavior at school, as I was understandably having trouble adjusting. I remember vividly, though, what happened when I got off the school bus that day and entered my home. After being beaten by a belt, I was informed by my grandfather that he would be calling me out sick from school for the next few days. During that time, I was to remain in bed in my room. I couldn't use any electricity, including the lights. To ensure this, my grandfather had turned off the breaker switch to the power in my bedroom. I wasn't allowed to eat unless I was invited to do so, and I wasn't allowed to get up to use the bathroom unless he came in and permitted me to do so. He warned me with complete sincerity that I had better do absolutely nothing but lie still on my bed, and he made clear that he would periodically check in on me.

As I'm sure you know, children of this age are bouncing with energy, so this was particularly difficult for me, especially since I was still somewhat afraid of the dark. So, for several days, I lay there with nothing but my mind to keep me company and on a forced fast, eating one meal every other day. While this is something no child should go through, it caused something in me to awaken. I realized that I could flow some sort of force out of my hands, and if I put my hands together, they would create a ball of invisible energy that made it feel like my hands were two opposite sides of a magnet pushing away from each other. I would begin sensing and seeing presences in my room, most of them just sort of passing by, but also a few who would stop and observe me for a bit before going on their way.

Dreaming became my refuge during this time, a means to escape the solitary confinement of my bed. I began wondering what happened as I fell asleep. How did I go from this waking consciousness to being within a dream? Pondering this led to paying close attention and becoming lucid during the transition between states of consciousness. Behind my eyelids, I would see moving blobs of color as if they were being painted with watercolor. Those shapes would swirl and eventually create what looked like a kaleidoscopic mandala that would then begin to take over my field of vision with my eyes closed, until I was entirely dreaming. If I needed to use the bathroom, since I couldn't get up or call my grandfather, I would visualize him coming into my room and saying I could take a bathroom break. With practice, this skill became more and more efficient until I could call him in my mind, and he would enter within a few minutes. I hadn't realized it yet, but I had touched magick, and magick had touched me, and I would never be the same.

Two years later, through a series of synchronicities, I got ahold of a copy of *To Ride a Silver Broomstick* by Silver RavenWolf. I began devouring any of her books I could get my hands on. Since my grandparents were very strict conservative, religious folks, I had to keep this part of my life secret. If I hadn't, my story might be completely different, and this book and my previous one would most likely not exist. I shudder to think what would have happened to me had my books and covert witchcraft tools been discovered, or had I been foolish enough to be honest about my interest in it at that time in my life.

When I think back to my original draw to Witchcraft at that age, there were several motives for why I had immersed myself into it. First, I realized that I had experiences that didn't fit my religious indoctrination, which I had already questioned. Second, magick had become a form of escapism for me, in the same way that many people retreat into fiction and fandoms. Most of all, though, the allure of power at a time when I felt the most powerless in my life was perhaps the most seductive aspect of Witchcraft to me. Magick did allow me to escape, and it did empower me, but not in the ways that I had expected when I had begun my early exploration of it.

While I don't remember the first spell I formally attempted casting, or which of my spells manifested first in my childhood dabbling, I do remember the first spell that I had cast where my willpower was utterly unshakeable and it worked undeniably. A few years had passed, and I cast a spell never to be bullied again with my mindset on my grandfather; it was some adaptation of the "Bully Frog Banish Spell" provided in Silver RavenWolf's book *Teen Witch*.[4] Within a week, it had manifested. My grandfather came in to give me a beating and I remember, as he stood over me and I was cowering on the floor by my bed at this grown man towering over me with a belt in his hand, that

---

4. RavenWolf, *Teen Witch*, 208.

something suddenly shifted in him. He froze for a second, sighed, and said, "You're hopeless. I can't even beat sense into you." He turned around and left my room, and went to sit in his recliner in the living room. To this day, I still don't understand how he acted in such an unexpected way that was not typical of his behavior. Later that night, he gave me the emotional manipulation statement he often said to keep me hostage. "I swear, if you don't get in line, I'm going to call your social worker and have them take you away again." For years this tactic worked, as the only thing I had feared more than my grandfather was the thought of having to go through the foster care system again.

However, it didn't work this time. I remember that a force of some kind palpably came over me, and suddenly I was filled with the spirit of courage. Like David staring down Goliath right in the eyes, I said with a voice of calm and centered strength I had never experienced in my life, "Do it." Every ounce of my being had meant it, and that steadfast conviction had been conveyed. I remember the shock in his eyes and his expression. Testing me again, he said, "I'll call her right now," as he reached for the phone, staring me in the eyes in a contentious showdown of will, hoping that I would back down. I didn't budge. Angry at my reaction, he had called right in front of me. I silently prayed in my head to the Goddess that I could escape but not end up in foster care. A couple of days later, my social worker arrived to talk to me. She had informed me that my father's brother in Southern California had synchronically reached out to them without my knowledge, saying that he and his wife would take me in until my father went through the legal battles to get full custody of me again.

The bully spell worked. My prayer to the Goddess worked. Magick works. Through witchcraft, I learned that I don't have to be a passive character in my story, a victim of circumstance. I discovered that I could be the author of it and direct the course and direction that my life story narrative takes. Witchcraft has continuously transformed me and my life. It can do all of this for you as well. That is why I am so passionate about teaching and sharing witchcraft with others. It's also why I have written this book: to share with you what I've learned since my initial interest in witchcraft and how I understand magick to work, along with my observations, tips, and troubleshooting. I want you to take control of the narrative of your life when it seems that everything is hopeless and working against you. I want you to be empowered through witchcraft as I have been.

The Mysteries of Magick

In witchcraft, we have a term called "the Mysteries." The Mysteries are great truths that you come to actualize through experience. You can sort of intellectually understand the Mysteries to some degree but can't fully come to know them as truths until you experience them directly. One of the best quotes regarding the Mysteries as experiential comes from an unlikely place: Frank Herbert's novel *Dune*. In the novel, the protagonist Paul Atreides is talking to Thufir, a *Mentat* and the head of security for the Atreides family. In the Dune universe, a Mentat is a person who has developed the ability to use their mental faculties for complicated computations, since computers and "thinking machines" were banned by humanity. Within the novel and its sequels is a secretive organization of nun-like women called the *Bene Gesserit*. They have undergone physical and mental conditioning to develop superhuman powers and abilities similar to magick and psychic ability, for which they are often called witches by others. Paul tells Thufir about a conversation he had with the Reverend Mother of the Bene Gesserit, "She said the mystery of life isn't a problem to solve, but a reality to experience. So I quoted the First Law of Mentat at her: 'A process cannot be understood by stopping it. Understanding must move with the flow of the process, must join it and flow with it.' That seemed to satisfy her."[5]

A wisdom phrase among elders in witchcraft is "Guard the Mysteries. Reveal them constantly." So, before we explore magick any further, I want to reveal one of the Great Mysteries of the path of witchcraft that I will repeat several times throughout this book. Are you ready for it? You might want to be sitting down for this one. Here it is. We are all One and the All is you. That's it. Was that underwhelming? I'm sure you're expecting something way more profound than that. Something more mysterious and secret. However, I have come to believe that all witchcraft and magick are based on that Mystery. So, what exactly does that mean? To unpack it, let's discuss what witchcraft is. Whenever I'm interviewed, one of the most common questions I'm asked is what exactly witchcraft is or isn't. You'd think that would be an easy question, but it isn't; this is due to the diversity of witchcraft practices and the fact that there isn't a Pope of Witchcraft telling us what it officially is and isn't. But there must be something that unifies witchcraft. For me, that answer involves the Mystery

---

5. Herbert, *Dune*, 40.

that I had just revealed. I have come to know witchcraft as the art of connection and relationship, and working with that connection and relationship through cause and effect to create inner and outer changes.

Witchcraft forges relationships through connection. Reality can be viewed as existing in layers. The most basic forms of this idea in occultism are referred to as the macrocosm and the microcosm, the larger Universe and the smaller Universe. Let's look at the human body and mind to give an illustration of this. I, Mat Auryn, am an individual autonomous person. Within me is a microcosm of individual living cells. If we could talk to one of these cells within me, I'm pretty sure it would have no concept of who I am as a whole. It would also most likely refute the idea that it and another cell were the same cells or the same being, just as you and I would agree that we are different individuals and not the same human being. However, the cells are part of an intricate system that composes me on a grander level, whether they are aware of it themselves or not.

Likewise, you and I are part of systems that make up larger forms of consciousness on higher levels. This is a truth for all things in the Universe, visible and invisible, physical and nonphysical, not just the cells in my body and not just humans as a whole. Everything is interconnected with everything else. As we zoom out to the macrocosm, everything unifies. As we zoom in to the microcosm, everything differentiates and separates. However, on the most fundamental level of reality, we are all One; Everything. This individuation and unification occur in a repeating pattern throughout the different levels of reality and consciousness. This idea is the heart of the Hermetic axiom of "As above, so below. As within, so without."

Witchcraft, then, is orienting ourselves to approach and connect with everything in the Universe as both smaller individual and larger cohesive forces—including within ourselves. We build and strengthen relationships to benefit ourselves and others mutually, and to influence change on both the microcosm and the macrocosm. Again, this concept is easy enough to grasp intellectually, but it takes on new levels of meaning once this spiritual orientation is enacted, leading to experience. For this reason, most witches are active animists. We interact with all things as individual spirits in their own right, whether that's an herb, a stone, a non-physical intelligence, or even your pair of shoes. This approach of animism is acknowledging the animated essence inherent in and unique to all things. In the witch's eyes, everything has consciousness on some level; everything can be connected to, and a relationship can be forged in which we assist one another.

The Anchoring Grounding Technique

Exercise 1

Anchoring (A Grounding Technique)

Before we move on to any of the workings ahead, it's important that we cover a grounding technique. Grounding assists us in assuring that we aren't overloading our system with energy. It keeps us healthy, balanced, and safe before we engage in any sort of meditation, magick, or energy exercises. This technique is also good for any situation in which you're feeling a bit overwhelmed or drained by your environment, such as being in loud noisy places, or feeling a bit spacey. Grounding should be performed before and after any energetic technique from spellcasting to meditation to psychic readings. Neglecting to do this will create problems down the road over time.

Begin by relaxing as much as possible. Visualize a tube of energy descending from the bottom of each of your feet. If you are sitting down on the ground, you can envision it coming down from each thigh. These two tubes of energy go into the earth and connect to create a loop. From there a chain keeps forming, descending deep into the earth. At the bottom of the chain, visualize an anchor. Feel the anchor sink into a very solid and sturdy part of the earth below you, keeping you safe and secure and steady. Affirm to yourself that any excess energy beyond what is appropriate and healthy for you is automatically flowing from your body and energy field down into the golden chain and anchor, like electricity traveling down a lightning rod. If at any time you feel overwhelmed with energy or emotion, send it out of your body and down through your feet into the chain strengthening it and empowering it.

When you are done with whatever magickal technique, meditation, or energy work you have performed, ground once again by affirming and visualizing any excess energy beyond what is appropriate and healthy for you leaving your body and energy field and re-entering your grounding chain. Then visualize the energy chain dissolving into Earth, helping it to heal and to be available for those who might need it.

Exercise 2

The Heart of Presence (A Centering Technique)

The second most crucial energy technique after grounding is centering yourself. Centering and grounding tend to be lumped together a lot, as they're rightfully often used together. However, understanding the difference is essential, and I like to separate the techniques when teaching any meditation or energy work to get a better feel and understanding of the processes. Centering is focusing your awareness and energy on your spiritual center at the present moment. The purpose is to essentially bring awareness to where you are in relationship to the greater metaphysical reality so that you have a vantage point to work from. It ensures that your thoughts and energy are focused and fine-tuned to here and now and not scattered or distracted.

After you have grounded yourself, close your eyes and bring your attention to your breath.

Visualize your auric field around you in the shape of an egg of white light. As you inhale, visualize this energy shrinking and condensing at your heart center in the middle of your chest. As you exhale, visualize your aura expanding from your heart center back to that egg-shaped aura around you. With each inhale, feel your mind focusing; with each exhale, feel yourself relaxing. Continue this breathing and visualization for about thirty seconds. Bring your awareness to the fact that you are the center of your reality within physical space from your vantage point, and that your heart is the center of your physical and spiritual essence within the metaphysical space of your reality. Affirm that you are right here, right now. All your attention is in the present moment at this time and this place.

Are Physical Items Necessary for Magick?

In *Psychic Witch*, I proposed that all you need to cast effective magick is the power of your mind. I am often asked why anyone would use candles, herbs, and other tangible physical items if we can cast spells effectively with just our minds. The honest answer is, it's easier to do so with items (which we call *materia* when working with them). Learning to work with energy and perform magick without physical objects will make your spellcasting stronger when you do.

However, the conscious mind only has so much storage capacity, just like RAM on a computer. The more things you're holding on to mentally, the more difficult it can be to focus our mental and psychic energy to cast a spell. When using materia in our magick, we free up some of our internal RAM and use that freed-up data space to perform more elaborate rituals and spells.

Another reason is that we are composed of multiple parts; many witch-craft traditions refer to these parts as the Three Souls, comprised of the Lower Self, Middle Self, and Higher Self. When we are moving about in ritual, holding spell items, working with tools, and lighting candles, we engage our Lower Self. We are giving our physical animal aspect of ourselves something to do to keep it pre-occupied and in alignment with the intent of the working, therefore helping bring all parts of ourselves into the working of the magickal goal at hand.

Exercise 3

❧

Walking Communion

This is a walking meditation and energy exercise that I've been doing for well over two decades. It's ridiculously simple, but some of the simplest exercises and practices can be the most powerful. This exercise establishes connection with the self and the other through acknowledgment, the most basic step of forming relationship. A skilled psychic witch can switch perspectives from unity to separation and can work accordingly based on one's magickal or psychic intentions. In this exercise we will be blessing through our intent and gratitude.

> *As you go on your walk, walk slowly and take your time. Mentally greet every plant, animal, and person that you come across. Thank them for the role that they play in the larger system of our planet. Mentally bless them with health, strength, and happiness. Don't just mentally think these things toward them, try to find the space within you that genuinely feels gratitude and love and project that.*

An adaptation worth incorporating in your life is to spend time acknowledging things that you come across daily in your home and work as individual entities. Thank them for the role they have within your life and how they assist you in it. This may feel super silly at first, but you are acknowledging and addressing things in your life as expressions of Spirit separate from yourself that you interact with daily. This is a major step in enchanting your life.

Spells versus Prayers

Sometimes spells are compared to prayer. There's some truth to this, and there's overlap. However, I define them a bit differently. Understanding the difference between a prayer and a spell can help you understand the mystery of effective spellcasting. Let's start with the similarities. Both prayers and spells are methods to manifest an outcome or goal by using means that are metaphysical and spiritual. For me, that's where the similarities end.

To make it a little bit more convoluted, what one group views as a prayer another group can view as a spell and vice versa. For example, a devout Christian can use a psalm in the Bible as a prayer, while a folk magick practitioner can use the same psalm as a spell. So, what makes one prayer, and what makes the other a spell? Let's use a metaphor to help clarify the difference.

Let's say that both prayers and spells are about using a car to arrive at your destination. Prayer is petitioning a spiritual entity—whether that's a deity, a spirit, a saint, or whoever—to drive the car, and trusting that they know the best route to get there. You know the expression, "Jesus, take the wheel"? That's the perfect example of prayer and fits perfectly with our metaphor. With prayer, you're requesting another entity to do the heavy lifting for you and trusting that they know the best way to get there. You are a passive recipient in the process. To stay with our metaphor, you're sitting in the passenger seat of the car and simply requesting where you would like the car to go.

With spells, you are becoming an active participant in achieving your goal. You are metaphorically stepping into the driver's seat, taking personal responsibility and direct involvement. Even when involving deities and spirits in spellcasting, the goal is still partnership with you directly engaging in the energy work. In this sense, divinity is your GPS, guiding but not driving for you.

In other words, prayer often involves supplication—it's a petition from a place of humility and surrender; you're asking the animated powers, be they spirits or gods, to perform their will regarding your request. You're essentially asking them to do the work for you on their terms, trusting that they know how to achieve it a manner that is best for you. Even spells that petition the assistance of those higher powers involve uniting your will with theirs, and so are not the passive affairs that simple prayers would be.

There's more of the witch's will and energy in a spell than in most forms of prayer. But on a deeper level, the witch understands that they themselves are a part of the Universal Mind, Star Goddess, or however they define the ultimate animating reality, even in spells that involve reverence and adoration of that power. The witch steps into their divinity and sovereignty, and weaves their will and energy with any deity or spirit they call upon during spellcasting. I am not saying that prayer doesn't have its place in a witch's life or that it isn't also potent. It absolutely does and is. It's just that prayer isn't necessarily on your terms regarding what will happen and when.

However, this boundary between prayer and spells can be blurred between passive and active energy work. For example, in the folk magick traditions of Appalachia, there's a technique of praying that Orion Foxwood refers to as "praying true." This practice is when one unites with divinity as "creator and creation."[6] We also see this technique of praying true in action in forms of prayer such as those in Charismatic Christianity, where prayer is used to invoke the Holy Spirit and where worshippers are given authority as instruments of the Holy Spirit to perform miracles on behalf of it. We also see this in folk magick traditions such as Braucheri[7] and American Conjure,[8] where prayer and psalms are often paired with symbolic acts, blurring the lines between prayer and what we would call spells.

The main difference to me lies in the relationship between unity and separation, and the different vantage points of each. Prayer is from the vantage point of petitioning powers that you acknowledge are separate from you; you are requesting things from a place of need so that they may enact your requests as they deem appropriate. It is you in the microcosm, addressing the macrocosm. Spells are from the vantage point of acting from your own place of divinity, of seeing you and the divine macrocosm as united. Petitionary spells in which deities and spirits are invoked blur the lines, often working from a place of personal authority and power but requesting and working with powers that you acknowledge as separate from you, and acknowledging their divinity but telling them exactly what you want and how you wish for it to unfold. In my story at the beginning of the chapter, I had employed both spellcasting and prayer at different times for similar goals. To illustrate the similarities and differences between prayer and spellcasting, let's perform one of each to see how they feel to you.

---

6. Foxwood, *Mountain Conjure and Southern Rootwork,* 79–80.
7. RavenWolf, *HexCraft: Dutch Country Magick.*
8. Bogan, *The Secret Keys of Conjure.*

Exercise 4

❦

Prayer for Blessings

Spirit guides, allies, ancestors, and divinity
I ask for guidance for what is appropriate for me
I ask for your blessings upon this day
I ask to make known my True Will's way
Blessings of protection, blessings of wealth
Blessings of happiness, blessings of health
Blessings of wisdom, blessings of peace
Blessings from the North, West, South, and East
So that the work of my will may be unimpeded
So that my impact is beneficial where it is needed.

Exercise 5

❦

Spell of Reclaiming Your Power as a Psychic Witch

Magickal timing: Nighttime, preferably during a full moon. Your birthday is also an excellent time for this.

Materia:
- one white chime candle
- cinquefoil

Purpose: This is a spell to call back your power as a psychic witch. It's common in life to have our power taken from us by others. It's also normal to have given away aspects of ourselves and our energy intentionally and unintentionally to others, places, or at certain events in time. With this spell, you will be calling back your full power, grabbing it, and proclaiming your ability to be the author of your life's narrative, and becoming sovereign in the course that it takes. This spell only uses a white candle and cinquefoil. Cinquefoil is often used in magick to grab things with their "five fingers."

Directions: Using a nail or other sharp object, carve your name into the side of the white candle. If you also have a magickal name or other names you've been known by in life, such as a "dead name" or your maiden name, or names from previous marriages, you can also carve those into your candle along with your current name. Form a solid ring of cinquefoil around the candle about two inches from the candle itself. Ground and center. Light the candle and say:

> *By flame of candle lit this night*
> *I claim the force of my birthright.*
> *At this place, this very hour*
> *I call back my witch's power.*
> *As moth is drawn to moon's soft light*
> *I lure back my power and second sight.*
> *I call back my lifeforce wherever it be*
> *In person, object, in land or in sea.*
> *I grasp the power to shape my destiny*
> *I accept the crown of my own sovereignty.*

Exercise 6

Sigil to Unlock Inner Vision
By Laura Tempest Zakroff

Magickal timing: New moon to full moon

Materia:
- blue or purple candle (short or tall votive size recommended)
- marker for drawing or instrument to carve sigil on candle
- a favorite oil for anointing candle and self

Purpose: This sigil is designed to help you remove emotional and/or mental barriers you may have that are blocking your ability to access your inner vision. It provides foundation, protection, support, clarity, and direction—while helping to clear away obstacles.

Directions: There are many ways to work with this sigil—it can be applied to the body, placed on your altar, used as a meditational focus, worked into other spells, or anything else that seems in line with the intent and focus. One of the simplest and easiest things you can do is to incorporate it into a candle spell. This can be a working unto itself, or you could use it as preparation for divination or similar activity.

Sigil to Unlock Inner Vision by Laura Tempest Zakroff

While you could photocopy the sigil and glue it to a candle holder, it's best to draw or carve it directly onto the candle so that you can feel the energy in the shapes and lines. Start with the circle, then the crescent moon, triangle, the double-spiral line, then the asterisk stemming from the top of the triangle, and lastly the three dots. Place the candle in a sturdy holder. Next take the oil you've selected and anoint your third eye, the inside of both of your wrists, and the sigil on the candle. Settle yourself before the candle and light it. Gaze at the candle in such a way that you can see both the light and the sigil in your vision, and let your eyes relax/unfocus. Then close your eyes and see that light within yourself, becoming brighter and brighter, expanding until it reaches out through your body. If you're going to perform divination next, when you feel ready, open your eyes and begin that work. Let the candle burn for as long as you're doing that working or feels necessary.

Exercise 7

❦

Witch's Wheel Sigil for Wisdom

Magickal timing: Anytime

Materia:
- a piece of paper
- a writing utensil
- a traced, printout, or photocopy of the Witch's Wheel (you can find this easily online by searching)

Purpose: The Witch's Wheel is a simple method to create a sigil. In this exercise we will create a sigil to gain wisdom. You can use this method to create a sigil of anything that you desire. While less intuitive or artistic than some methods, it was the first method I had learned and as such I want to share it with you as it's probably the quickest sigil method out there.

Directions: The first thing you want to do is write out a short and simple statement of what your intention is. The more clear, succinct, and short the statement, the better. Our intention is to increase our wisdom, so the simple statement of "INCREASE WISDOM" is perfect. Start by finding the "I" and drawing a small circle in that space. From that circle draw a straight line to each letter, ignoring spaces between words. On the final letter "M" draw a horizontal line to finish it.

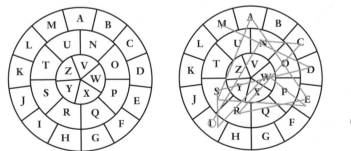

Creating a Sigil with the Witch's Wheel

Exercise 8

❧

The Spare Sigil Method
for Magickal Empowerment

Magickal timing: Anytime but preferably on a full moon

Purpose: This is one of the most famous sigil creation techniques. This technique was created by artist and occultist Austin Osman Spare. Spare, who has become a great influence on chaos magick, claimed to have first learned magick from an elderly woman named Mrs. Patterson, whom he said came from a line of witches from Salem who didn't get caught during the witch trials. This is most likely not historically true, as we know that the victims of the Salem witch trials were not actual witches, but rather victims of the mass hysteria and zealotry of other people. There's also no evidence of such a woman ever existing. Like other such historical claims by witches and magicians, there's two main possibilities, the first and most obvious being that he completely made her up, perhaps due to a need to legitimize his magickal practices. Another possibility, and I do think it's completely possible, is that Mrs. Patterson (whom he affectionately referred to as his Witch Mother) did indeed exist but was either a spirit or a thoughtform rather than a person interacting with him. Regardless, Spare's magickal methods have been popular for so long because they work, and witches use what works.

Directions: Unlike the Witch's Wheel method, you want to be very clear about your statement and it should be a full sentence starting with the words "It is my will…" Go on to be very specific about what you want, avoiding any negative words like "not" or "don't" or "never." It's also important in this method to ensure that your statement is so clear that it won't backfire or manifest in undesirable ways. So in this example we will be making a sigil for magickal empowerment. But we want to make sure that this magickal empowerment doesn't harm us or manifest in negative ways. So since we have things that we want our sigil to avoid, we then have to rework it into a statement that is positive and write it out. So if we start with the phrase "It is my will to be magickally empowered in a manner that is safe, healthy, and balanced," we would then cross out all repeating letters until we are left with the letters GKPF.

**IT IS MY WILL TO BE MAGICKALLY EMPOWERED
IN A MANNER THAT IS
SAFE, HEALTHY, AND BALANCED**

~~IT IS MY WILL TO BE MAGICKALLY EMPOWERED
IN A MANNER THAT IS
SAFE, HEALTHY, AND BALANCED~~

GKPF

Determining Your Sigil's Letters

We then take those remaining letters and begin forming them into a single symbol. After we do that, we then stylize it as a whole symbol using our artistic creativity until it's unrecognizable as letters at all. When first creating the sigil, it's important to go through the whole process of writing the statement out and eliminating letters. The reason is that you are actively engaging your left hemisphere of your brain, the logical and analytical side, and then converting it to the right hemisphere of your brain and engaging your artistic and intuitive faculties, translating the statement from being something consciously understood to something that engages the subconscious. After you create it the first time, you don't have to repeat the process. Just draw out the sigil itself.

Transforming Your Letters into a Sigil

The Witches' Alphabet

Theban Script is a magickal alphabet commonly referred to as "the witches' alphabet." The alphabet was first published in the book *Polygraphia*, a book on magickal alphabets written by Trithemius in 1518. Later it was presented in Cornelius Agrippa's *Three Books of Occult Philosophy* where he credits it to Honorius of Thebes, which is where the name "Theban" comes from. Honorius of Thebes is a legendary, possibly mythical, figure from the Middle Ages. The legend goes that during the time when the Catholic Church was destroying all works on magick throughout Europe, a band of magicians and wizards came together to have their sacred texts and grimoires translated into a secret code to remain safe from inquisitors. They elected a master among them, Honorius, to create the new cipher, and he wrote seven volumes on the highest magickal arts in his new alphabet, with the help of an angel named Hocroell. The legend states that the magick within these volumes was so powerful that only few could be entrusted with the books.[9]

Occultist David Goddard, in his book *The Sacred Magic of the Angels*, also suggests that the script is angelic and seems to connect it with being of a lunar nature. It later was published in *The Magus* by Francis Barrett in 1801; Barrett revived interest in Agrippa's work and from Barrett's work many witchcraft traditions and occult orders began including it in their magick. Since then, full grimoires and Books of Shadows have been written in Theban and witches use it in much of their magick, inscribing it on tools and candles, as well as writing out petitions to different deities and spirits in the script. While we may never know this alphabet's true origins, what we do know is that countless magickal practitioners have been using it since at least 1528 when it appears in *Polygraphia*. Not only does this show that there's an effectiveness behind employing these letters, but it also means that they're highly magickally charged as a thoughtform from repeated magickal use.

---

9. Jenkins, *The Theban Oracle*, 23–31.

૪ A	૧ B	ᴟ C	ᴟ D	૨ E	ᴟ F
ᴜ G	૪ H	ᴜ I/J	ᴟ K	૪ L	૨ M
ᴟ N	ᴟ O	ᴟ P	૧ Q	ᴟ R	૪ S
૨ T	৸ U/V/W	ᴜᴟ X	ᴟ Y	ᴟ Z	૪ End of sentence

Theban Script—The Witch's Alphabet

Exercise 9

❧

Crafting a Poppet of Yourself

Magickal timing: Anytime but preferably on a new moon

Materia:
- fabric and cotton (alternatively you can purchase blank poppets online or at most witchcraft-focused metaphysical shops or craft supply shops for fairly cheap)
- needle and thread
- a small square piece of paper
- personal links of yourself
- sigil to unlock inner vision
- Witch's Wheel sigil for wisdom
- your name (or magickal name) written in Theban

Purpose: A poppet is another word for a doll. Using dolls in magick is probably as old as magickal practice itself and spans ancient Egypt, Chaldea, Greece, Rome, China, and parts of Africa and Europe. Creating a poppet of yourself is one of the most efficient ways to cast magick on yourself. The poppet becomes a surrogate for a specific individual and in this case it's yourself, so anything you do magickally to the poppet you are doing magickally on yourself. In many cases, casting a spell at a target is easier than casting on ourselves. The poppet helps us to remedy that, by being an energetic mirror of ourselves. The poppet uses sympathetic magick, which is magick where you are declaring one thing to be another. It also uses "contagion magick," which is magick that creates an energetic link between two things because it uses something from that person such as hair, blood, spit, a signature, or an item owned by the person. These items are also referred to as "personal concerns," "tag locks," or "personal links." Since this is a poppet of yourself, you want to be sure that you take care of it and that it's in a well-protected space where others won't meddle with it. You also want to ensure any magickal workings that you perform on your poppet are done one at a time. You don't want to overload your poppet with different magickal instructions all at once, but rather keep it focused in its workings.

Directions: Begin by creating sacred space by either casting a circle or preferably using the Threefold Space casting taught later on in this book. If you are an arts-and-crafts type of person, assemble your poppet without fully sewing it together. If you bought a blank poppet, cut it open (usually in the back or the butt area). Place your personal links along with your name written in Theban, the Sigil to Unlock Inner Vision, and the Witch's Wheel Sigil for Wisdom inside the poppet, then sew the poppet shut. The whole time you are working on your poppet you just want to be mindful of what you're doing and what your intention is. When your poppet is ready to empower, hold it in your hand and say the following while envisioning it glowing with life force:

With witch's breath upon your form
No longer a doll but now transformed
By air and fire, water and earth
Awaken now little one, newly birthed.

By the power of divinity
Outside and within me
By witch's word I now decree
You are (name) to me.

Upon this hour, upon this night
Between us a link is fastened tight.
What I do to you, I do to me
Enchanting us both equally.

Breathe on the poppet's face nine times. Now any magick that you do on the poppet will be done to you.

To dismantle the doll, make the following declaration, seeing its energetic glow dimming.

You once had a name
We once were the same.
My energetic links I recall
Now you're simply just a doll.

Then cut it open and dismantle it, taking out all your personal links you placed into it.

Spell Remains

What do you do with your materia after you've cast a spell? Well, it depends. The first main consideration is the nature of the spell that was cast. Was it to draw something to you? Was it to banish or get rid of something? Next you want to consider whether the spell is a long-term or short-term working. For example, a spell to get a new job is probably going to be a short-term spell, while a spell for wisdom or psychic clarity is most likely going to be a long-term spell. The next consideration is what items were used in the casting. The last but definitely not least consideration is the environmental impact of disposing of the materia.

If I cast a spell to draw something to me, I want to hold on to the spell materia as much as possible. I'll take the materia, including wax remains, and either put it into a spell sachet or a spell bottle and do so as a final spell to give it all an extra boost and maintain the spell's energy in my home. This is particularly true if this spell is meant to be long term or permanent. If the spell is temporary, I try to properly get rid of the remains after the spell has come to fruition.

If the materia is reusable, such as crystals or other tools, I will energetically recycle it using the energetic composting technique taught later in this book. If I want to get rid of the materia, I will hold my hands over the objects, thank them for their assistance, and make a declaration that their magickal purpose is over. I usually say something like, "Spirit of basil, thank you for your assistance in this working. Our work is done for now. I send you blessings in gratitude. May there always be peace between us."

Food materia I will place in the compost bin and any glass (such as candles) or paper I will recycle, unless the paper was for removing something, then I will burn it in my cauldron. Herbs I will bury or sprinkle in the front yard if it's for a spell to attract or manifest something or if it's protective. Herbs used in long term spells I will sprinkle or bury in the backyard. Be mindful of the ecology of your area before sprinkling herbs about; you want to make sure it's safe for your local wildlife. Regardless of where I place the herbs in my yard, I will bless them for future endeavors. For example, if I did a money spell and am disposing of the herbs, I will say something along the lines of, "May these herbs bless this household with the energy of prosperity."

If the herbs were used to banish something I will throw them in the compost. Any and all salt I will throw away. Please don't ever put salt on or in the ground as it will ruin the soil; this holds especially true for casting salt circles. Please don't ever cast a salt circle on any form of soil. Everything else I will also throw away, but I try to make that as minimal as possible. The bottom line is you want to be resourceful and reuse as much as possible and waste as little as possible, both physically and energetically.

Chapter 2
UNDERSTANDING SPELLCASTING

⁓∞⁓

While there isn't necessarily a wrong way to cast a spell if you can achieve your desired results, there are definitely more efficient ways to cast them. What I mean by this is that magick can work independently without doing it in a specific ritualized manner. Many people can cast spells and have them manifest without necessarily going through any traditional procedures. Specific approaches such as shifting your consciousness, finding ways to engage your imagination, sincerity, enthusiasm, immersion, having solid magickal goals, harnessing your willpower and intentions, partnering with your materia, and keeping silent are beneficial for successful spellcasting. While that may seem overwhelming at first, I'm going to help walk you through these aspects. Try not to feel overwhelmed by these various approaches. Instead, try to approach the information here as something you integrate into your practice at a comfortable pace for yourself and see how your magick improves.

Intuitive Improvisation

Sometimes not everything goes precisely as you plan during a spellcasting ritual either. You might forget certain words or miss a step in the process, or something else unforeseeable might happen. This has happened to me, and it's bound to happen to you if it hasn't already. Don't worry, the fabric of reality isn't going to start deteriorating because something went wrong in your ritual. When something does go wrong, I suggest you just roll with the punches. Ritual is part theatrical performance, even if the audience is just you and the spirits. Just like performing in a play in front of a live audience, trust your intuition and improvise when you forget a line or when something goes wrong. A couple of years back, I was a presenter at Pantheacon, one of the biggest Pagan and witchcraft conferences in the United States at the time, held in California. People from all over the country and sometimes the world would fly in to attend Pantheacon to take workshops and participate in group rituals from teachers and authors of the witchcraft and Pagan world. At this particular event, along with teaching, I also had to help in leading a ritual for Black Rose Witchcraft.[10]

I was pretty nervous as this was a larger group than any ritual I had even attended, let alone one that I had to help lead. I have been to some pretty big rituals where there've been a lot of participants, but this was larger, as the Black Rose Witchcraft rituals were always popular at Pantheacon. To make matters even more intimidating, not only were former and current instructors and mentors of mine from various traditions in the audience of participants, but Selena Fox was there as well, which intimidated me beyond belief. Selena was intimidating not because she is an intimidating individual—on the contrary, she's one of the most approachable and friendly people I've had the pleasure to meet—but rather I was intimidated because she is somewhat legendary in the witchcraft world. Selena was instrumental in bringing awareness to what witchcraft actually is in the public eye, helping to dispel horrible misconceptions about it. She is also historic in fighting for legal rights and equality for modern witches in the United States including, but not limited to, having the pentacle be included as a religious emblem on the graves of veterans who were Wiccans, witches, or Pagans. Not only that, but she has also been leading rituals and practicing witchcraft for way longer than I've even been alive. The level of respect I have for this legendary elder in our community is monumental.

To drive home how intimidated I was by her presence, here's a little story. At the previous year's Pantheacon gathering, I was on the elevator going

---

10. To learn more about Black Rose Witchcraft visit Modern Witch University at www.modern witchuniversity.com.

down to the lobby of the hotel where the conference was being held. The elevator stopped at another floor on the way down, and Selena came on. She gleefully stepped in, shot a friendly smile, and pushed the button for her floor. It's probably the only time in my life when someone's presence made me completely lose the ability to speak. My mind raced between "Holy shit, that's Selena Fox!" and trying to figure out something to say to introduce myself. She left the elevator before my brain decided to give me back the power of speech. Now, a year later, here I was going to be helping to lead a ritual in which she would be participating without knowing she was going to attend beforehand. No pressure, right?!

The Black Rose ritual we planned involved music that would be played over a PA system. The music was a crucial element of the rite itself, as it would help build energy during a part in the ritual when participants were to walk in a circle around the central altar. We had tarot cards from several decks all mixed and spread across the altar face down, of which participants would come one by one and pick a random card for a message. Unfortunately, as has been my experience in ritual, when there's a lot of magickal energy being raised by several people, the electronics can go haywire. That's precisely what happened.

As people began to walk in the circle to build power, the sound system decided to turn off completely, and it wasn't even Mercury retrograde! Everyone just stopped in their tracks where they were and began looking around. The ritual mood was being threatened, and the energy-raising had jolted to a halt. Thankfully, in a moment of panic, I quickly tuned in and got the intuitive nudge of what to do, which is a good thing since I had to act quickly or the whole ritual was in danger of being ruined. Yelling so everyone could hear me, I shouted, "Okay, everyone. Let's do a quick IAO to raise some energy!" The whole room filled with a thunderous EEEEEEEE AAAAAAAH OOOOOOH, and then I began clapping a beat which everyone joined in on, and we continued our walk around the altar and were able to finish the ritual. Whew! Crisis averted! Many people came up to compliment us on the ritual afterward, including Selena. Regardless of what unforeseen hiccup occurs during your own spells and rituals, it's important to take a moment to tune in, listen to your intuition, and speak from your heart as your spirit moves you to do.

Exercise 10

∾⧲∾

Collage Spell to Enhance Intuition
By Skye Alexander

Magickal timing: When the moon is in Cancer, Scorpio, or Pisces

Materia:

- scissors
- a piece of poster board or cardboard
- magazines or other sources for colorful images
- glue/paste
- colored pencils, markers, crayons, paints, etc. (optional)
- a glass of water (the glass should be clear, without any words or pictures)
- a dark blue or black cloth

Purpose: We've all heard the expression "a picture is worth a thousand words." To do effective magick work, it is essential to be able to clearly visualize your objective. With this spell, you create a picture that represents psychic power to you, in order to increase your intuition. It also engages both sides of your brain and strengthens your imagination. As you work, keep your mind focused on your purpose—the process is part of the magick and the more attention you bring to it, the better.

Directions: Cut a square, rectangle, or circle out of the poster board or cardboard. This will serve as the backing for your design, so make it large enough to suit your purpose (at least 4 × 6 inches). Cut out pictures that represent psychic power, intuition, or inner knowing from magazines or other sources. These might be images of the moon shining on the ocean, shadowy shapes in a dark forest, surreal landscapes, dream symbols, owls, black cats, or whatever resonates with you.

Configure the pictures you've chosen on the poster board backing in a design that feels right to you. Don't worry about your artistic talent—what matters is connecting with your source of insight and your innate psychic ability. When you're happy with the design, glue the pictures into place. If you like, you can write words or draw symbols that describe your intention on the collage you've created. Paint, sketch, or embellish the design; affix gemstone beads, shells, or other objects to it that relate to your objective.

When you've finished, open the circle and lay the collage face up on your altar (or another flat surface) where it can remain for at least an hour. Fill a glass with water and set it on the collage, so the images you've assembled will imprint the water. Cover the glass and collage with a dark blue or black cloth to prevent ambient energies from affecting your spell. Let everything sit for at least an hour, preferably overnight. Remove the cloth. Drink the imprinted water to incorporate the magick you've created into yourself. Display the collage where you'll see it often to remind you of your intention.

Getting the Balance Right

Do you remember the first time you attempted to cook? I sure do. I was in middle school, and we were having a class party. I decided that I'd make a batch of cookies. How hard could it be to cook? I opened up one of my aunt's big cookbooks and skimmed the ingredients and instructions. Overly confident, I gathered all the ingredients. Well, almost all of them. There were two things I couldn't find, vanilla extract and baking soda. That's fine. Baking soda sounded gross to put into a cookie to my adolescent mind anyway. I figured I'd just add some vanilla-flavored soda pop instead; it seemed about right to me. I decided I would just add extra sugar and chocolate chips so that they would be extra good. I also didn't realize that the sugar was powdered sugar until I added it. I shrugged it off, assuming that the type was inconsequential. So I dumped the whole bag of powdered sugar into the mixing bowl.

When it came to adding the chocolate chips, I realized we were out of those as well. It must have been all my sneaking into the kitchen when alone and stealing fistfuls at a time to eat. We had to have some sort of chocolate, though. After scavenging all the cupboards, I finally found an old box of chocolates hiding in the back. I had never heard of laxative chocolates, but I figured chocolate was chocolate. Right? Feeling triumphant about my discovery, I crushed it up and added it to the mixing bowl. What was next? Ah. The flour! I heavy-handedly dumped half the bag of flour into the bowl. Baking cookies is such a piece of cake! What else did the cookies need according to the recipe? Oh right! Eggs. Another gross-sounding ingredient to put into the batch, as my mind went to scrambled eggs. But the recipe called for it, so maybe I'll just add one egg so that I don't overpower the batch with breakfast flavors.

Now it was time to stir it all up. There weren't any clean mixing spoons as they were all soaking in the sink to be washed later. I submerged my hand into the dishwater and grabbed out a mixing spoon, shook it dry. It looked pretty clean to me. I proceeded to stir the batch of cookies with my unsanitary mixing spoon. I knew I would surely impress everyone in my class once they got a taste of my delicious cookies. When I had done stirring it into a goop, I took globs of the concoction and pressed them flat with my hand onto a cookie sheet.

Next, the instructions stated that I had to pre-heat the oven to 375 degrees and wait about ten minutes. I needed it to go much faster, so I figured if I turned the dial on the oven to the max, surely it would cook much faster. That's pretty logical, right? While waiting, I decided to play on the household Nintendo 64 game console for a few minutes and come back to check on it later. So I left the messy disaster in the kitchen and headed to the living room to play my game. The game I was playing was terrific. So terrific, in fact, that, like UFO abductees, I experienced missing time while immersed in the game. Ten minutes could have passed, or hours could have passed. I will never know for sure, as time completely ceases to exist when a child is engrossed in a video game.

It wasn't until the fire alarm started the terrifying screeching that I ran into the kitchen to find it filled with black smoke coming from the oven. As I ran to turn off the oven, my uncle and aunt came home from work at that exact moment. I spent the rest of the night cleaning the kitchen as a fair punishment since I had made such a huge mess. Needless to say, no one had gotten to taste my cookie abomination attempt. We ended up going on an emergency cookie run at the local store and grabbed some from the bakery to bring to school the next day. It's a good thing the batch burned, or I'd probably be the most unpopular kid at school after feeding my classmates a bunch of laxatives!

With this experience, I could have concluded that trying to make cookies doesn't work at all, or that it was just something other people could do but that I couldn't, since my initial attempt had failed. The problem, though, was that I didn't follow the instructions correctly, and I didn't have an experienced cookie-baker to assist me. I also didn't make proper substitutions for ingredients I was missing. In my arrogance, I had just assumed that baking cookies was easy, and that the recipe itself wasn't that crucial to follow.

Following the instructions of a recipe exactly to the letter doesn't always work out that great either. Sure, a dish would be created as it was meant to be. That doesn't mean that it will always be to my liking. But with practice, experimentation, adjusting for my preferences, and making proper substitutions, I can eventually tailor it to my taste. Magick, like cooking, requires a balance of following procedures and modifying and garnishing them to your preferences. It also requires the help of someone more experienced to help guide you in successful spellcasting. That doesn't mean you have to seek out a formally established tradition of witchcraft and be trained in person, though there's merit and significant benefit from that. It means asking someone who knows what they're doing to guide you, including through books, and I hope that I can be that guide for you.

The Science and Art of Magick

"Magick is a science and an art"—this statement is the common denominator of our standard definitions provided by occultist Aleister Crowley, with many variations and adaptations since he provided his. He defined magick as "the science and art of causing change to occur in conformity with Will."[11] Science in this context is the study of theory, mechanics, and experimentation based on past wisdom. Think of it as the recipe instructions. The art aspect is the experience, the mystery, the individual soul expression, and the connection to the magick. Think of that as the modification, garnishing, and presentation of the dish to your liking.

The witch seeks to balance thought and action, study and practice, research and experience, understanding and application. If we only accumulate knowledge and never apply it or practice it, that knowledge doesn't do much and never develops into wisdom through experience. Suppose we rely solely on experience and personal gnosis (direct spiritual revelation) and neglect the wisdom and insight of older occult books. In that case, we are prone to hit the same pitfalls and roadblocks that occultists of the past did, and we will lose centuries of wisdom and insight that could help us be more proficient at our

---

11. Crowley, Waddle, and Desti, *Magick: Liber Aba*, 126.

magick. It's like trying to conduct a science experiment without understanding the science that has come before. On the other hand, if we neglect reading newer books on occultism, we lose out on innovation, progress, and growth in the occult arts. Using the science metaphor again, it would be like being stuck in Isaac Newton's science period and missing out on modern scientific developments.

In *Magick Without Tears*, Aleister Crowley responds to a letter asking why she, the reader, should study magick in depth. Crowley responds by writing, "Why should you study and practice Magick? Because you can't help doing it, and you had better do it well than badly."[12] He then uses a very dry golf metaphor that is confusing if you aren't a serious golfer. You might be, but I'm not. So let me use a different metaphor to shed some clarity on this. Let's say that you want to grow an apple tree. You can throw the seeds on the ground, and there is a possibility that that will eventually turn into an apple tree. However, through observation and studying the mechanics and the processes behind how apple trees grow, we as a species have understood how to guarantee the best results when growing apple trees. Understanding the various factors and conditions a tree needs can achieve the desired results with much more success. For example, when we know the pH balance of the soil, sunlight, shade, watering levels, and when and how to prune the tree, we apply that knowledge through the procedure. Likewise, in magick, we use specific techniques, procedures, and steps to ensure that our magick will be the most effective in its results.

Exercise 11

❧

Candle Spell to Listen to Your Intuition
By Astrea Taylor

Magickal timing: Anytime you need to check in with your intuition

Materia:
- an essential oil that brings out your intuition
- a chime candle in a color you associate with your intuition

---

12. Crowley, *Magick Without Tears*, 42–43.

- a candle holder
- matches or a lighter

Purpose: Many people feel there are times when they can't access their intuition, or they're confused about what it's saying. Often, this happens when our intuition is at odds with the way society tells us we should behave. This candle spell removes blocks to intuition and facilitates a closer relationship with the intuitive body—the energetic body double that reacts to all the energies around you.

Directions: Go somewhere you can relax and have some space away from the world for about ten minutes. Put five drops of the essential oil onto one of your palms. Inhale deeply. Allow the aroma to spark your intuitive senses. Rub the oil onto the candle while thinking about your intuition. Close your eyes and envision the candle becoming one with your intuition. When you're ready, place the candle in the candleholder and light it.

The flame of this candle sparks my intuition.
Any energy that is not mine is now burned away from me.

Stare at the flame and feel it ignite your intuitive body. Feel your intuitive body as a flame that encompasses you and reacts to the energy around you. When you're ready, think about a situation into which you want more insight.

I open my awareness to my intuition about this situation.

Notice what comes up in your intuitive body—feel all the sensations that arise. You may feel emotions, tension, tightness, expansiveness, warmth, or several other feelings. Without judgment, notice what you feel and where you feel it. If you experience tension during this exercise, don't try to release it. Listen as it tells you how you really feel. Continue listening until you've heard all your intuition has to say. When you're done, take a deep breath and give yourself a hug to melt away any tension.

I honor my intuition. May I be more in touch with it, now and in the future.

Blow the candle out. You can relight the candle anytime you wish to reconnect with your intuitive body.

Shifting Consciousness

Before a witch can become reliably proficient in the use of magick to any real effect in the world, they must first learn to master the world within. The microcosm of our mentality serves as the fertile ground from which the fruits of our magickal intentions create changes on the macrocosmic level of the world. And this, in a nutshell, is how the late Doreen Valiente, the "Mother of Modern Witchcraft," saw it. Valiente often discussed the integral power of the mind and its place within magick, even to the exclusion of ritual tools often deemed necessary by occultists and grimoires, when she said, "the greatest adepts in the magical art have also made it clear that all these things are but the outward trappings. The real magic is in the human mind."[13]

The mental component of magickal operations has long been cited by occultists, especially so in the concept of the *magickal Will*. This is to what Aleister Crowley referred in his famous definition of magick: "the science and art of causing change in conformity with Will." Later, Dion Fortune would make this mental component of magick even clearer when she augmented Crowley's definition, stating that magick was "the art of causing changes in consciousness in conformity with the Will."[14]

The difference in these two statements, though subtle, is nonetheless profound. It is a powerful key into the inner secrets of witchcraft: in order to be able to connect to the magick around us, we must first learn to connect to that within. We must light our inner Witch Fire; the spark of magick and divinity through which we will develop our psychic talents and learn to commune with forces outside of ourselves, and toward this end we engage in what the witches of old called *fascination*.

Though in ordinary vernacular the word has come to mean a state of intense and compelling interest or attention, its original meaning sheds light on how the term has been used magickally. From the Latin *fascinates*, "to cast enchantments, to charm, or bewitch," "To fascinate is to bring under a spell, as by the power of the eye; to enchant and to charm are to bring under a

---

13. Valiente, *Natural Magick*, 13–20.
14. Valiente, *Natural Magick*, 13–20.

spell by some more subtle and mysterious power. This difference in the literal affects also the figurative senses."[15]

To magickally engage in fascination is to bring another into a subtle trance state in which their figurative, imaginal, or psychic senses are controlled for a particular purpose, much like as in modern hypnosis. For the practicing witch this art is focused more on developing one's own inner talents, rather than trying to bring another under their control. This practice enables the witch to be both the hypnotized and the hypnotist, and in trance tapping into and developing their psychic and magickal abilities.

In her classic work *To Light a Sacred Flame*, author and teacher Silver RavenWolf writes, "To fascinate your mind basically means to put your mind in the alpha state."[16] Studies of the human brain have identified various brainwave states, measured in hertz cycles and labeled with letters of the Greek alphabet. The "alpha state" is one in which we regularly engage, moving in and out of such states throughout the normal course of any given day. We naturally shift into the alpha state when we are daydreaming or deeply engaged in an activity such as reading, a reality that makes the alpha state the easiest to control. Being in the alpha state is optimal for the art of magickal fascination, allowing one to combine the roles of hypnotized and hypnotist, and allowing one's conscious mind to direct and control the unconscious. In this state we psychically tap into information that we are constantly receiving and can begin the process of translation from the unconscious into our full consciousness.

It is no wonder that many witchcraft circles refer to the alpha state as "ritual consciousness" and great care is taken to learn how to enter into this state at will as a precursor to whatever magick is to be done. We shift into alpha as the preliminary act of our magickal rites. Even in those traditions that do not use the language of brainwave states there is usually some technique or procedure at the beginning of a ritual or ceremony that serves this purpose of moving into magickal consciousness. This state empowers our ritual actions. A circle cast while in ordinary consciousness will not serve the same as one cast while in the right frame of mind. In alpha, we "walk between the worlds" operating on various levels of consciousness and reality at once and

---

15. Century Dictionary.
16. RavenWolf, *To Light a Sacred Flame*, 48.

embodying the connective liminal state referred to in the Hermetic axiom, "As above, so below. As within, so without."

Once this skill has been mastered and the witch can step into and out of the alpha state at will, the witch will have opportunities to tap into even deeper states such as the more deeply immersive theta, characterized in our most vivid dreams and given occult expression in astral journeying, direct spirit contact, and other psychic phenomena. While dreaming in theta, our body becomes paralyzed lest we physically act out our dreams. This shows the intensity of the theta state and offers a hint as to its difficulty in terms of control. Being closer to the dream state than alpha, theta can lure us away from our conscious mind and into a space in which we lose all control or sense of self. Through time and practice one can learn to better control this state, but it is through working with alpha that these skills will be developed.

The failure to master the theta state is by no means a judgment of one's magickal potency. Our magickal goals can all be achieved working through alpha alone. However, it will not be as immersive as it would be were we working in theta. But while theta requires us to operate under certain restricted conditions, alpha can be engaged during the normal course of our day.

Being able to enter into and maintain a light trance state is essential for both magickal and psychic work. Both witches and psychics can enter into this state without conscious awareness, but when it is consciously realized it can be shaped and controlled, leading us to some powerful places both magickally and psychically. Try not to be deterred by the use of the word "trance"; what may sometimes carry an air of mysterious and mystical obscurity is in fact just the normal operations of the human mind, which constantly moves and shifts in relation to the environment.

So, if imagination and dreams are part of our magickal consciousness then why don't all our imaginations and daydreams manifest in the world the way our spells do? The missing component is that key given earlier and often spoken of by occultists as an essential element to the working of magick: the Will. The capitalization here gives us a clue that this is not just our ordinary willpower or drive, but is instead our True Will, when we are aligned with our Higher or Divine Will. Changes in consciousness happen naturally all the time, but when they are focused and directed through the trained magickal Will they are given the impetus to cause change in the world.

Carl Jung's pioneering work in psychoanalytical studies was founded on the belief that the numinous could communicate through the unconscious mind, most often through the dream state. He spent years studying and analyzing the dreams of his clients and privately experimenting with the shifts of his own consciousness toward the direct interface with the spiritual mysteries of his own unconscious. Likewise, the witch's art of fascination bridges the gap between the worlds of conscious and unconscious, the human and the divine, the inner and outer. Above and below.

Exercise 12

∞

Color Breathing—A Simple Way to Enter Alpha

Try entering into the alpha brainwave state before engaging in magick or divination to see the difference for yourself. Once you've entered alpha, pay attention to any thoughts or sensations that come to you while you're divining or performing your spell or rite.

1. Ideally, get into a comfortable sitting position with either your feet flat on the floor or your legs crisscrossed.

2. Straighten your back so that you're sitting with your spine, neck, and head aligned in a straight column.

3. Consciously relax your mind and body as much as possible while ensuring that your back, neck, and head are still as straight as is comfortably possible.

4. Bring your attention to your breath and begin taking steady, deep, rhythmic but comfortable breaths. If you still feel any tension or discomfort within your body, bring your awareness to that part of your body and visualize your breath reaching that part of yourself and relaxing it deeper with each breath, releasing any tension stored there.

5. Close your eyes and keep your awareness on your breath.

6. As you inhale, visualize that you're inhaling the color red. See the red air filling not just your lungs but your whole body with red light.

7. As you exhale, visualize that you're exhaling the color red all around you in an egg-shaped energy field of your aura.

8. Keep inhaling and exhaling the color red for a few moments. If you're having trouble visualizing the color, quickly run through your mind objects that are that color, such as an apple, lipstick, a firetruck, etc. This will often jolt the mind to visualize the color if you're having trouble conjuring it in your mind's eye. Then return your focus to the color breathing visualization.

9. When you feel you have the color red established in your visualization, filling your body and your aura, continue by moving on to these different colors after red in this order: orange, yellow, green, blue, purple, white.

10. Once you've completed this visualization exercise, affirm to yourself, "I am in the alpha state of consciousness, where I am fully in touch with my psychic and magickal abilities."

11. Let the visualization fade, and when you're ready, open your eyes and perform whatever witchy task you set out to do.

Difficulty with Focus and Visualization

Just like anything worthwhile, witchcraft and psychic development both take work, and that work is done through making a consistent effort. Effectively bending and changing reality in your favor is not something that will be quick and easy to become adept at. Even the most seemingly "basic" and "simple" and "foundational" practices take extreme effort and can become highly potent when that effort is made to be proficient at them. However, for some people this is more difficult, and for others who are neurodivergent it's not as simple as just putting in effort.

As a community of witches we should be mindful of those who are neurodivergent, and be aware that not all the same techniques and tactics are going to work for everyone in the same manner. As such we should try to accommodate this and create as inclusive a learning environment and spiritual community as possible. I have had many friends, students, and readers with varying degrees of distractibility, including ADHD, all of whom learned to meditate and get better at focusing with some accommodation.

Meditation isn't about how well you can concentrate; it's training the mind to focus. The process is the meditation. However, meditation isn't one size fits all and there are many ways to meditate other than sitting down and focusing on clearing your mind.

Some of my neurodivergent students have had success with variations such as moving meditations: swaying their bodies while standing or sitting (including rocking back and forth gently), or walking, dancing, running, or creating art. Some folks need to listen to music while they meditate. Essentially, anything that can get you into the flow, allowing that mental chatter to fall away, is a form of meditation. You also don't need to be neurodivergent for these methods to work for you. Finding what works for you as an individual is more important than trying to put extreme effort into something that barely works, or doesn't work at all. What is important is that you're finding how you connect to these practices in the manner that is most effective for you. Remember that in the end, this is your path, your life, your magickal practice, and it needs to work for you alone. This may take some experimenting and brainstorming but it's well worth it when you find a practice that works for you, as the benefits of meditation in all areas of life, including your magickal life, are many.

Scheduling your meditation in the hour following your medication schedule (as prescribed by your doctor) can be a useful tool. I want to be crystal clear that magick and psychic ability are never a replacement for therapy or medical treatment. Physical disability doesn't make you less of a psychic or a witch, just as being neurodivergent doesn't make you less of one either. Actively using all available resources to take care of yourself—physically, mentally, emotionally, and spiritually—is in alignment with the spirit of the witch. It's taking sovereignty and responsibility for your health and your life.

While many have difficulty with visualization, imagine what it must be like for those who suffer from aphantasia, which is the inability to visualize imagery in your mind. In these instances, our best and only recourse is to focus elsewhere, and build on other strengths. That's why I also focus on all the other clairs in *Psychic Witch* so that you can operate from your strengths instead of visualization if it's more difficult or impossible for you. This way, you can tailor it to your natural psychic and neurological predispositions. In a nutshell, if you can't visualize a ring of energy when you cast a magick circle in your Witch Eye, try to feel it, hear it, smell it, taste it, know that it is there, or a combination of these, preferably trying to invoke all of these senses simultaneously.

Elizabeth Autumnalis, a close friend of mine who is a fellow initiate in the Sacred Fires Tradition of Witchcraft, is one of the most talented psychics and witches I know. A few years back we were camping in the woods of New Hampshire. We were walking through the woods one night down a dirt path with only moonlight to guide us. We were on our way to meet up with some friends at a ritual bonfire when we encountered a spirit. As we were walking and chatting, I saw something in my peripheral vision. It was a pair of eyes peering from behind a tree, and I could make out an outline of a tall figure. While there were a lot of active nature spirits all around there, this one was very different and was specifically focused on us. We both stopped at the same time and were both staring at it. "Do you see that?" I asked and Liz confirmed it. I tuned in to see if it was a threat or not; it wasn't. The spirit was more of a guardian of the area and was scoping us out and sizing us up to see if we were a threat. I pulled up the screen of my mind to see what the spirit looked like. We made a few casual statements to it, telling it that we are just respectful visitors that weren't a threat, and continued our stroll to the bonfire. Once we arrived at the fire we began talking about it to our friends. We both described the spirit exactly the same. Here's the thing, though: Liz didn't actually "see" it. Not as an image in her Witch Eye, and not with her physical eyes. Yet she was able to describe it in just as much detail as I could.

Sometimes it helps to talk about what you're picking up with your inner senses, to just start describing it. Often as you start speaking and describing what you're sensing psychically, the information will start coming through with more and more detail as you speak, even if you aren't literally "seeing" it in your Mind's Eye. If you're really stuck with bringing information you're perceiving clearly, just start describing what you do sense. This is a helpful psychic technique whether you have aphantasia or not.

My theory is that Liz is still receiving psychic information from "the noirs," a term coined by Ivo Dominguez Jr. that refers to the processing of information at a subconscious level as opposed to the conscious level of the psychic "clair-" abilities.[17] Noirs are the psychic senses that don't show up in

17. Dominguez Jr., *Keys to Perception*, 49–53.

clear or perceivable manners that relate to our primary five senses of sight, sound, touch, taste, or smell. Rather, they're "dark" as the name suggests. It's a psychic impression that is brought to us that doesn't filter through those clairs. It's what people often refer to as claircognizance; I would put intuition into this category, as well as being in the realm of the noirs. As such, the noir senses often bypass the clairs of the Middle Self's awareness, yet information is still conveyed. Some other examples of this in action would be the divinatory and mediumship processes that rely on the ideomotor phenomenon, which is when your subconscious mind is controlling motions such as the use of a pendulum, a spirit board, or automatic writing. That is noir in action. You're receiving the information and processing it by other means that bypass the conscious mind.

It's interesting to note that people with aphantasia dream in images like those of us without it.[18] This suggests that dreams are involuntary faculties of imagination, aside from lucid dreaming in which you are controlling the imagery of the dream. It also suggests that aphantasia isn't the inability to see images, but rather it's the inability to conjure images in the mind's eye on command. I know many folks diagnosed with aphantasia who, with consistent effort, have been able to slowly begin to see images on command in their mind, it's just much more difficult for them than for others.

When it comes to dreams, we often forget them quickly upon awakening. As the conscious mind becomes alert when we wake up, it prioritizes what is important to process, which usually has to deal with starting our day. Shortly afterward our dreams fade unless they made a strong emotional impact on us, or we train our mind to bring that information to the forefront. One method to do this is to consistently record our dreams immediately upon waking, training our minds to focus on and retain our dream experiences. This is also one of the steps that is involved in becoming a lucid dreamer. Therefore, it doesn't surprise me that a technique that I found helpful for folks with difficulty seeing images in their mind, including those with aphantasia, is the technique that I described before of verbally describing what they're trying to visualize. For example, if you're trying to visualize a dog, begin by verbally describing what a dog looks like in as much detail as

---

18. Whiteley, "Aphantasia, imagination and dreaming."

you can while you're attempting to see it in your mind's eye, even if the image isn't coming through clearly in the moment.

There are many things we all struggle with when it comes to spiritual and magickal practice; that's why it's a practice. We get better at it through consistent effort. Truthfully though, there is no quick-fix-fast-food-path to psychic or magickal proficiency. It all takes work. Some of us have to work harder than others in certain areas, just like everything else in life. But everyone has the capacity to be psychic and engage in magick. As I stress in my first book, you don't criticize yourself for lack of focus and you don't give up. You acknowledge that you lost focus and bring it back, understanding that this act in itself is strengthening your focus. If you have trouble focusing or visualizing, I strongly encourage you not to give up. Keep trying. You may even discover new techniques on your own that help you. Be gentle with yourself, but I encourage you to persevere.

To help provide some tools for those who struggle with concentration or visualization I reached out and listened to many folks with aphantasia and ADHD who are also seasoned magickal practitioners. After many conversations with folks that have these conditions, here are some techniques I've developed to assist you with getting into a meditative state. I have experimented with it myself and reached out to friends with ADHD and aphantasia to test this out, get feedback, and ensure it worked as well for them as it did for me.

Exercise 13

❧

Entering Alpha by Pendulum

Magickal timing: Any

Materia:
- a pendulum of some sort

Purpose: This is a method of entering into the alpha brainwave state of consciousness for those who may have difficulty with concentrating; it is particularly helpful for those who have ADHD, as well as folks who have trouble visualizing. Have you ever seen those old-fashioned hypnotists that use a pocket watch to hypnotize someone? Essentially, all they're doing is getting the person to solely focus on one thing, inducing alpha with the movement and then inducing theta through suggestion. All trance states are a form of hypnosis. The key factors in this are who is doing the hypnotizing, who is leading you into that brainwave state, and what is being done once there. For this however, we're just going to bring you into alpha using a modification of this technique with you leading the session.

Most witches and psychics already own a pendulum for divination, and you can buy fairly cheap pendulums at your local metaphysical store or online. If you don't own a pendulum, you can use a pendant at the end of a necklace chain, or you can tie a key or something else that has a bit of weight to the end of a string. The pendulum doesn't have to be fancy, but like all tools, investing in one that you really like and continuously put energy into through use is beneficial.

Directions: First, take a deep breath and shake out all the nervous tension and energy that you may be holding on to. Take another deep breath and relax. Hold your pendulum in front of you so that the stone or whatever is at the end of your pendulum is at eye level. Take another deep breath and relax a bit deeper. Begin to swing the pendulum side to side and follow it with your eyes. Now keep your hand still and keep your eyes solely fixed on the pendulum as it's swinging. Mentally or internally state, "I am relaxing and entering the alpha state of consciousness" in a calm, relaxed, soothing, but firm voice. Keep repeating this as your eyes stay focused on the moving pendulum as it begins to slow down and the swings become smaller and smaller. Do this until the pendulum stops or you can feel that your mental processes and awareness are starting to shift. You should feel relaxed and slightly dissociative, like when you're daydreaming. You are in the alpha brainwave state. It would also be a good idea to pair this with the psychic prompt method of using your free hand to cross your fingers (like you're making a wish) to begin training your brain to shift at your command through a Pavlovian response. If you don't feel a shift, then try to repeat it a few more times until you do. If not, try the following two methods.

Exercise 14

❧

Entering Alpha—The Pool Method

Magickal timing: Any

Purpose: This technique is designed specifically for people who have difficulty visualizing, or an inability to do so due to a condition such as aphantasia. This method, as well as the next one, is focused more on sensory and physical sensations connected to clairtangency. This is because most of the people that I've talked to that have aphantasia, or extreme difficulty with visualizing images, have told me that they can feel things by imagining physical sensations way easier than visualization.

This and the following method have both resulted in success for people who have difficulty in these areas. The reason I include two different methods is not just to give variety but because I have found that about half of the people do better with the pool method and the other half do better with the sun showers method, depending on the predisposition of their clair senses.

When I use the word "imagine" in these, know that I'm not necessarily saying to form an actual image in your mind but rather to conjure up the feeling in your body.

If you have trouble visualizing and conjuring up physical sensation, what I would encourage you to do instead is to know that it's happening. This in itself is also imagination and is also going to help you to build those senses. For this exercise, it may be helpful to slowly enter and submerge yourself the next time you go swimming or take a bath (without doing the meditation) to get acquainted with the physical sensations so that you can conjure them through your memory.

With these two exercises, it would be beneficial to hold your psychic prompt every time that you engage in it to solidify that Pavlovian response once again.

Directions: Begin by closing your eyes and taking a deep breath, and relax. Imagine that you are at the top of the stairs leading into a warm pool of water. Imagine that you take one step down into the pool. As you do, imagine what that feeling of stepping down one step feels like. Imagine how the warm water up to your ankles on that second step feels. Feel the warm water relax your feet. Take another step down and feel the warm water up to your knees, relaxing them. Take another step down and feel submerged in the warm water up to your waist, easing the tension of your lower body up to your waist. Take another step down and feel the warm water up to your solar plexus right at the bottom of your rib cage, as everything relaxes up to that point in your body. Take another step down into the pool and feel the warm water begin to relax everything up to your shoulders. Now take one last step into the water, knowing that you can breathe in it and feel your whole body as it is submerged in this warm relaxing imaginal water. Take a moment to think about this state of deep relaxation as you are entirely immersed in this pool of energy. When you are ready, take a deep relaxing breath and open your eyes slowly. You are now in the alpha brainwave state of consciousness.

Exercise 15

∽

Entering Alpha—The Sun Showers Method

Magickal timing: Any

Purpose: Everything from the "purpose" section of the last exercise applies to this one. The main difference is that this one is also invoking the senses of hearing and smelling if those are stronger for you, or in case invoking several senses enhances the immersion of this technique. If you were having difficulty conjuring the physical sensations, you could do what you did with the bath in the last exercise, except that in this case you will be in your shower and slowly decreasing the pressure of the water. If you do this, however, just like using the bathtub the previous exercise, be sure not to add the meditation to it. You are getting familiar with how your body feels under different water pressures so that you can draw on this memory when you engage in the meditation exercise.

Directions: Close your eyes and take a deep, cleansing, and relaxing breath. Imagine that you are standing in the rain, and it is raining heavily. Imagine what the rain feels like against your body. Imagine what the rain sounds like around you. Imagine what the rain smells like. Take another deep breath and exhale; imagine that the rain is lightening up a bit. Focus on the bodily sensation of the rain against your skin as it begins to decrease in its intensity. Focus on the smell of the rain. Focus on the sound of the rain as it reduces. Take another deep cleansing breath and relax a little bit deeper. Now imagine that the rain is just a light sprinkle against your skin and focus on that sensation. Focus on the sound of just a drizzle all around you. Focus on the smell of just a light rain all around. Take another deep breath and relax a little bit deeper.

Imagine that the rain has completely stopped. Feel what your body feels like after you've been standing in the rain even though it isn't raining anymore. Feel the water dripping off your body. Listen to the silence around you that occurs right after it has been raining. Smell the smells around you. Take another deep breath and relax even more profoundly; imagine that the clouds have parted, and the sun is above you shining brightly. Feel the sensation of the sun's warmth against your skin, drying all the water that was on you. Imagine the sounds of a relaxing sunny day. Perhaps some birds are chirping. Maybe you hear children laughing or talking in the distance. Take one last cleansing and relaxing breath and open your eyes. You are now in the alpha brainwave state of consciousness.

Exercise 16

∞

Moonlight Key Necklace

Magickal timing: Full moon

Materia:
- one hundred beads (preferably moonstone)
- string (for the beads)
- a key or key charm (preferably silver)
- a white or silver candle

Purpose: This is a technique that I have found is helpful for folks who have trouble concentrating and focusing; it will also be employed in later workings in this book. Some common feedback I received about *Psychic Witch* was that people struggled with the very first exercise, "Preliminary Focus." Essentially this is a technique of training the mind to focus your mind and enter into the meditative state of alpha brain waves. In the exercise, I suggest that people start a countdown from the number one hundred to zero three times in a row, and if you lose focus to start over again. In the book, I also discuss how these practices should be thought of like a workout and that you shouldn't start with something too intense right off the bat. So, it's okay to work up to one hundred. For example, you could count down from the number ten to zero three times without losing focus. Then when you have mastered that, move up to twenty-five as your starting place, then fifty, then seventy-five, then one hundred. However, this is still difficult for some people who struggle with visualization and concentration in general. So, I've decided to give an alternative in which you can keep your eyes open and focus on physical objects while simultaneously enchanting an item to assist you in these areas. The Preliminary Focus is a practice that I still feel is a crucial foundational skill, so I don't encourage completely abandoning it in favor of this or the Color Breathing technique, but rather use this as a stepping stone to achieve the alpha state so you are able to tap into that state of consciousness as thoroughly as possible.

Directions: On the full moon, gather all your items together. Begin to string fifty beads one at a time. As you string each bead state: "*To focus, to know, and to see, clearly.*" As you do, focus on your desire to be able to visualize, to focus, and to know psychic information clearly. After the fiftieth bead is placed, string the key and state:

> *Hallowed be the key that unlocks the Mysteries.*
> *Hallowed be the key that opens perception to me.*

String the remaining fifty beads one at a time on the other side of the key, with each bead focusing on your desire, while stating, "*To focus, to know, and to see, clearly.*"

Tie the ends together or use clasps to complete the necklace's creation. Place it around your white candle, so that it creates a ring around it.

Light the white candle. Hold your hands over the candle and state:

Upon this full moon night
I charge the key of lunar light
To unlock the receptive state
And open the psychic gates.

Let the candle burn fully down.

To enter the alpha brainwave state, count the beads one at a time, starting with a bead next to the key and moving away from it, stating, *"I am opening to a calm, receptive, meditative, psychic state"* as you count each bead. If your mind wanders, simply repeat the bead again before moving to the next. Try to relax your mind and body just a little bit more with each bead. When you get to the key after all one hundred beads have been counted, hold it and state, *"I am in a receptive, meditative, psychic state."* Repeat this process of counting and affirming each bead and the key three times.

Now wear the necklace for whatever psychic or energetic practice that you're going to engage in. Not only will this practice anchor your mind psychologically and serve as a Pavlovian trigger, but the constant use of it with psychic and energetic practices will retain an active charge that will make it easier to slip into the state. Eventually, you'll be able to just put on the necklace and automatically enter into that state of consciousness. I suggest starting with your eyes open, and as your practice strengthens, perform the counting and affirmations with your eyes closed, trying to see the number in your mind's eye as you go through each bead. If you can't, that's okay; just move to the following number. With time, you should strengthen your focus and visualization and begin seeing the numbers. Don't give up or be too hard on yourself.

If you work with the goddess Hecate, like I do, you can also consecrate it in her name and petition her for assistance. You don't have to do anything super formal to include her, just ask from your heart with sincerity and she will listen. Hecate is the goddess of witchcraft, and the key is a sacred symbol to her, with Kleidouchos (meaning key keeper) being one of her sacred epithets. The number three is sacred to her as a triple goddess, and one hundred has loose associations with her as well, with the prefix "Heka" meaning "afar" or "distant" as well as the number one hundred such as the Hekatónkheires of Greek mythology, the hundred-handed ones. Moonstone was also originally named after the goddess Hecate by Jean-Claude Delametherie, who named it Hecatolite. Due to this it has modern associations with the goddess as well.[19]

Sincerity and Enthusiasm

Two of the essential keys to magick that I don't see discussed nearly enough are enthusiasm and sincerity. Enthusiasm is the energy you put into your magick. Looking at the root of the word "enthusiasm" can give us insight into why it's so important. The word enthusiasm comes from the Greek roots "en," meaning "in" and "theos," meaning "a god."[20] It is to be inspired and exhilarated in the ecstasy of a god. I believe enthusiasm to be an effect of being in alignment with one's True Will. True Will, in a nutshell, is one's divine purpose in life. It is the reason we have incarnated, and that's different for each individual. Enthusiasm is the energy you put into your practice to meet that purpose.

Sincerity is the quality of heart that you bring to your magick. It is the attitude you bring to your practice, the way you approach it. Sincerity is the heart of the magickal mindset. Looking at the root etymology of sincerity can also give us a clue to its power. Sincerity comes from the Latin "sincerus," meaning "whole, clean, pure, and true."[21] It is the state of being that isn't tainted by pretense. It is being in the right relationship with your motives for engaging in the magickal path.

It isn't uncommon to lose sight of enthusiasm and sincerity in magick. Still, it's a sign to evaluate that something is out of balance and to determine how you can re-spark those qualities within your practice. Perhaps you're burned out in your practice, and it's beginning to feel like a chore instead of something that fires up your spirit. This tends to signify that you need to slow down and strip your magickal practice down to the bare minimum, if not take a temporary break from it completely until you find your enthusiasm for it again. This can also happen when our magickal practice takes over most of our lives and isn't balanced with living and enjoying life. A lack of sincerity

19. Kynes, *Crystal Magic*.
20. Harper Douglas, "Etymology of enthusiasm," Online Etymology Dictionary, accessed November 28, 2021, https://www.etymonline.com/word/enthusiasm.
21. Harper Douglas, "Etymology of sincerity," Online Etymology Dictionary, accessed November 28, 2021, https://www.etymonline.com/word/sincerity.

might also indicate that you're engaging in magick or spiritual practice with the wrong motives. Perhaps you are operating from a place of pure ego, more concerned with going through the appearances of being a witch in the eyes of others than being sincere about your practice itself and why you are engaging in it. Another possibility is that you're engaging in spells and practices because you feel you have to but have no actual desire to do them. By evaluating your levels of enthusiasm and sincerity, you can discern how aligned you are in your practice and figure out how to come back into alignment with it again. Without these two approaches, it is unlikely that your spiritual experiences of magickal results will be that fruitful.

These approaches are the springboard which everything should be built upon.

Magickal Immersion

A secret component to proficient spellcasting is to immerse yourself in the magick by engaging the imagination fully. When you're immersed in magick, you're as much in it as you are in the physical world. The rest of your life is suspended. You can't think about anything else. You are the witch at that moment, and you are the spell itself. It's a kind of psychic self-hypnosis. Many people who do magick have a hard time getting into this state, and it's also one of the reasons we enter into altered meditative states before performing magick, such as entering the alpha brainwave state, which is connected to the imagination. It's also one of the many reasons I am constantly emphasizing the foundational practices of magick, regardless of where one is on their path of experience with the arts of witchery. They may be doubting their magick and not feeling in alignment with their abilities. This is where, contrary to what most people may tell you, roleplaying is beneficial in witchcraft. It's a way of stimulating yourself in a magickal way, to get into the zone and become the spell itself through alignment.

The way roleplaying works is that you're not just playing a character, but you're playing yourself. It's akin to method acting a glorified version of yourself as a powerful witch. Just like Method acting, roleplaying is about being fully immersed in a character. You may be worried about deluding yourself or losing yourself into fantasy through this immersion. I understand this, and I am a strong proponent of skepticism and critical thinking, except while engaging in the act of spellcasting itself. While performing a spell, you need to have faith in your abilities and in the magick itself. This is best achieved through this immersive state. This profoundly immersive magickal state helps to remove any self-imposed limitations that you may have ingrained within yourself that are creating blockages, which helps in allowing your magick to flow stronger.

Silver RavenWolf poetically refers to this as the Witching Hour, which she describes as "when all of your being urges you to get up, get moving, and get working! Confidence that you can easily step from the problem at hand to the success that you desire seethes around you. And you know, to the depths of your soul, it is time for magick: the moment your power has matured."[22] I find her use of this term for this concept to be such a beautiful and poetic name for this state of immersion. The Witching Hour in folklore is a time when witches and spirits were thought to be at their most potent. Legend puts this time anywhere from midnight to 4:00 a.m., depending on which tradition, culture, or era is discussing it. The most popular times to place this at is either midnight or more commonly, 3:00 a.m. RavenWolf's notion that this isn't a specific time on a clock, but rather anytime you're in this profoundly immersive magickal state, is a powerful one. Discussing it further, she writes that, "If you believe that the universe is a sea of potential within and without, above and below, then you have the secret to all power, all magick, all success."[23]

Roleplaying and its effect upon a person's personality and psyche, as well as its relationship to ritual magick, is a topic that scholars are exploring at the moment.[24] When it comes to casting a spell, not only do you want to roleplay as a powerful spellcaster, but you want to immerse yourself into the spell itself. I usually break this down by connecting inner aspects to the seven planes of reality and seven energetic bodies of the individual.

Physical Immersion: Wearing ritual clothing or jewelry. These are robes or garments that you only wear when performing magick and are set aside for those purposes alone. This helps to allow those clothes to not only act as a form of immersing yourself into

---

22. RavenWolf, *The Witching Hour*, 1.
23. RavenWolf, *The Witching Hour*.
24. Bowman and Hugaas. "Magic is Real."

the right state, but it also acts as a psychological trigger. Physical immersion also includes the material ingredients of your spell, whether it's herbs, candles, crystals, tools, or statues. These all help to immerse you into the act of spellcasting.

Etheric Immersion: This is immersing yourself into your environment on both a physical and energetic level. In spellwork, it's the act of establishing a space for your magick to become a container of the energy you will be raising. It is ensuring that the space is clean physically, purified energetically, and feels sacred to you. This also includes entering into meditative and altered states and connecting with our inner sacred space as much as our outer.

Astral Immersion: The astral plane of reality is directly related to willpower. This is the act of engaging the will with control and confidence, knowing that what you are performing creates a chain of cause and effect that will manifest the spell's desire.

Emotional Immersion: This is invoking the emotional energy of the spell's goal while performing the act. For example, if you were casting a love spell, you would focus on the feelings of what loving and being loved feels like while casting the spell. If you are casting a spell to enhance psychic ability, you will focus on the emotion of peacefulness and emotional availability.

Mental Immersion: This is immersing yourself into the goal of your spell through thinking positive thoughts in alignment with the spell's purpose, as well as vocalizing the goal during the spell somehow. Part of this immersion is not just the words themselves but how you deliver them. This is the magickal voice, a way of speaking that, just like your magickal robe, is set aside except for the act of spellcasting or ritual. This isn't just one tone of speaking, but several depending on the desire of the spell; however, it is always one that is steady and firm, regardless of what the spell's intention is.

Psychic Immersion: This is engaging your inner senses and projecting them into your physical reality to enhance the spell at hand.

It's the conjuration of engaging the imagination to see, hear, smell, taste, and feel things you personally associate with your spell's desire. For example, when casting a spell for psychic ability, I might visualize silver sparkling energy around my candle. I might conjure the smell of jasmine, the taste of vanilla, the feeling of silk against my body, and the sound of owls hooting. These are all sets of symbols that I personally associate with psychic ability. By tuning in and projecting that into the spellwork, I'm telling my subconscious to activate the energetic pathways within me that align with psychic ability.

Divine Immersion: This is having complete faith while performing my spell that the deities or spirits I'm petitioning and working with are indeed listening and assisting. While working, I have full confidence in myself and in my own divinity as a co-creator who can directly affect reality through my magickal power. It's then letting go of the spell and not obsessing or dwelling on it afterward by allowing the immersion to end with the casting of the spell.

Strategic Magickal Goals

Spells accomplish goals. Having a well-planned goal to aim your spell at is going to assist you in manifesting what you desire that spell to accomplish. This may sound like common sense, but it tends to be something people don't give enough thought to when planning their spells. Most new spellcasters fall into two camps: those who are too short-sighted in their goals, and those who are not far-sighted enough to magickally reach a large goal. Having the right goals with spellcasting can make or break a spell. The biggest influence on my magick in this regard comes from Jason Miller's books and courses.[25] Because I have found the focus on the goal during the spell-planning stage so important, I wanted to ensure that I cover some pointers to help your spells to reach the next level.

---

25. Miller, *The Elements of Spellcrafting*.

There are five main areas that are important to look at when it comes to crafting your goal. While I will use psychism as the goal of the spellcasting in this example, these five focus areas apply to all spellwork regardless of what type of magickal goal you have. The main areas we need to be focused on when crafting spell goals are precision, openness, realism, enthusiasm, and strategy for larger goals. Your spellcrafting goal should be one or maybe two sentences at most, but formulating the language of this goal correctly should take a considerable amount of time to get just perfect when you're planning your spell.

The first step in spellcrafting a goal is precision. You need to be completely clear and specific about what it is you want the spell to achieve. It's important to give this a lot of thought; it's easy to think we know what we want without meditating on it, only to end up realizing you weren't specific enough. This still happens to me. Let me give you a recent example that immediately comes to mind. I recently did a spell to assist me in having laser-like focus without distraction. The spell manifested and I found that my focus was so well honed that many hours would fly while I focused on the task at hand without me realizing it. So what was the problem? The problem was I was focusing on the wrong things. I spent a week organizing our massive home occult library alphabetically by author without a single distraction—but this wasn't the reason I had cast a focus spell, which was to focus on writing this book. I wasn't clear enough in my spell about what I wanted that focus to be on or for how long.

The next part of goal setting for your spell is the exact opposite of the last one; it's about striking a balance between being precise about our goal and allowing fluidity in regard to how a spell can manifest. Magick always wants to find the path of least resistance to manifest, which is why we want to be precise about how it will manifest. On the other hand, if we make it too precise, we make it difficult for the spell to be achieved. The key is to find the sweet spot between being adequately specific without being so specific that the spell has difficulty manifesting. Each time we specify our intent we are narrowing down the stream of what will manifest to ensure we're getting what we truly want—but when we are too rigid with how it should manifest, we are increasingly limiting the potential to get what we want and in the time frame that we want it. In this case, your goal may be choosing a path of the most resistance while there may be several other ways in which it may potentially come about.

Another crucial consideration in formulating your goal is to discern if your goal is within the realm of possibilities to occur at all. This boils down to evaluating your life and situation and comparing it to the plausibility of the goal being achieved to see if it's easily enchantable. If it isn't, it's about then determining how you might make it more enchantable. While magick can and does sometimes achieve the miraculous in terms of things that would seem impossible, it's much more effective if you can cast a spell that isn't bordering on impossibility. If you're casting a spell to be an expert at mediumship, but you don't make time in your routine to meditate, do psychic development sessions, or sit down to perform a mediumship session itself— the spell is most likely not going to do much. Your current life situation isn't enchantable in this scenario.

If you are casting a spell to become a famous rockstar but don't know how to play an instrument or sing and don't have any desire to learn, or you don't want to be noticed by others, your life isn't enchantable for that request. Likewise, if you try casting a spell to be able to physically fly through the air as a superhuman power, the odds are so stacked against you that I can assure you that this won't happen. The situation just isn't enchantable.

If your goal is so far out of reach, the key is to approach it strategically. Have a larger magickal working for your final goal but cast smaller stepping-stone spells that help you achieve it, which makes your life more enchantable. Instead of reaching for something huge that is unlikely to manifest, break the spell down into several mini spells that will lead to your final goal. When one of those spells has manifested, move on to the next one until you eventually reach your major goal.

The last component to be mindful of when planning your spell goal is to evaluate your excitement level. Are you excited about the spell you're planning? If not, then why are you casting it? It sounds a bit silly to ask this question, but it's a very important one. If you are not excited about the spell, there's an obvious lack of desire and will for it to work. Your excitement is a part of your manifestation of the spell. It denotes how much energy you are putting into it. If you are not excited about the spell goal, why should the Universe or any spiritual allies be?

This touches back on the previous topic of enthusiasm and the power within that state of mind. If you aren't excited about the spell, it indicates that you need to rethink why you are casting the spell in the first place.

Jason Miller sums up the importance of enthusiasm in magick perfectly in his book *The Elements of Spellcrafting*: "A good goal is inspiring. It lights a fire in the belly. It is a reason to charge into the temple at dawn, or head to the graveyard at 3 a.m. Just because we are not going for the impossible or highly improbable doesn't mean that we can't strive for greatness."[26]

Desire, Intention, and Will

We may have the thought (intent) to do something, but until our brain sends electrical signals through the nervous system to perform that action, it will always remain a thought. That electrical activity between thought and action is in a metaphorical sense that force of will. It's the step between thought and action that transitions the two. It doesn't doubt or second-guess itself; instead, a decision has been made, and a force is moving that thought into being an actualized reality.

In this metaphor, the conscious mind of intent is directing the will. That isn't always the case. Will is something we often do unconsciously, but to bring awareness to willpower will help you to understand how to tap into it and make it a conscious tool that will assist in every area of life, and this is especially true when it comes to the casting of spells. Keeping with our metaphor, when our intention and will are in sync, we can walk from point A to point B without much thinking. When they aren't aligned, we either don't move as in the previous examples, or our will is on autopilot. An example of this metaphor is when we are talking on the phone and pacing without realizing it. Our actions are no longer conscious but now unconscious.

Will is an energy and one we should familiarize ourselves with and be able to harness and direct if we want to be proficient spellcasters. We become familiar with identifying the force of will through observing it. We harness and strengthen our will through engaging with it consciously, and this is done through discipline and dedication. By learning to recognize and work with our personal willpower, we can then begin to slowly learn to recognize

---

26. Miller, *The Elements of Spellcrafting*, 28.

and enact our higher True Will. That doesn't mean that intention is useless. Intention is a huge factor in magick as it helps us to determine what our magickal goals are.

Exercise 17

∽

Identifying and Strengthening the Will

Magickal timing: Starting on the new moon to full moon

Materia:
- a notebook or journal
- a pen

Purpose: This is a practice that is meant to strengthen the will by creating a simple disciplined routine. This practice also serves for identifying will as an energetic force through observing the subtle space between thought and action.

Directions: Starting on the new moon every day until the full moon, set a five-minute timer and write in your journal. It's even better to try to pick the same time every day to perform this exercise.

The key is to do absolutely nothing else until the timer goes off. It's okay if you don't even know what to write in your journal. If you feel stuck, you can simply write, "I am writing in my journal to observe and identify the force of will within myself." What you write isn't as important as writing itself.

However, I choose journaling as an example for this exercise because I have found journaling to be one of the most powerful things that the witch can do daily, and this will help to make it a daily habit. So, if it's not about what we are writing, what is the point of this? It's to observe how your mind goes from having the thought to write something down to the action of making those pen strokes. As you write, you want to find that space between thought and action because that is the energy of will that you need to focus on and identify.

Partnering Instead of Using

Another successful key to spellcasting is how you approach materia being used in your spells. It's a very Western colonial mindset to see the ingredients in your spell as just that, ingredients to use. Witchcraft is about connection. You are connecting to the self, spirits, nature, and the cosmos. It's about seeing these as all the same and paradoxically different. We are all one, yet all individually unique. Even two of the same herb or crystal are going to be unique and slightly different. We connect through the power of honoring and respecting. This is why most witches tend to be animists, seeing everything as alive and endowed with spirit.

The term "animism" was coined by Western anthropologists immersed in a Christian worldview to describe unfamiliar spiritual and religious beliefs that they viewed as "primitive" and that included a belief in the spirit within seemingly inanimate objects. However, if we look more closely, we find the practice of animism to be almost universal regardless of culture. Even pre-Christian European pagans engaged in animism. Animism is believed to be the oldest religious belief in the world.

I believe that animism is a natural orientation for humans that we are trained out of. We even see modern examples of people engaging in animism almost every day without realizing it. One example is the way vehicles, whether they are ships, bikes, or cars, are given names, pronouns, and spoken to. Another example is electronics, particularly when they are beginning to fail, or when they are frustrating us. It's common for people to start talking to that device, yelling at it, or even pleading with it to work as if it were a person.

When we think of cars, ships, and electronics, we may believe that they can't possibly have a spirit since they are far removed from the natural world and composed of different parts. Just because something is comprised of various components or has undergone processes of transformation that remove it from its natural state does not mean that it does not have an inherent spirit within it. If we were to look at human beings, we would see that we too are composed of various elements and even various individual biological life forms, from single cell bacteria to the trillions of cells that compose the human body, yet we have an overarching singular consciousness as a single body. When we bake a pie we're using unique ingredients, but once it is a pie, it is no longer just those ingredients; it is now a pie. Spellcrafting is like this as well. While we use different materia in our crafting, it usually acts as a component to something new in something whole and something that has a spirit of its own. For example, if you're making a spell oil it incorporates different essential oil materia. Once the oil is finished, it's no longer those elements of essential oil that created it; it's now something unique, a spell oil. I find a powerful approach in magick is to honor and treat each materia as its own individual spirit (like cells that assist in a function) and then the finished product as its own spirit as a whole.

We also see children naturally engaging in animism, often talking to toys, plants, and seemingly inanimate objects and treating them as being alive and autonomous. Observing children and how they interact with the world is key to both magickal and psychic ability, and this is a great example of it. Approaching the world through an animistic point of view will significantly heighten your psychic ability because you are opening up new possibilities of the dialogue between you and the world around you, both seen and unseen. Remember, they aren't *just tools* or *ingredients*. They're allies that assist in bridging the inner and outer worlds of magick.

When it comes to spellcasting, the easiest way to connect with the material components of your spell is to acknowledge them individually, ask them for their assistance in the working, and thank them for their support. This simple approach shifts the dynamic of the energetic relationship between you and the ingredients you use in your spell, and you should notice the difference in effectiveness between partnering with materia spirits for a spell and merely using ingredients in a spell. Another great way to honor the spirit of the materia that you are working with is to try to make sure that it's ethically harvested and ethically sourced to the best of your ability. This isn't always completely possible, but you should strive to make better choices when you can. The following is an exercise that I use to connect with a materia for the first time so that we are familiar with one another.

Exercise 18

Connecting with Materia

Hold the object in your hand if you have it with you. Ground and center yourself and enter into an alpha state. Bring your awareness to your Cauldron of Warming (see Chapter 3 for an explanation of the Three Cauldrons) located below your navel. See it swirling with the energy of your Lower Self as if someone had been stirring it with a ladle or spoon. Imagine that it's beginning to overflow inside you as if you were hollow. As it overflows it begins filling your body with this awareness from your feet all the way to the top of your head until you are completely filled with this energy.

Vocally or mentally state, "I wish to vibrate in harmony with the spirit of (name of object) in perfect love and perfect trust."

Scan your inner awareness; what do you sense? Do you see any imagery? Perhaps you smell or taste something. Perhaps you feel or hear something. Visualize the spirit of the object in your Witch Eye. Introduce yourself. Take a moment to commune with it, ask it questions, and get to know it.

When you are done, thank it. Visualize all the energy from the cauldron that filled your body returning back to the cauldron.

Now repeat this process two more times, once with your Cauldron of Motion of the Middle Self located at your heart center, and then with your Cauldron of Wisdom of the Higher Self located at your head. Notice if you have any different experiences with your senses. Did the spirit of the object have the same form or a different one? Did it act differently or convey different information based on which soul you approached it with?

Exercise 19

Cleansing and Charging a Tarot Deck Spell
By Theresa Reed

Magickal timing: One full moon, one new moon

Materia:
- your tarot deck
- sandalwood incense (I prefer stick incense)
- silk cloth
- black tourmaline crystal
- dragon's blood incense
- rose quartz crystal
- selenite crystal

Purpose: This is a two-part spell to clear negative energy from your tarot deck and recharge it with positive, healing vibes. There are many reasons why you may want to cleanse your tarot deck.

Some of the most common are:
- you've done too many readings with the same deck
- you wish to clear your deck after a particularly negative reading
- you've been gifted a brand-new deck
- you inherited someone else's deck (Grandma left you her Thoth)
- your readings feel "blah"
- you haven't touched your deck in eons

Frankly, you don't even need a reason to use this spell. Consider it good spiritual maintenance that will keep your tarot readings humming like a well-oiled machine.

Directions: On the full moon, gather your tarot deck, sandalwood, silk cloth, and black tourmaline crystal. Open a window and sit near it. Light the incense and allow the smoke to envelop your tarot deck for about a minute.

Put the incense aside and hold the deck between your hands. Close your eyes and recite these words out loud or silently to yourself:

> *Under the full moon's glow*
> *I command all negative energy to go.*

If you prefer, you can choose your own words. What's important is that you command the cards to release any and all energy that is not conducive to your readings. Lay the cards on the silk cloth, put the black tourmaline on top, and wrap it up into a neat little package. Put the wrapped deck under the light of the full moon and leave it alone until the new moon. (During this period of rest, I will use a different tarot deck for readings so that the one that is being cleansed has plenty of time to get clear.)

When the new moon arrives, gather the deck, dragon's blood, and the rose quartz. Unwrap the deck. Light the dragon's blood and slowly waft the smoke around the cards for a minute or two. (Dragon's blood is protective and also attracts good energy.)

Next, take the deck in your hands and hold it to your third eye. Repeat these words out loud—or silently:

The new moon brings fresh energy
My tarot deck is ready to work for me.

Once again, feel free to change the words as you see fit. What's important is that you set an intention that feels positive. Set your deck on the windowsill with the rose quartz on top. Allow it to rest for one day under the new moon. It's ready to use. Keep a selenite crystal on your cards between readings. This will neutralize most energy and keep your deck clear.

Exercise 20

❧

Spell-Checking with Divination

Magickal timing: Any

Materia:
- A tarot deck

Purpose: It is always wise to get a consultation before casting a spell. For the witch there is perhaps no greater consultant than that of divination. Divining before casting a spell can give you insight into whether you have the green light to go or whether you should go back to the drawing board and re-craft your spell. One of the quickest forms of divination for a spell is simply to consult a pendulum for "yes" and "no" questions. Pendulums are great "training wheels" for learning to listen to and trust your intuition. After working with a pendulum for a while, you'll find that you already know what a pendulum will say before you use it.

However, if you're looking for more insight into your spell, divining with a more complex system can help you come up with the best "plan of attack" and help troubleshoot your spells. It should be no surprise that my preferred tool of divination is tarot. I thought I would share how I "spell-check" before performing a spell to ensure success.

Directions: I begin by getting into a meditative state and shuffling my cards, focusing on my desired goal. For example, if I wanted to do a spell to receive a job promotion, I would focus on that goal of a job promotion itself while internally projecting out a petition prayer. This is the one that I use, but feel free to adapt it to your spiritual path:

> *With the guidance of Divinity*
> *I shuffle these cards seeking clarity.*
> *Gods and guides with eyes to see*
> *Reveal the best path of magick for me.*

Then I lay out the cards into a four-card spread:

Position 1—*Which type of magick*
Position 2—*Advice on the magick*
Position 3—*Possible blockages*
Position 4—*Outcome if you perform the magick*

For position one, I divine the type of magick to perform based on the elemental suit that comes up. This helps me get a general idea of what the cards are recommending and incorporate it into my spell. I gain further insight based on the card itself. If I get a Major Arcana card, I refer to its astrological attributions and then translate that to the element that rules it. Here are some examples of elemental associations with types of magick:

Pentacles (**Earth**)—*Herb magick, crystal magick, poppet magick, and knot magick*
Cups (**Water**)—*Potions, elixirs, flower essences, and washes*
Wands (**Fire**)—*Candle magick, sex magick*
Swords (**Air**)—*Chanting spells, incantations, petition spells, affirmations, and meditation*

This is purely an illustration of correspondences; use your intuition and really look at the images on the cards. They might have something to tell you despite not being a "traditional" meaning of the card. The tarot "speaks" in various ways, including symbolism of imagery.

Chapter 3
APPROACHING
THE MYSTERIES

I n *Psychic Witch*, I discussed the threefold models such as the triple souls, the three alchemical essentials, the Three Cauldrons, and the tripart cosmology of the Witch's Tree. These concepts are crucial to how I approach both psychism and magickal ability, creating foundational components just as important as concepts such as the elements, planetary powers, and astrological influences. As such, I feel like it's important to review these concepts for those unfamiliar with them and to bring some further insights, perspectives, and understanding into these concepts for those who are already familiar with them. They will be important for connecting with the mysteries of magick for proficiency in spellcasting through direct experience for the work in this book, as well as having a map to identify and understand what those experiences are, and a framework to make sense of what levels of reality we are operating from and which parts of ourselves are interacting with those levels of reality. By using these threefold models, we can begin to build a framework of the aspects of our selves and how we correspond and relate to the metaphysical universe on inner and outer levels. There are also important foundational concepts to understand in metaphysics and occultism regarding the relationship of consciousness, energy, reality, and divinity. I feel that these concepts are best summarized by the seven Hermetic Principles, a union of ancient occult wisdom complemented by innovative insights from spiritual movements such as Theosophy and New Thought. These principles are sometimes referred to as the Master Key to approaching the Mysteries and realizing the inherent power of mind over matter. One of my witchcraft teachers, Laurie Cabot, placed emphasis on the Hermetic Principles, referring to them as being the core basis of how and why witchcraft works.[27] In all my occult studies, various concepts continually return me to those basic ideas, worded in various ways, that are outlined by the Hermetic Principles.

The Three Souls

Many witches view the self as being threefold and refer to it as the three "souls" to drive home the point that these are divine aspects of ourselves, even if we wouldn't normally consider them to be. Depending on which tradition of witchcraft you're working with, these three souls are known by various names and may have slight differences in the finer details of what each soul embodies and how it is defined. The main division tends to be Higher Self, Middle Self, and Lower Self. The Higher Self is what we generally refer to as "soul" in modern day usage. It's the divine part of us that is pure and a spark of Source itself. The Middle Self is our personality, our mind, and our sense of "self." The Lower Self is the instinctual aspect of ourselves. Some traditions consider the Middle Self to also include the body, and some consider the Lower Self to include the body. Likewise, some traditions view emotions as being a Lower Self aspect while others view them as a Middle Self aspect. The way I reconcile this is that the emotions of the Lower Self are what we feel, those raw unprocessed feelings that we feel in our bodies. The Middle Self's emotions are when we process these feelings, can name and describe them, and to some degree control them.

As with all things in occultism, these ideas are just maps and models to help us understand the energies and concepts we're working with, and none of them are perfect or absolute. If we get too hung up on these maps as being literal or absolute truth, we begin to confuse the map with the territory. Essentially, we need these maps for our Middle Self to make sense of things perceived by the Higher and Lower Self. We can also look at the Three Selves as having connection and parallels with the three forms of consciousness of a person: the Middle Self being the conscious mind, the Lower Self being the

---

27. Cabot and Cowan, *Power of the Witch*, 198.

subconscious mind, and the Higher Self as being the superconscious mind or collective consciousness. The common terms used in mainstream spirituality, though a bit watered down from their witchcraft tradition parallels, are Mind, Body, and Spirit.

The Three Cauldrons

A helpful tool for working with the three selves is using the Three Cauldrons model. The Three Cauldrons are energy centers where we process energies and work to transmute and transform them. The Three Cauldrons come from an Irish bardic poem called *The Cauldron of Poesy*. The poem describes three cauldrons contained within a person. Through working with the Three Cauldrons, I've found that they also "brew" energies in the sense that they process energies and then combine and filter that energy out in different forms from what was originally received, just like you would add ingredients to a brew and the combination creates something different than its individual ingredients. The Three Cauldrons also serve as focal points for the Three Souls, functioning as energetic containers within us that make it easier to focus upon and work with our Three Souls.

The first cauldron is the Cauldron of Warming and is situated beneath the navel. The Cauldron of Warming is fueled by environment, movement, sexual activity, and connection with nature. It's the Cauldron that brews etheric, creative, generative, and vital energies within a person. The second cauldron is the Cauldron of Motion, situated at the heart. *The Cauldron of Poesy* states that this cauldron is born on its side and through great happiness or great sorrow is either tipped right side up or turned upside down in people. This cauldron is where we process emotional energy, and it is fueled by things that evoke emotions from us, such as art, film, music, and poetry. The Cauldron of Motion is the cauldron that brews astral energy. The third cauldron is the Cauldron of Wisdom, situated inside the head. *The Cauldron of Poesy* states that this cauldron is born upside down in a person and turned right side up in those who cultivate great wisdom and spiritual connection within their lives. This cauldron is fed through the accumulation and integration of wisdom, divine connection, and spiritual practice. The Cauldron of Wisdom is the cauldron that brews psychic, celestial, divine, and transcendent energies.

In the Blue Rose line of the Faery Tradition of Witchcraft, and also in Black Rose Witchcraft, the Three Souls are given symbols.[28] The Lower Self is given the symbol of the moon, which in astrology represents the unconscious aspects of ourselves. The Middle Self is given the symbol of the sun for the conscious aspects of ourselves, just as the Sun represents the individual's personality and sense of self in astrology. The Higher Self is given the symbol of the star, to represent that consciousness beyond our sense of self. For me, this is a perfect symbol set, as it shows the energetic forces that each of the Three Cauldrons works with under the domain of that symbol.

What I mean is that the Lower Self or Cauldron of Warming deals with what is referred to as sublunar energies. Sublunar is a phrase coming from Aristotelian ideas of energies below the sphere of the moon in his geocentric model of the cosmos. While we know the universe isn't geocentric, most magicians work with magick in that manner, viewing where they are as the center of the universe for the purpose of ritual. The sublunar energies are the four classical elements of etheric energy: earth, air, fire, and water. The Middle Self or Cauldron of Motion is given the symbol of the sun and refers to everything under solar influence, which is our solar system and a reference to the astral energies of the seven classical planets. The Higher Self or Cauldron of Wisdom is given the symbol of the star, so this can be seen as a reference to "the stars" or rather celestial energies like constellations such as our zodiac, and star systems far beyond, like the Pleiades. The Cauldron of Wisdom is fueled by the energy of the Three Rays, which are embodiments of Divine Will, Divine Love, and Divine Wisdom and are the trinity of divine energy. These three rays also express themselves as the astrological modalities of mutable, cardinal, and fixed. The combining of the four elements and three modalities is expressed in our zodiac, as divided by the four elements with each of the three expressed as an astrological sign. For example, the zodiac's water signs are Scorpio (Fixed Water), Pisces (Mutable Water), and Cancer (Cardinal Water).

---

28. Faerywolf, *Betwixt & Between*.

The Three Alchemical Essentials

In alchemy there's the concept of the three alchemical essentials, which were seen as keys to the alchemical process. We must remember that alchemy is a spiritual system with spiritual metaphors, a way of encoding spiritual knowledge that didn't seem religious in nature to safeguard the information from religious authorities who would kill these spiritual explorers for heresy. These three essentials are Mercury, Salt, and Sulfur. These three forces were seen as being within all things and their interactions created transformation. Energetically, we see parallels to the three divine rays, the three modalities, and the Three Souls. This is symbolized on Baphomet[29] with the burning torch above, symbolic of Sulfur, (the fire of the soul), the caduceus of Mercury below, and the head of consciousness and mind (Salt) between the two.

Alchemical	Astrological	Divine Ray	Three Souls
Sulfur	Mutable	Divine Wisdom	Higher Self
Salt	Fixed	Divine Love	Middle Self
Mercury	Cardinal	Divine Will	Lower Self

The Three Worlds of the Witch's Tree

Another pivotal concept is that of the Axis Mundi, the World Tree. The World Tree is a map of the three primary realms of existence using the tree as a model. Traditionally the World Tree is seen as a massive oak tree, but this varies among different Pagans and witches. The main idea is that there's a great cosmic tree with its branches in the Upper World, its trunk in the Middle World, and its roots in the Under World: three separate divisions of reality, all connected and part of the same metaphorical tree. The Upper World is the realm of the collective unconscious, transcendental divinity (the divinity that transcends our physical world), and that of greater cosmic forces. The Middle World is our physical reality, the overlapping etheric reality, the mighty dead, the gateways between realms, and imminent divinity (the divinity inherent in the physical world). The Under World is a term for the realm of the ancestors, the astral, chthonic divinity (the divinity associated with the

---

29. For more information on Baphomet, see *Psychic Witch* 106–9.

Under World), deities of primal power, and our inner world. Populating each realm are spirits and divinities of different types that have their own autonomy and individuality. These three worlds correspond to the Celtic realms of Land, Sky, and Sea. Land is the Middle World, Sky is the Upper World, and Sea is the Under World. Witches also identify with this World Tree and see it within them. This is called the Witch's Tree, and it serves as a tool for exploring the different realms of the World Tree via inner psychic means. The connection of the World Tree and the individual Witch's Tree within each witch is summarized by the Hermetic axiom "As within, so without."

Exercise 21

Journey to the World Tree

Get into a comfortable, relaxed position where you will not be disturbed. Close your eyes. Enter alpha. Ground and center yourself.

You notice a silver mist on the ground at your feet. The mist begins to swirl around your feet, slowly spiraling around your body and moving upward. It completely surrounds you and engulfs your vision until all you can see is the thick silver mist. As the mist begins to slowly fade away, you find yourself in a forest.

Before you is a vast and powerful oak tree; this is the Axis Mundi, the cosmic World Tree. It's so immense that it almost appears as if its massive trunk is a giant pillar holding up the very sky itself. From your point of view, you can see the towering branches high above you, though you can't see how far the branches reach. It seems as if they reach up to infinity. High in the branches, silver and blue stars seem to hang like ornaments, decorating it with a celestial and otherworldly glow. At the base of the tree you see giant roots woven in and out of each other. Some of the roots are bigger than you. Some of the roots are bigger than buildings. Take a few minutes to observe the tree and take in its details.

All oak trees have a dryad, a tree spirit that lives within them, and the Axis Mundi tree is no different. The dryad of the Axis Mundi is the Anima Mundi, the cosmic world soul. As you approach the tree, you place your hand upon its trunk, feeling the texture of the bark. You call out to the Anima Mundi and request entry with your hand upon the tree. Almost immediately, in response to your call, you feel her presence in the tree, though you don't see her. Take a moment to connect with this energy and see if there are any messages, images, or insights that come to you as you feel the Anima Mundi. When you are finished, thank the spirit of the World Tree. Turn around and away from the tree to see a silver mist. Step back in the mist until it's all you can see. Allow the mist to fade away as you begin to move your fingers and legs, or anything to bring you back to bodily awareness. When you're ready, open your eyes and ground and center yourself once more.

The Hermetic Principles

The *Kybalion* is controversial, as it claims to be sharing ancient Hermetic knowledge. It was ghost written by "Three Initiates," which is thought to be a pen name of William Walker Atkinson, the publisher of the book, who was known to write under various pen names and pseudonyms.

Some folks feel it isn't true to pure ancient Hermeticism, and they are right. Most things considered to be of the Hermetic tradition claim to be authored by Hermes Trismegistus. The *Kybalion* doesn't make this claim; rather, it is dedicated to Hermes Trismegistus. Researchers such as author Mary K. Greer point out that many of the *Kybalion*'s principles seem to be based on the introduction to a translation of *Kore Kosmou*, also known as *The Virgin of the World of Hermes Mercurius Trismegistus*,[30] translated by Theosophists Anna Kingsford and Edward Maitland. This paired with concepts from Theosophy and New Thought create the framework of ideas which the *Kybalion* presents.

Regardless of how ancient or pure to Hermeticism the *Kybalion* is or isn't, it is definitely not a perfect book, and at times is deeply problematic. As such, like any occult text, it shouldn't be taken as gospel. Like many Victorian and post-Victorian occult books, we can gain value from them while also understanding and discussing which ideas, comments, and statements are problematic with transparency and honesty. Despite some of its deep flaws, the *Kybalion* is also rich with insight, particularly for those who are new to occultism and magick. In fact, the *Kybalion* itself defines itself as Hermetic in the usage of the word as sealed (like the expression "hermetically

---

30. https://marykgreer.com/2009/10/08/source-of-the-kybalion-in-anna-kingsford%E2%80%99s-hermetic-system.

sealed"), which was a common term of the time of its authorship; today we would use the term "occult," meaning hidden knowledge.[31] So I feel it is a moot point whether the book is from an ancient tradition or modern traditions. What it is, is sharing a view of occult philosophy regarding how the universe works and how humanity can understand it to co-create reality. Some of the most powerful and wise witches that I have had the honor to study under embraced and taught the *Kybalion*'s Hermetic Principles as an important foundation for the magickal path.

The Principle of Mentalism

The first Hermetic Principle in the *Kybalion* is the Principle of Mentalism. This principle states that the universe is mental—held in the mind of THE ALL. The elemental forces, the building blocks that compose all of reality in occultism, are within the mind of the All. This principle tells us that everything in existence is a mental construct of the Great Divine. It implies that everything on its most fundamental level is unified. Consciousness is the basis of everything: matter, energy, and spirit. It implies that we exist within the Great Divine and are ourselves part of it. Being within and a part of the Great Divine implies that everything is inherently divine, including us—who have minds ourselves. Being a part of the Divine Mind and possessing our own minds suggests that we, like the Great Divine, are able to create reality using our own divine mental energy. That's because according to this principle our thoughts are energy, and if we can harness that mental energy and direct it, we can begin to understand our own divinity as co-creators of reality. This reflects Dion Fortune's definition of magick, as being the science and art of causing changes in consciousness to occur in accordance with the Will.

The Principle of Correspondence

The second Hermetic Principle in the *Kybalion* is the Principle of Correspondence. This principle states: "As above, so below; as within, so without; as in the microcosm, so in the macrocosm."[32] This states that everything on one plane of reality affects another. It also states that, just like the Principle of

---

31. Anonymous, *The Kybalion*, 9.
32. Anonymous, *The Kybalion*, 16.

Mentalism, the All is within the all and that the all is within the All. Or, to put it more clearly, everything is within divine consciousness and divine consciousness is within everything. Everything is part of the Great Divinity, and the whole entirety of the Great Divinity is within all things. Everything is fractal in nature like a hologram, being parts of the whole and containing the whole pattern within the part. This suggests that the microcosm is an atlas of the macrocosm, and vice versa.

Furthermore, this principle suggests that things in different planes of reality are linked together by energy that corresponds between them. Working with plants or stones that hold a certain elemental, planetary, or celestial vibration allows us to work with and tap into those greater energies to create change via magick. This principle also suggests that what we do internally is intricately linked to our physical world and to higher planes of reality, and vice versa.

The Principle of Polarity

The third Hermetic Principle is the Principle of Polarity. This suggests that everything in the universe has an opposite and that one thing and its opposite are actually the same thing but different parts of that spectrum. Hot and cold, light and dark, reception and projection, righteousness and wickedness, happiness and sadness, life and death, and so on. Everything is not only linked to its opposite but is a complementary aspect that when combined makes up the entirety of what the thing actually is. The *Kybalion* expresses this by saying that "Everything is Dual; everything has poles; everything has its pair of opposites; like and unlike are the same; opposites are identical in nature, but different in degree; extremes meet; all truths are but half-truths; all paradoxes may be reconciled."[33] The last line is one of the main goals of alchemy and occultism: the reconciliation and reunification of energies that seem like they're separate but are only two halves of one side.

One of my all-time favorite movies as a child was the movie *The Dark Crystal* by Jim Henson and Brian Froud. The movie perfectly exemplifies this principle as a concept. In the movie there are two main species of creatures that are opposite but complementary: the evil, aggressive, selfish, and

---

33. Anonymous, *The Kybalion*, 19.

ignorant Skeksis and the gentle, pacifist, selfless, and wise Uru Mystics. The point of the movie is that these beings used to be a singular species, the UrSkeks who divided into the two separate halves.

The Principle of Vibration

The fourth Hermetic Principle is the Principle of Vibration. The Principle of Vibration states that "Nothing rests; everything moves; everything vibrates."[34] This means that nothing is truly still and that everything is vibrating or moving at different rates. We know through science that even the most solid-looking matter is composed of moving and vibrating atoms and molecules. This suggests that everything in the universe, physical and non-physical, is vibrating. When we remember the Principle of Mentalism, we realize that everything is composed of consciousness and thought. That means that our thoughts also have a vibration to them, and many spiritual, metaphysical, and occult practitioners refer to the vibration of something. Unfortunately, sometimes this is used to label things as "good" or "bad" vibrations, which leads to a whole host of problems including spiritual bypassing.

The Principle of Rhythm

The fifth Hermetic Principle is the Principle of Rhythm. This states that "Everything flows out and in; everything has its tides; all things rise and fall; the pendulum-swing manifests in everything; the measure of the swing to the right, is the measure of the swing to the left; rhythm compensates."[35] We know from the Principle of Polarity that all things are only a part of their opposite and that there's a spectrum within these two poles. The Principle of Rhythm states that everything is in a state of flowing from one pole to the other. This can be likened to the *Star Wars* phrase of "balance in the Force." The idea is that energy is flowing from one spectrum of the pole to the other and that one expression of energy will eventually give way to its opposite. We can think of this symbolically like the waxing and waning of the moon, as the moon increases in light, only eventually to decrease to darkness and vice versa. This paired with the last principle implies that nothing is permanent, and it will

---

34. Anonymous, *The Kybalion*, 17.
35. Anonymous, *The Kybalion*, 21.

eventually give way to its opposite in compensation, like a pendulum swinging back and forth. This also gives insight into the concept held by many witches that all things are cyclical: time, seasons, moon phases, rebirth, etc.

The Principle of Cause and Effect

The sixth Hermetic Principle is the Principle of Cause and Effect. It states that "Every Cause has its Effect; every Effect has its Cause."[36] This means that everything that is, is an effect of a previous cause and everything creates an effect. Nothing that occurs is without consequence. This isn't the idea that if you do good you'll get good back and if you do bad you'll get bad back. Rather, this idea isn't moralistic. This ties back to the fact that everything is moving and that everything is intricately linked with everything else. A stone thrown into a pond creates a ripple. Likewise, no thought, word, or action that occurs does so in a vacuum. Everything creates change one way or another, for good or ill or neutral, because everything is interacting with something else. The *Kybalion* refers to this principle as a law, and states that "Chance is but a name for Law not recognized," meaning nothing is random; everything occurs for one reason or another due to something else.[37]

The Principle of Gender

So now we come to the most controversial of Hermetic principles and for very good reason. The Principle of Gender states that "Gender is in everything; everything has its Masculine and Feminine Principles; Gender manifests on all planes."[38] There's a lot to unpack here. With a lot of older occult and classical text we must be discerning and honest, while still salvaging what we can work with from the wreckage. A book can be both incredibly insightful and helpful at points and highly problematic during others, and this includes most of our foundational texts in occultism. Our task as readers in the modern age is to pan through these older texts, sifting through the rubbish of problematic personal and cultural biases and ideologies of their

---

36. Anonymous, *The Kybalion*, 23.
37. Anonymous, *The Kybalion*, 23.
38. Anonymous, *The Kybalion*, 117.

time period to find the golden nuggets within them and what applies to us now. The *Kybalion* is no exception.

Much of early Victorian occultism used the principle of gender in their metaphysical concepts, with some being more literal with it than others. The *Kybalion*, influenced by those traditions and written in post-Victorian times, adopts a lot of that heteronormative language. Although it is a bit more progressive in comparison to the well of influences the author drew from, it still falls completely short as a metaphor in modern times with our current understandings. The *Kybalion* affirms that the principle of gender does not mean the sex of something (or someone) but refers to the energetic functions of generation and creation. However, it then proceeds to say that sex is merely a material manifestation of the gender principal in action.[39] This is incorrect and muddies the waters of what the author is trying to explain, as this line of thinking is rooted in problematic ideas of gender essentialism.[40] Using gender as a metaphor in occultism to describe the complementary and opposing forces within all things in the universe falls short because we know that scientifically sex and gender are not synonymous nor binary, but rather a spectrum of uniqueness throughout nature, which includes people as well. The principle also falls short using gender as a metaphor because one gender is not inherently more "passive" or "receptive" or "darker" than another; this view relies completely on gender stereotypes and sexism.

The author of the *Kybalion* seems to be trying to tap into an idea that was progressive for his time without the framework we have now and using the flawed metaphors of what came before. For example, the *Kybalion* asserts that the focus of the seventh principle is more akin to "'attraction and repulsion' of the atoms; chemical affinity; the 'loves and hates' of the atomic particles; the attraction or cohesion between the molecules of matter" or even "the very Law of Gravitation."[41] It is a labor of love at times to think beyond the literalism of such works, but the possibilities are endless once we've done so. Life and death, creation and destruction, receptivity and projection, positive and negative electrical charges: these polar complementary and opposing forces

---

39. Anonymous, *The Kybalion*, 117–118.
40. Magdalene, *Outside the Charmed Circle*.
41. Anonymous, *The Kybalion*, 122–123.

such as the projective force of life, and the receptive force of death—these forces are alive within our lives and alive in our magick.

In the context of psychism and magick, the *Kybalion* discusses the Principle of Gender as being embodied in the concepts of "I Am," which can be broken down into two parts according to the book—"I" and "me"—and which assist us in coming to know our "I Am."[42] It relates the concept of the projective "I" with the conscious mind (or in our framework, the Middle Self) and the receptive "me" with the subconscious mind (or the Lower Self).[43] The *Kybalion* also associates "I" with willpower and "me" with the physical body and physical appetites.[44] This section is decoded much easier to me when framed in the Three Soul Model, and seeing "I Am" as the Higher Self containing within it the Middle and Lower Selves. When these parts are aligned and in balance, we can masterfully engage in both magick and psychic ability where the conscious mind can interpret and translate the imagery of the subconscious mind and likewise energize impressions of mental imagery into magickal manifestation.[45]

Exercise 22
✒
Mental Transmutation Meditation

Magickal timing: Any

Items:
- Moonlight key necklace (optional)

Purpose: This exercise is an active meditation I've created employing the Hermetic Principles for the purpose of "Mental Transmutation" as described throughout the text of the *Kybalion* and I've had a lot of great success with it. If you wish to use your moonlight key during any mental transmutation, it will strengthen the key's ability as well as make this exercise more effective, but it's entirely optional.

---

42. Anonymous, *The Kybalion*, 126.
43. Anonymous, *The Kybalion*, 124.
44. Anonymous, *The Kybalion*, 127.
45. Anonymous, *The Kybalion*, 136.

Directions: Begin by deciding what you would like to transmute; it could be an emotion, a belief about yourself, a thinking pattern, or a bad habit. Once you've chosen what you would like to transmute, enter into alpha, ground, and center yourself. For this example, we will transmute beliefs about being psychically closed off to being psychically open, but you can modify this exercise to anything else you wish to transmute.

With your eyes closed, begin by assessing how whatever you are transmuting feels. For this example, focus on how you might feel psychically blocked or closed off. Conjure up an image in your mind of what it looks like. Hold that image in your Witch Eye and then see a lock over the image. Mentally name the lock "psychic ability." Take a moment and imagine this aspect of yourself that you're transmuting as a vibration, perhaps as a physical vibration, a musical note, a visual of a wavelength, a color of light, or a combination if possible.

Allow the image, the feeling, and the vibration to fade. Now conjure up your idea of what the opposite polarity of this would be. In this case, it'd be the state of being psychically open. How do you imagine that would feel? Try to conjure up those feelings inside you, roleplaying those feelings for a moment. Now conjure up an image of what you think that might look like. Hold that image in your Witch Eye and see a key over the visual. Name the key "psychic ability." Like before, take a moment and imagine what this transmutation would be like as a vibration in contrast to the previous vibration. How are they different?

Allow the image, the feeling, and the vibration to fade again. Now conjure up both images in your Witch Eye side by side, seeing the aspect you wish to transmute with a lock over it, and the desired transmutation with a key over it. Acknowledge that the lock and the key are two complementary and opposite parts of a whole, just as the area you wish to transmute (in this case being psychically blocked) and the desired transmutation (being psychically open) are opposite poles of a spectrum (of psychic ability as a whole for this example).

Now conjure again that feeling of how being psychically blocked feels as a vibration within you. With your eyes still closed, take hold of the moonlight key around your neck if you are incorporating it into this exercise. Mentally put the key into the lock and turn the key. As you unlock the lock it releases the vibration of the transmutation. Feel the original vibration you're feeling and the vibration unlocked simultaneously. Feel the vibration within you slowly conforming and synchronizing with the vibration that has just been unlocked. The unlocked vibration holds its vibration as the vibration you feel begins to shift. For example, the music note begins to adjust to the desired music note, the color shifts to the desired color, the wavelength conforms with the desired wavelength, the emotion conforms with the desired emotion.

Once you have mentally transmuted the energy, make a mental or verbal declaration of what you have just performed, such as "I have transmuted my psychic ability to a state of openness. I integrate this into myself and my life." When you are done, ground and center yourself again, exit alpha and slowly open your eyes. Note the difference in how you felt before the exercise versus how you feel now.

Exercise 23

❧

Energy Transmutation Candle Spell

Magickal timing: Any

Materia:
- one white chime candle
- one black chime candle
- one grey chime candle
- corresponding incense sticks (optional)

Purpose: This spell is to transmute any situation from one end of the polarity to another. The best example that I've seen of the principles of transmutation being employed in a specific spell is one of my personal favorites, "The Swifting of Energy" from the brilliant Dorothy Morrison's book *Utterly Wicked*.[46] The spell's purpose is to take curses, hexes, or any other negative energy someone is sending you and transform that energy to fuel your goals. This spell I'm sharing here was inspired by the Swifting of Energy spell and

---

46. Morrison, *Utterly Wicked*, 132–136.

is much more simplified than hers, but I definitely recommend checking out the version she teaches.

Direction: Line all three candles in a row about an inch or two away from each other somewhere safe. Place the black candle on the left to represent the starting energy and the white candle on the right to represent the desired end result of the energy. Place the grey candle in the middle to represent the transition between the beginning and end of the energy's transmutation. For this example, let's do this spell for mental clarity. Begin by verbally naming the black chime candle as the current situation. You could do this by pointing at the candle and saying "Candle, your name is my unclarity." Then do the same for the white candle stating, "Candle, your name is clarity." Then point to the middle grey candle and say, "Candle your name is transition."

Light the black candle and state the charm:

> *As this candle drips and burns*
> *By will and word I now affirm*
> *The light, the flame, it will remain*
> *As each candle it's fed is changed.*
> *The start and the end, two halves of the same*
> *Beginning to shift with the movement of flame*
> *As three candles are burned and dismissed*
> *The energy achieves a full spectrum shift.*

When the black candle has burned almost all the way down (and most chime candles last around two hours) move the flame to the next candle. I do this by using an incense stick that corresponds to my desired goal as an added boost. For example, for this example of mental clarity I might use a lemongrass incense stick and light it using the flame of the black candle, then use it to light the grey candle. When lighting the grey candle, repeat the charm. Do the same when the grey candle is almost out, using the incense (or whatever means you have of transferring the flame) to light the white candle, repeating the charm.

Chapter 4
CLEANSING AND PROTECTION

T he popular expression "cleanliness is next to godliness" has merit when it comes to magick. Just like cooking, surgery, or performing scientific experiments, you want to ensure that your work area as well as the instruments you're working with are cleansed and sanitized so that they're not contaminated with unwanted influences. The most important instrument or tool in magick is yourself: mind, body, and soul. We want to ensure that we are clear channels of energy and working in an environment where the energy that is raised and directed is held in the equivalent of a clean container. In the last chapter we looked at the triple aspects of the self. Now we will look at how those aspects of self accumulate the need for cleansing and how to cleanse them, as well as cleansing our environments of imbalanced and undesirable energies.

The Higher Self never needs cleansing. As stated, it's always in a state of purity. We cleanse our Middle Self through meditation, focus, and altering our consciousness, essentially cleansing our mind and bringing it into a state of openness and receptivity. When we talk about cleansing in magick, we're often referring to cleansing the Lower Self's aspects: the body, emotions, and energy. The Lower Self is also referred to as the "sticky self" because it's constantly picking up energies that it encounters like a sponge. Many names refer to this type of energy, but within witchcraft it is often referred to by its ancient Greek name of *miasma*. Miasma is essentially energy that is viewed as a sort of heavy energetic debris.

I don't believe that miasma is necessarily good or bad, and it is not equivalent to the concept of sin in certain religions. It's sort of like how being dirty
doesn't make someone a bad person. It's also unavoidable, just like being dirty
is inevitable. We naturally build up uncleanliness, both physically and energetically, just through daily living. As witches, though, we tend to engage in
practices that often bring us into contact with more miasma than the average person as we dive into deeper and more profound energy work. Witches
get their hands dirty, both physically and energetically. Why is it important to
cleanse this miasma, though? As stated, this energy is heavy and can essentially
clog up the works, so to speak. It can make it more difficult to move energy
and directly engage with it, which we want to avoid if we're trying to cast spells
or engage in practices like mediumship or astral projection where we need to
be energetically clean.

Like dirt, miasma isn't just something that collects around people but
also gathers around objects and locations. For me, psychically, miasma seems
like a film around things. When it's heavily collected, it's like a slimy smog.
Have you seen those old black and white photos of spiritualists performing a mediumship session, and they supposedly capture ectoplasm on film?
Whether genuine photos or not, and let's be honest, it's very doubtful that
they are, they are a great illustration of how I perceive miasmic buildup.

Certain events and activities have greater miasma levels, just as certain
things and activities make you dirtier in the physical. Again, there isn't a
judgment of good or bad connotations to them, just like it isn't bad that your
hands get dirty from working in your garden or taking out the trash. Like
these examples, a good rule of thumb is to see anything that would cause
you to wash your hands or bathe or make you feel dirty in the physical will
often also collect miasma that needs to be cleansed. This ranges from physical
uncleanliness, to wearing dirty clothes, to being in filthy living conditions.
Think about how those things make you feel emotionally. Emotionally and
psychologically, we feel much more relaxed, happy, and have a better sense of
wellbeing when we are showered, in clean clothes, and our homes are clean.
Since, in my experience, miasma is directly related to the Lower Self, evaluating things connected to our bodies and emotions will help us to understand
when we're building up miasma. Emotional states that bring us distress in

any way can attract miasma or may be a direct result of the miasma itself. Again, none of these things are necessarily good or bad in themselves; they're experiences that every person has, and fairly regularly.

Rites of passage such as your birth, death, and so on are traditionally activities that generate great amounts of miasma, whether one is directly engaging in those activities or coming into direct contact with them. The same is said about illness as well as energy healing. It's been my experience that even spellwork, astral projection, divination, and mediumship build up miasma, as we encounter external energies that collect on us like debris. Luckily cleansing miasma is extremely easy, especially since physical cleanliness is half the battle.

The Difference Between Cleansing and Purification

When I use the words cleansing and purification, I differentiate between these words in terms of different levels. Whether you choose to differentiate these words as I do isn't as important as understanding the difference of intensity and regularity of the two ideas. The primary difference between cleansing and purification, in a magickal context, is that cleansing is a more casual clearing of energy, and purification is a more thorough deep cleaning. To think about it in terms of housekeeping, cleansing is akin to dusting, sweeping, and removing clutter. Purification is more like mopping, scrubbing, and steam cleaning your carpet. If we were to think of it in terms of personal hygiene as a metaphor, cleansing is washing your face with soap and water, and purification is more like going to the spa for a deep cleansing facial.

While cleansing and purification are essential, you should keep in mind the difference in regularity and functions. I tend to do purifications only once a moon cycle since I do regular cleansings of self and space. I do cleansings regularly, before I engage in any magickal or psychic practice, or if I'm feeling particularly energetically dirty. You don't have to get obsessive with cleansing and purification. Treat cleansings like washing your hands. You wash your hands before you eat, but probably don't take a shower before you eat every meal; you probably shower regularly, just not nearly as often as washing your hands. Likewise, it would help if you were cleansed before engaging in spiritual activities. You will notice a massive difference in your flow and connection to the energy you're dealing with.

Exercise 24

ⵦ

The Cleansing Elixir

Magickal timing: Anytime

Materia:
- a glass
- drinking water

Purpose: This is my version of the Kala rite. I originally learned the Kala rite from Storm Faerywolf, who teaches a few different versions of it in his book *Betwixt and Between*[47] and in his witchcraft school Black Rose Witchcraft at the Modern Witch University.

The Kala rite is a foundational practice in the Faery/Feri tradition of witchcraft. Essentially the ritual is one of transmuting energy that you have instead of releasing it. It allows you to transform your blockages as well as mental and emotional energy that is not serving you into something that empowers and heals you.

Directions: Begin by filling up a glass of water. Take that water and hold it to your belly, the cauldron point of the Lower Self. Focus on your Lower Self, also known as the "sticky one" that absorbs and holds on to emotions and psychic energies. As you hold the water to your belly, feel all your negativity and blockages welling up inside of you.

Begin to breathe in a slow and steady manner, envisioning this negativity like a toxic sludge or blackened smoke beginning to leave your body and energy and fill the water between your hands, through the direction of your breath through your willpower.

Next you will be calling upon the great Source/Spirit. In the Faery tradition, they tend to use the Star Goddess as the name of this force. Feel free to replace "All-Powerful Spirit" with whatever your notion of the Great Mystery may be.

Raise the glass of negative energy up to your heart, the cauldron point of the Middle Self. In a firm and powerful voice, call out:

---

47. Faerywolf, *Betwixt and Between*.

I call upon the All-Powerful Spirit
Whose body composes reality
Who was, and is, and ever shall be
The endless one of eternity!

Feel the presence of Source begin to surround you. You are composed of this force, as is everything, as is nothing.

Next, focus on your Higher Self, that part of you that is Source and has never left Source.

Bring your focus back to the glass at your heart. Focus on your intention of transforming the glass, and in a firm and powerful voice, call out:

Spirit, transform with your divine light,
The contents of this glass I hold.
Cleanse it. Perfect it. Make it right.
From darkened lead to brilliant gold!

Envision Spirit beginning to merge with you and empower you, making your aura glow with a fire-like energy of divinity. For added potency you may want to perform "Soul Alignment and the Witch Fire" (Exercise 60 in my book *Psychic Witch*). As your Witch Fire burns, raise the glass to your forehead, the cauldron point of the Higher Self.

Ignite in me the ancient Witch Fire
Release in me what needs to go
Transmute this water by my desire
As the Cosmic Power starts to flow!

With your will and imagination, see the darkened water begin to spark and glow, slowly turning into crystalline waters of healing. Then proceed to drink the water. To finish, state:

Impurities healed
The magick sealed
As above, so below
By my Will, I make it so!

Exercise 25

❧

Clearing Psychic Gunk Tub Tea Spell
By Adam Sartwell

Magickal timing: This is a mostly as needed spell and can be done at any time. It can be made stronger by utilizing the waning moon. This type of cleansing is stronger when the moon is in the water signs of Cancer, Scorpio, or Pisces.

Materia:
- tablespoon dried or fresh hyssop
- tablespoon dried or fresh lemongrass
- tablespoon of dried or fresh lavender flower
- large mason jar
- boiling water
- a handful of Epsom salts
- optional: 6 drops lavender essential oil for each usage

Purpose: Psychics can sometimes be very sensitive to the energies we encounter. Whether it is our work environment, a party, or a day of reading at a psychic fair we can come home with leftover energies and patterns that are not ours. This tub tea spell has served me well in getting me to relax and let go.

Directions: Get out your mason jar and start heating up your water to boiling. Hold the dried herbs one at a time in your hand imagining them full of light and energy. In your mind or out loud call on the essential spirit of that plant to come forth and help you cleanse and clear yourself. Pour the herbs into the mason jar and fill to the top with boiling water. Place a plate on top of it to hold in any essentials from the herbs that might escape through steam. Let this steep for at least fifteen minutes; past then it can be used or steeped for longer but no more than a day. Strain out the herbs and you can use this right away, or save for up to two days in the fridge.

Add this mixture to a warm bath. You can put the whole thing in the bath for a stronger cleansing or if you are being gentle with yourself you can get three baths out of the tub tea. It is all up to your preference on whether to do one strong cleansing or three gentle ones. Add the handful of Epsom salts to your bath for extra cleansing and optionally some lavender essential oil.

Over the prepared bath hold out your hands and imagine the water filled with cleansing light.

Say this chant or something of your own devising:

By Crone, Mother, and Maiden pure
Cleanse and clear me of what I endure
Herbs, salt and Goddess divine
Leave me only with what is mine.

Slip into the bath, imagining it absorbing all the gunk you have picked up and neutralizing its energy. Say the chant again while in the bath and relax. You can do any cleaning meditations to enhance it more while in the bath. When you get out of the bath as you pull the plug say the chant for the final time, imagining all that gunk going down the drain.

Exercise 26

Psychic Enhancement Bath Salt

Magickal timing: Full moon and/or on Mondays

Materia:
- 1 cup Epsom salts
- 1 cup sea salt
- 10 drops lavender essential oil
- 10 drops jasmine essential oil
- 5 drops mugwort essential oil
- 3 drops peppermint essential oil
- 1 large bowl for mixing
- 16 oz. (or larger) mason jar for storage

Purpose: Magickal baths can do more than just cleanse your energy, they can also bring in specific energies at the same time, soaking your body and infusing that energy into your aura. This is my go-to bath formula when I need that extra boost of psychic connectivity. There are a few traditional rules when it comes to spiritual or magickal baths. One is that you don't use soap or shampoo or anything like that. Your physical body should already be cleansed; if not, then take a bath or shower before taking your spiritual bath. There are a few reasons for this, but mostly it's because you're engaging with ritual and separating this act of spiritual bathing with mundane bathing. It's also traditional to air dry instead of using a towel with magickal baths. See it as an act of the energy absorbing into you instead of wiping it away or soaking it into a towel. I normally just stay in the bathtub and meditate for a few minutes until dry. If you can't take a bath or don't have a bathtub, you can modify any spiritual bath into a shower by adding the salts into a pitcher of warm water instead of directly into the bathtub. Then while in the shower, slowly pour it over your head ensuring at least some of the water covers your whole body.

Directions: To make this formula add the 2 cups of salt to the bowl and mix thoroughly. Add the essential oils to the salt, ensuring the drop amount is precise. As you add an essential oil, ask it for its assistance in creating this for each oil you use. For example: "Spirit of lavender, I ask for your assistance in creating this Psychic Enhancement Bath Salt" then repeat the same with jasmine, mugwort, and peppermint.

With a spoon begin to stir clockwise, mixing it thoroughly. As you do say,

> *I stir this salt within this bowl*
> *I stir this salt with my Three Souls.*
> *Plant spirits four, assist with this spell*
> *So that psychic senses are heightened well.*

Keep repeating this as you stir until you intuitively feel that you're done mixing it. Store it in your mason jar. When you take a bath, use about two handfuls of salt. As you add the salt to the water say:

With this salt, I transform this water. No longer is it just water, but an elixir of psychic enhancement, so that whatever is dipped within it is infused with its energy.

Then soak.

Exercise 27

❧

Spiritual Vermifuge
By Christopher Penczak

Magickal timing: Dark moon or waning moon nearest to the dark; otherwise a Tuesday for Mars or Saturday for Saturn

Materia:
- garlic (powdered or fresh) in a small bowl
- charcoal disc
- incense tongs
- incense burner such as a small cauldron or brass bowl with sand or salt to disperse the heat allowing you to safely hold it

Purpose: Just as our physical body can get infections in the form of pathogens, our subtle bodies have corresponding infections. While this can sound scary to a new practitioner, it is simply a fact of life for everyone, though most people unaware of their subtle bodies are unaware of subtle infections unless they have corresponding physical infections. Just as the material world has bacteria, viruses, and in particular, parasites, so too do the subtle levels. These creatures, while unpleasant, are not evil. They only cause problems when our natural subtle immune systems are too depleted to effectively deal with them. While you would think psychics, witches, and healers would have a strong natural immunity, we are also the groups most likely to overextend our vital energy doing magickal projects and can be more susceptible to these infecting forces.

Psychic bacteria that passes from human to human is usually cultivated in humans' first, unwanted thoughtforms that are projected and multiplied from imbalanced and unhealthy thoughts and ideas that take root and are fed emotional energy. They are sometimes referred to as thought viruses and rule our mob mentality. They can be even more powerful in the days of social media. The true psychic equivalents of viruses are usually from the nonhuman elemental realms, attachments of energies from elemental spirits, land spirits, and faery beings, usually when humans have been in the wrong place at the wrong time, doing the wrong thing in nature, often desecrating it, knowingly or unknowingly.

Psychic parasites are entities that drain our vital and psychic life forces to live, often keying into strong emotions. They are akin to physical tape worms, ticks, and leeches. They can be unknowingly passed from a client to reader or healer. Prolonged depression, fear, and anger are often forces that attract them, and prolonged drug and alcohol abuse stemming from such feelings can create easy access. Thankfully, herbs that have antimicrobial and antiparasitic properties—with antiparasitic herbs being known as vermifuges, as they "fumigate" vermin from the system—have similar spiritual properties. Some of the best herbs include agrimony, black cohosh, black walnut, peppermint, tansy, thyme, turmeric, and especially wormwood, but an easy, very effective, and fairly safe one is garlic. Fresh garlic cloves or dried garlic powder is easily accessible for most of us and incredibly effective for all forms of basic psychic infection.

Directions: Ideally perform this as the moon is waning near the dark moon to banish harmful forces. If you need it during a waxing moon phase, then try to time it for a Mars day (Tuesday) or Saturn day (Saturday), to best evoke the powers of garlic. If you are using fresh garlic, peel and mince the garlic with a knife so you have small pieces of garlic, though you might find dry garlic powder from the kitchen spice rack is actually better to use.

Light your charcoal, the kind traditionally used for loose granular incense, and carefully place the disc upon the sand or salt in your incense burner without burning yourself. Use incense tongs if necessary. A cauldron with a handle is ideal for the incense burner, allowing you to pick up and move the vessel. Hold the garlic in a small bowl and enchant it by feeling your subtle energy in your hands mix with its own vital life force, warm and fiery, and say:

I call upon the spirit of garlic to lend its might.
Release me from all known and unknown
Spiritual infections, parasites, and attached entities.
I ask this for my highest healing good.
So mote it be!

Then sprinkle the garlic upon the charcoal. If it's fresh minced, go sparingly at first, as the wet pieces will sizzle a bit. Add more as you go. The released energy is more important than the smoke. Do not directly breathe in the smoke as it will be quite acrid, but gently spiral with it fairly close to your body, rotating your body counterclockwise, and with each complete circle, extending your arm a little further out, creating a spiral of smoke and fiery garlic plant spirit energy around you. When you feel the spiral is as wide around you as it can be, pause in the center. Place the incense burner down. Take a deep breath in and when you exhale, exhale forcefully, exhaling any and all unwanted psychic pathogens and parasites into the newly created garlic spirit energy around you. Imagine them either breaking down or feeling far away from you because of the energy of garlic. Do this three times, with three deep breaths and forceful exhales. Pause and notice the difference in how you feel.

Place a little more garlic upon the charcoal and hold the incense burner out at arm's length. Start slowly spiraling by turning your body clockwise and gradually draw the incense burner closer to you, creating an inward spiral. When you reach the center, pause and focus upon your own psychic protection shield being infused with the blessings and magick of garlic, to ward off future infections and parasites. Say this to complete the spell:

I thank the spirit of garlic and ask for your
Further blessing to be infused in my aura.
Protect me from future infections and attachments.
Blessed be.

Ground yourself as needed at the end, perhaps drinking a bit of water to balance the fiery energy.

Repeat this ritual spell as you feel necessary.

Exercise 28

∞

Sea Salt Fire Purification

Magickal timing: This spell can be performed at any time.

Materia:
- sea salt
- a fireproof surface
- a cauldron or fireproof dish (preferably one with legs elevating it)
- a high percentage proof of alcohol
- matches

Purpose: The Sea Salt Fire Purification is my go-to method of cleansing a room when I need to wipe the energy out of an area completely. This technique will remove almost all of the miasma within a room, so it may also nullify objects and spells you have about, and you will most likely need to recharge and re-empower them after this. This technique is also beneficial if you're having trouble removing a spirit that doesn't want to leave, since this will cut off the energy supply it's feeding off of and using to manifest in this plane of reality.

Most people think of salt as a magickal cleansing item, and it definitely can be. The truth is, it's a highly versatile mineral susceptible to however we work with it. Salt is a crystal, and just like crystals, it can be programmed in various ways. Since salt's crystalline structure is that of tiny cubes, being the Platonic solid associated with the element of earth, they have a strong influence on the physical and etheric levels of reality. Salt is also the Middle World's alchemical element through correspondence with the Middle Self.[48]

While performing this ritual, please be extremely careful and always consider your safety. The flame from this burning is enormous and should never be left unattended. This technique shouldn't be a standard form of cleansing. Instead, think of it more like a deep cleaning of energy. If you maintain healthy cleansing habits, you shouldn't need to use this often. This technique should be used when you need more powerful cleansing methods such as after a severe

---

48. Penczak, *The Three Rays*, 63.

illness, a death, intense emotional energy, a haunting, or when there's just an extreme amount of negative energy stuck in an area that isn't lifting out.

Directions: Fill your palm with sea salt and direct your awareness to it. Though not required, to increase the empowerment of this, perform a Soul Alignment and direct your personal Witch Fire into it.[49]

I ask the spirit of salt to partner with me
to cleanse and purify the energy of this room.

Place the sea salt into the cauldron. Pour alcohol into the cauldron, enough to cover the sea salt but not so much that it's drowning in alcohol. Take a match and strike it stating:

As my words do proclaim
As this salt is lit aflame
Discordant energies on this plane
Are burned away without remains.

Drop the match into the cauldron. As the salt and alcohol mixture is lit, visualize the flame drawing all the discordant energy toward it like a vacuum and burning it away as it comes near. Remember that it's very likely to burn away energy that isn't discordant either. You will notice a complete shift in the room. Be sure to open a window to bring in some fresh energy from outside.

Exercise 29

The Cinnamon Purification Rite

Magickal timing: This spell can be performed at any time

Materia:
- powdered cinnamon (*Cinnamomum verum*)

---

49. See Exercise 60 on page 132 of *Psychic Witch*.

Purpose: One of my favorite forms of quick purification before ritual or spell work is a super simple method that I originally learned from Jack Grayle's courses and book[50] that uses ground cinnamon. His method was inspired by the PGM. The PGM is an abbreviation for the Greek Magical Papyri. The Greek Magical Papyri is a Roman-Egyptian collection of spells of eclectic syncretism sorcery from the third century BCE. Not only is cinnamon purifying and sanctifying[51] but the PGM states "The deity is pleased by it and gave it power."[52] The deity it's referring to is mentioned as the "Aion of Aions" or what we could simply think of as Spirit (with a capital S), Source, or even Baphomet in a modern occult context, or however you may conceptualize the highest power within the universe.

This is the modification and greatly adapted version of this cleansing that I use in my own practice. The great thing about this purification is that it doesn't involve burning anything and ground cinnamon is super easy to carry with you wherever you may be. You can even grab some from your grocery store in the small containers and keep it in your car or in your purse or backpack.

I have also found that through consistent use of this method, the clairtangency in my hands seems to strengthen and along with it the power of psychometry, which is gaining psychic information through touching things.

Directions: Sprinkle about a dime-sized amount of cinnamon into your palm. Ground and center yourself.

With the cinnamon in your palm begin rubbing your hands together. Say:

> *I call to Cinnamomum verum, the plant spirit of cinnamon.*
> *I ask that you fully cleanse my physical body to be worthy of the gods.*

From here on, you want to take your hands and brush them around your aura starting around your head down to your feet.[53] Repeat this action with each sentence.

---

50. Grayle, *The Hekatæon*, 21.
51. Blackthorn, *Blackthorn's Botanical Magic*, 117.
52. Betz (translator), *The Greek Magical Papyri in Translation*, 175, 182, and 188.
53. For a review of the various layers of the aura (the etheric body, astral body, and so on) see Chapter 14 *of Psychic Witch*.

May my etheric body be as pure as my physical body.
May my astral body be as pure as my etheric body.
May my emotional body be as pure as my astral body.
May my mental body be as pure as my emotional body.
May my psychic body be as pure as my mental body.
May my divine body be as pure as my psychic body.

Place your palms together at your chest and state:

May I be purified and cleansed on all levels. May my Lower Self
be as pure as my Middle Self and my Middle Self as pure as my
Higher Self and my Higher Self as pure as the gods themselves.

Take one of your cinnamon-dusted fingers and draw an equal arm cross-roads on the back of your neck starting with top to bottom stating:

As above, so below.

Then left to right:

As within, so without.

And finish by affirming:

I am cleansed.

There shouldn't be much cinnamon on your hand, but if there's any excess go ahead and dust your hands off or wash your hands.

The Importance of Shielding and Warding

It is important to take responsibility for our own thoughts, emotions, energy, and actions, rather than constantly pointing at others. Often we are our own worst enemies, and I have seen many people fall into a paranoia that someone was working negative magick on them when they essentially cursed them-selves. By ensuring that we live a life of integrity and ethics, we reduce our chances of accumulating and perpetuating drama and unbalanced energies in our lives, whether magickal or otherwise. Living a life of integrity is one of the best defenses one can have in their magickal practices.

This doesn't mean we shouldn't focus on our protection or that if we are just good people or think only positive thoughts that we will be fine. Bad things can happen to good people, and anyone who suggests otherwise is foolish. In his 1970s classic *Mastering Witchcraft*, Paul Huson advises the reader that "The moment that you set foot upon the path of witchcraft a call rings out in the unseen world announcing your arrival."[54] Doreen Valiente, also suggested the similar dangers of magick: "Many people will tell you that occultism, witchcraft and magic are dangerous." She assures us that it's worth it, though, continuing to state that "So they are; so is crossing the road; but we shall not get far if we are afraid ever to attempt it. However, we can choose either to dash across recklessly, or to use our common sense and cross with care, and so it is with magic."[55] She then continues to explain that magick can be a high-risk force, just like electricity, atomic power, television, the power of the press, or anything else that has power, and argues that magickal power, like those mentioned, can also be helpful and enhance our lives.

This is why we don't want to rush into magickal, psychic, or any other energetic practices without any care or concern for safety. Magickal practices should be thoughtfully and respectfully engaged. This includes taking protective precautions. You could hurt yourself severely when baking a cake if you aren't wearing oven mitts when taking it out of the oven. Do not let hubris or overconfidence make you think that you can just pull the burning hot cake pan out of the oven with your bare hands. Likewise, don't rush into energy work without protections because you feel you're too skilled to need any protection. Being a good driver doesn't mean you don't need to wear a seatbelt.

While in an ideal world we wouldn't have to protect ourselves from other people or spirits, unfortunately we sometimes do. One of my greatest lessons is that assuming that just because I have good intentions and don't want to harm or control other people, that doesn't mean that other people are coming from the same mentality or have the same motives. The world is a dangerous place filled

---

54. Huson, *Mastering Witchcraft*, 136.
55. Valiente, *Natural Magick*, 11.

with dangerous people, and this includes the non-physical as well. Sometimes we do need to defend ourselves, and ignoring protection is straight-up naive.

Some people will sometimes interchange the words "shielding" and "warding," but there is an important difference between them. Shielding is what it sounds like, adding a layer of protection around oneself, an object, or a place. Warding is inherently apotropaic, which means that it actively repels negative energies and forces. To ward something literally means to turn something away. Think of shielding as a turtle shell and warding as the bright colors on venomous animals that signal and warn other animals to stay away. Another way to think of the difference is that moats around a castle are a form of shielding that makes it harder for invaders to enter, while gargoyles positioned on or around the castle are intended to be apotropaic, designed to intimidate people and spirits, decreasing the probability of an attack.

Exercise 30

∞

Seal of the Nine Heavens
By Benebell Wen

Magickal timing: Waning crescent moon, as close to the dark moon as possible; this is associated with yin energy, which is when spirit presence is most empowered

Materia:
- red candles (you'll need as many candles as it takes to adequately illuminate your ritual space during an evening hour)
- sandalwood or cedar wood incense
- red vermilion ink
- medium to paint the seal onto

Purpose: The seal features stylized oracle bone script that are the four characters of Jiu Tian Xuan Nu's name (九天玄女), also known as the Lady of the Ninth Heaven (or Nine Heavens). She was a protégé of the Empress Mother of the West, considered a dark goddess, where this protégé of the goddess mastered the occult arts and warfare. Later, she herself became the patron goddess of the Yellow Emperor. According to lore, the Lady of the Nine

Heavens taught the emperor's court magic and military strategy. Through the dynasties, she has embodied different powers to different people, though she is beloved by occultists in particular for her association with ceremonial magic and witchcraft. The Lady of the Nine Heavens is considered a dark goddess, like her mentor, one who does not shy from retributive justice. Yet she is also considered beneficent and merciful through her connections to Kuan Yin.

The ritual rendering of her seal by an occultist who possesses integrity, honor, beneficence, loyalty, and moral excellence, and who knows of or intuits imminent psychic threats of harm from another, can call upon the Lady of the Nine Heavens for protection. This seal can also break or sever any malefic attachments on your personhood. Your artistry in rendering the seal is not as important as your sincerity, so do not worry about the aesthetic value or line accuracy of your sigil.

Directions: In a darkened room at a late hour, illuminate your space by candlelight only. From one of the candle flames, light the incense. Incense smoke connects the human and celestial worlds. You will be inscribing the seal's design onto a smooth surface, which you can then keep on you as a talisman. Consider a disc of wood, a flat round stone, or a cabochon.

Inscribe the first character of her name (九), meaning Nine. As you write out the character, recite or form the pronunciation with your mouth, "Jiǔ."

Then, saturating your next words, prayer, or thoughts with the sincerest emotion you're feeling, confess what is troubling you and the nature of your purpose for calling upon the Lady of the Ninth Heaven. Speak or express your feelings in your native language.

Inscribe the second character (天), meaning Heaven. Recite or form the pronunciation "Tiān."

Formally request divine protection. Use words of reverence and respect. Here, also offer why a greater good is served if you are protected and kept safe. This does not need to be a quid pro quo pact; rather, it should be a reiteration of the good you do for the world around you and a renewed vow to continue to serve those in need.

Inscribe the third character (玄) to the left of the second, as we are writing to form a circle with the seal, clockwise. This character means "of the Mysteries" or "the Occult." There's an implication of darkness or the unseen. Recite or form the pronunciation "Xuán" (shwen, a "sh" sound that rhymes with "wren").

Visualize all the emotions you have been generating as threads or tendrils of energy that you are now collecting and binding together into a united force.

With intention, convert that united force into vindication. Feel how, starting from the crown of your head, running and surging through you down to your feet, you feel a divine empowerment intensify and engulf you, amplifying your personal power. This is the successful invocation of Jiu Tian Xuan Nu, who sent a wave of power and psychic invulnerability through you.

The final character (女) means Lady or Woman. As you write the character, recite or form the pronunciation "Nǚ" (say "ee" like "she" first, pucker your lips as if you're whistling, then add the "n" sound in front). As you do so, relax, unwind, loosen all tensions in your body and mind, and speak words of sincere gratitude to Jiu Tian Xuan Nu for appearing for you and endowing you with the power to protect yourself.

Moving clockwise, draw a circle around the four characters and as you draw the circle, recite "Ji Ji Ru Lu Ling" (急急如律令), a traditional esoteric Taoist closing to a spell, likened to "So mote it be." Set the painted seal on your altar and let it sit there until it has fully dried.

The painted seal is now empowered. It will deflect and disperse any arrows of baneful magic directed at you. If there had been malefic spirit attachments, holding the painted seal breaks those attachments and causes the malefic spirit to be evicted from your presence. (In the case of a malefic spirit attachment, once that personal attachment has been broken, then consider a ritual banishment of the spirit from the environs altogether.)

Even if you have not worked with the Lady of the Nine Heavens before, she will appear and honor the petitions of any practitioner who has integrity, honor, beneficence, loyalty, and moral excellence, and who has been unjustly harmed.

Exercise 31

∾

A Psychic Protection Kind of Evening
By Storm Faerywolf

Magickal timing: Anytime before sunrise, when the spell will end

Materia:
- a small clear quartz crystal
- a white candle
- matches or a lighter
- a piece of paper, roughly 2-inch square
- a pen
- a small cotton or muslin pouch on a string, or a tea infuser
- small amounts of rosemary, lavender, mugwort, salt, and whole black peppercorns
- a medium bowl half-filled with water
- a cauldron or ash pot

Purpose: This spell is intended to enforce a short-term, semi-permeable boundary around your consciousness to enable you to engage in psychic work while remaining protected from unwanted influences.

Directions: Gather your items. Begin by performing whatever grounding or centering exercise(s) with which you are most comfortable. Once complete, hold the crystal in your hand so that if you look through it, you are looking at the unlit candle wick. Light the candle and say,

From the darkness I conjure light
Within me shine and guide my way.

Imagine that the light of the candle is being transmitted to you through the crystal, and that this light is one and the same as the divine light within yourself. Focusing on this inner light, write your name on the paper in a reverent manner, holding the same attitude that you would for the giving of an offering to a god. Now, fold it up into a little square then draw a pentacle upon it. Now, press the crystal against it and CAREFULLY drip some of the wax over the whole thing in order to seal it all up. Make sure to completely cover the crystal and the paper.

Once dried, place it in the pouch or diffuser, along with a pinch of each herb and some salt. Close or tie it up. Cast a small handful of the black peppercorns into the bowl of water (representing negative forces), along with the lavender (positive forces), rosemary (cleansing/protection), and mugwort (psychic vision). Sprinkle a pinch of salt in a counterclockwise circle in the bowl of water. Lower the pouch or diffuser into the center of the water. Imagining that the crystal is still shining with your inner light. Begin stirring the water with the pouch/diffuser as you chant:

> *Light that shines from deep inside*
> *Act upon me now as guide*
> *Reverse all shade, repel all fright*
> *Defend my soul until first light.*

Continue repeating the final two lines of the spell as you raise power into the water. The positive forces are both within and outside your boundaries, symbolized by the pouch or infuser. The negative forces stay out. When you feel ready, raise the pouch or diffuser and catch some of the runoff water, using it to anoint yourself on the third eye, throat, the back of the neck where the skull meets the spine, and hands. Dip it back into the bowl and raise it up, again catching the runoff and now sprinkling some all around you. Keep the wax-covered charm with you for the rest of the evening. At sunrise the spell will be broken. The water may be poured around the home, while you may dispose of the herbs as you see fit. Dismantle the charm the following day, by retrieving the crystal (to be kept for future protection spells) and burning the wax-covered paper in your cauldron.

Exercise 32

⤨⤨

Evil Eye Bottle Spell

Magickal timing: On a Saturday

Materia:
- A blue glass bottle

Purpose: The belief in the evil eye is widespread, including both polytheistic and monotheistic religions throughout the world. The basic idea is that someone can send you harmful energy from holding jealousy or ill thoughts about you in their heart, which is transferred to you when they look at you. Written references to the evil eye go as far back as ancient Ugarit, and most likely, the belief in it goes even further back in history. However, the most extensive writings we have on the evil eye comes from Classical Greek authors.

Interestingly, there appears to be a recurring theme among different religions, traditions, and cultures about what averts the evil eye—that's the symbol of the eye, a hand, and deep blue color. Certain amulets to protect against the evil eye, such as nazar beads, incorporate both, depicting an eye and usually a deep blue color. Other amulets such as the hamsa charm incorporate all three. However, due to ancient cultural exchange, tracking down the origins of the hamsa and nazar charms is very difficult as they're found in many variations through the Mediterranean and Middle Eastern cultures, ranging from Judaism to Hinduism to Islam to Greek paganism.

Growing up, I was unfamiliar with evil eye amulets until I came across them in metaphysical shops. It wasn't until I was older that I realized the same logic used in charms such as the hamsa or nazar beads was very similar to a tradition I was taught as a child. While my family wasn't openly magickal, there were some practices they referred to as "superstitious" that they've held on to, despite being magickal in nature. Instead of being called magick, it was just "something you did." The interesting thing about these practices is that they talked about them equally as if they believed and didn't believe in them, but that it was "better to be safe than sorry." In retrospect, these seem like the remnants of old folk magick that persisted through generations but conflicted with the modern religious beliefs of my family.

One such practice was to keep the evil of others out by taking empty bottles made of dark blue glass and placing them on the windowsill where the sun would shine through. I've taken this practice and put more magickal intent behind it.

Directions: Make sure the bottle is clean and empty. Take the bottle and hold it in your hands, speaking to it:

> *Blessed bottle of deep dark blue*
> *Sing for me a song that's true*
> *A song that repels and protects*
> *Against energies my foes project.*

Place your lower lip against the edge of the top of the bottle and blow across it in a long exhale, causing it to make an elongated resonant sound. You can do this a few times if you wish, then declare:

> *This bottle of deep dark blue*
> *As rich as the sea and sky*
> *Will never allow through*
> *The forces of the evil eye*

Place the bottle on a windowsill to do its job.

Exercise 33

❦

Scraping Away Attachments and Cords

Magickal timing: Any

Materia:
- A dull blade of some sort, preferably a boline made of iron or steel

Purpose: Scraping is a technique that I learned initially from Aidan Wachter in his book *Six Ways: Approaches and Entries into Practical Magic.*[56] I have

---

56. Wachter, *Six Ways*, 148–149.

been using it since I first learned about it and have adapted it over time. This technique essentially cuts away any attachments, parasites, hooks, or energetic cords that you've either picked up on your own or that have been maliciously sent your way under other circumstances. This is particularly helpful if you feel that someone is draining your energy psychically, intentionally, or unintentionally.

For this exercise, you will need a dull blade of some sort, such as most athames for sale, or my preferred tool for this, the boline, a hand scythe used for cutting plants in witchcraft. You want to ensure that the blade isn't sharp as you will be working close to your skin, and you don't want to cut yourself. Aidan suggests performing this ritual about an inch away from your body. For me, this makes absolute sense as this is where the etheric level of your aura resides, which is the last place in multidimensional reality before something is physically manifested. The etheric is where the energy takes on a form the strongest and becomes the most permanent over time. So, by clearing from this level, you're clearing the other layers of the aura further out as well.

Directions: Throughout this technique, visualize that your boline is glowing with a black aura. Black is the color of Saturn and is associated with protection, removal, and energetic boundaries. Then, holding your boline in your right hand, very slowly sweep it over the left side of your body from head to toe about an inch or so over your body. Focus on your will and intent to slice away anything unhelpful attached to your energy. While doing so, chant:

> *Tool of Saturn, cut and clear*
> *Attachments that have thus adhered*
> *To my aura without consent*
> *Severed by will and strong intent.*
> *Be they parasites, hooks, or cords*
> *Or other thoughtforms of discord*
> *I scrape their influence off from me*
> *Becoming clean, and clear, and free.*

Now repeat this with the right side of your body with your boline in your left hand.

Once done with the scraping technique, take a moment to feel how clean and clear you are from these attachments and hooks. While doing so, visualize your energy body glowing white and becoming more assertive in its strength. It's increasing its immunity just as the body does after successfully fighting off a virus. Declare:

With this energetic clarity
I now increase my immunity
Against unhelpful energies
That attempt to attach to me.

Finish by shielding yourself.[57]

Exercise 34
❧
Psychic Witch Cord
By Devin Hunter

Magickal timing: New moon

Materia:
- cord at least as long as your height
- yarn (black, blue, purple, silver, or gold)
- black fabric pouch
- Psychic Protection Charm Bag herbs (mugwort, rue, black pepper)
- your own hair
- blue fabric pouch
- Clair-sense Booster Charm Bag herbs (lavender, yarrow, rose, bismuth)
- white paper
- a small bottle (with a closed handle or large mouth)
- Spirit Guide Bottle Spell herbs (rosemary, rosehips)
- bell or chime

---

57. For a review of foundational shielding, see Exercise 43 on page 79 of *Psychic Witch*.

Purpose: A "witch cord" is a magickal tool that has seen many names and permutations throughout history. In some traditions they are referred to as "witches' ladders" or "devil's tails" and in others as the slightly less intimidating "fairy ropes." They are a type of vertical hanging altar made of empowered rope or twine with multiple talismans, charms, and amulets tied or braided together, and they can be constructed for any number of reasons.

Witch cords are great in that they help us to tackle a goal from multiple directions, and fuse together the magic of several smaller (and interchangeable) workings into one large harmonious working. For our purposes, we will be making a psychic witch cord, which is made especially to boost natural psychic abilities, provide protection from astral nasties and, among other things, to assist in spirit guide communication.

Directions: To create a witch cord we first must take our "measure." This is an old witchcraft practice usually observed by covens during initiation wherein the measure was taken to ostensibly create a sort of crude magickal clone of the new member. This is usually kept by the presiding clergy and used to access that member magickally later if needed. For our purposes, you will be creating a measure that will be used as cord to which the amulets and other spells will be attached.

To make this central piece of the working, you will want to begin with a length of cord that measures your total height. This cord should not exceed ½-inch thickness or knotting will become an issue later on and will adjust the length too much. I recommend using black; however, feel free to use whatever color you feel best represents your psychic energy. Tie off both ends of the cord to prevent fraying. This represents the first measurement.

Grab one of the ends and wrap it once around your wrist, then tie a knot where the end meets the cord. This is the second measurement. To take the third measurement, take that same end and wrap it around your waist, tying a knot in the location where the end meets the cord. Do this again for your chest and neck to take the final two measurements. Once you have tied all six knots, you have taken your measure. Next, bless the cord by hovering it over your favorite psychic incense and saying:

Head to ground and all around,
My measure here I take.

Freely given, magically driven,
This work shall never break!

Fold the cord in half and tie a loop in the center so it can hang freely off a hook or doorknob.

Now, the rest is really up to you! What you attach to this cord can be anything from jewelry to spell bottles and charm bags, to tarot cards or art that you hole-punch. I sometimes even make my own beads by drilling shells and bark. The only limit is your imagination, and since we are talking about your psychic well-being, take this as an opportunity to get specific with your needs. That being said, here are four amulets that you should add to your starter cord. Remember, you can always change these out later and update the cord as your needs change. Once you make each of these, attach it to the cord using black, blue, purple, silver, or gold thread or yarn. You can tie them directly to the cord or you can get creative and weave them into the original braid of the cord. (Feel free to adjust these as necessary for your resources.)

1. **Psychic Protection Charm Bag**

   a. To a black fabric pouch add three pinches of mugwort, two pinches of rue, one pinch of black pepper, and a piece of your own hair.

   b. Empower by reciting the charm:

      Mugwort, rue, black pepper, too;
      Shield me now, let nothing through!

2. **Clair-sense Booster Charm Bag**

   a. To a blue fabric pouch add seven pinches of lavender, five pinches of yarrow, three pinches of rose, and one small piece of bismuth.

   b. Empower it by reciting the incantation:

      As clear as my vision on a sunny day,
      my psychic gifts never lead me astray.

3. **Spirit Guide Bottle Spell**

    a. On a small piece of white paper, draw an image of your spirit guide, roll it up, and then put it in small bottle (preferably with a handle or thick lip that will make adding it to the cord easier). If you are not familiar with who your guide is, draw what you think a spirit guide looks like. To that bottle, also add two pinches of rosemary and a pinch of rosehips.

    b. To empower the bottle, gently blow into the mouth of the bottle and then say:

    > *Spirit take this breath as yours,*
    > *Break all barriers and open doors.*
    > *Let us be together just as one,*
    > *Let us be together, there is work to be done.*

4. **ESP Enhancement Chime**

    a. Cleanse and empower a small bell or chime to help enhance your awareness of environmental shifts in energy.

    b. Empower it by reciting the charm,

    > *Keen to changes great and small,*
    > *I shall know them one and all!*

After adding each piece to the cord, spend a few moments visualizing the different parts all working together for the common outcome, which in this case is a psychic-empowered you. Visualize a white light emanating from your third eye and see it being absorbed by the cord, eventually absorbing so much that it emanates with that white light, and say:

> *One by one you join my cord,*
> *Meet me here for I'm your ward.*
> *By the powers and all they bless,*
> *By witches' will and nothing less;*

What is woven here in rhyme
Shall endure for all of time!

Hang the cord over your altar or in a location where you will visit it often. During the full moon, revisit the cord, connect to it, and feed it energy by performing the cord blessing above.

Exercise 35

∞

Lavender Lemon Psychic Connection Wash
By Lilith Dorsey

Magickal timing: Any

Materia:
- juice of 1 lemon
- ½ ounce dried or fresh lavender blossoms
- 1 tablespoon dried mugwort
- 1 tablespoon powdered myrrh
- 1 tablespoon powdered galangal
- 1 small piece fresh ginger root
- 1 cup spring water
- 1 cup tap water
- large glass jar
- saucepan
- white natural fabric cloth

Purpose: Spells can come in many different formats. Many draw their strength from the elements. Earth, air, fire, and water have their own special magicks and every psychic knows ways to use them to help improve their power. This particular spell is a wash that capitalizes on the immense power of water.

This formula starts with two main ingredients: lemon and lavender. You may be more familiar with these in your kitchen or garden. Lemon is known to bring about protection and purification, necessary components when you are attempting to connect with other realms, while lavender is a beautiful floral scent that is known to attract beneficial energy. Mugwort, myrrh, galangal, and ginger will all help to open you up to psychic energy. The last two wash ingredients are waters. Spring water, bursting forth from deep inside the earth, will refresh and rejuvenate your working. Tap water is a humble ingredient that in actuality represents your own special spirit of place.

This water will connect the wash to your home.

Directions: Gather all your ingredients together on your sacred space or working altar. Heat the waters in the saucepan to simmer. Just as it begins to simmer, remove it from the heat and add the lemon juice, lavender, mugwort, myrrh, galangal, and ginger. Let it sit overnight, preferably placed on a windowsill where the moon's rays will touch it and give an added blessing. In the morning, strain the mixture through your cloth into the glass jar. (If you wish, discard the used herbs on your compost pile or bury them in the earth.) Your wash is now in the jar and ready to use. A splash is all you need. It can be added to your floor-washes, cleaning sprays, or even your bath to bring about a heightened connection and psychic awareness.

Chapter 5
SPIRITUAL SHAPES
AND SPIRITUAL SPACES

D ifferent shapes move and hold energy in different ways. The key is instructing the shape in how it is to behave and which part of its nature you want to activate. This is similar, for example, to the spiritual properties of a stone or plant, which contain various aspects in regard to the powers they possess; the witch, when working with a stone or plant, instructs or requests which parts of its nature it wants it to bring forth for the magickal working to assist in their intention. There's a saying that the bane and balm grow on the same stalk, meaning a plant often holds the opposites of its power. A plant that heals can poison and vice versa. It's just a matter of which part you're working with. The same is true for shapes. They have the ability to work in one way, and also its exact opposite. This aligns with the Hermetic Principles, which state everything also possesses the potential for its opposite, and can (and does) shift in scale from one pole to another. A lot of this information regarding shapes I originally learned from the teachings of Ivo Dominguez Jr. and his book on the subject, *Casting Sacred Space: The Core of All Magickal Work*. If the information in this chapter interests you, I highly suggest reading that book for further study on these ideas.

When it comes to the shapes of spiritual spaces, we have to examine what the purpose of any sacred space is and contemplate what your goals and motives are in your magickal work that you've set out to do. Primarily it allows us to create a space that is set aside and sacred. Casting sacred space creates a container for the energy work and magick that is being performed within it, or it creates a nexus point of things we want to bring together. It also orients us in time and space. In other words, it gives us some sense of where things are in the world of spirit, so that we have a frame of reference of where we are working and how we can interact with primordial energies of the universe. We must map out where things are before we can attempt to use them, and sacred space often does this by declaring where those things are within the framework created.

Another crucial aspect of casting sacred space is that it protects us. Some folks may say that they don't feel the need to be protected by other spirits when performing workings, but sacred space doesn't just protect one from spirits, it adjusts the energies to be workable. Think of performing magickal ritual being similar as going into water. Perhaps a simple swimsuit or going nude is acceptable. Perhaps you'll want a snorkel or goggles. In some scenarios you're going to want diving gear and an oxygen tank. In rare scenarios you might want a shark cage. You also might need a submarine. All these things protect the swimmer from various things, not just a hungry shark. It's protecting the oxygen of the swimmer, making it easier to move about within the water, and also protecting the swimmer from the crushing pressure of the ocean's depths. It also helps if you have radar to help orient you and tell you where you are and where you're going.

Sacred space creates a liminal environment where you are entering into other worlds and energies. While the swimming comparison may sound drastic, think about how fragile humans are on the physical. Not only can humans only live within very specific conditions of temperature, pressure, oxygen levels, and so on—but being comfortable is even more delicate. Think about how uncomfortable it is in the middle of winter or summer if your heating and air are turned off. You can still exist in those temperatures but it's much more difficult. This is simply our physical existence; now think about how sensitive we are when it comes to nonphysical energies and locations when we're engaging in magickal ritual. Keeping with our water metaphor, sacred space allows us to come back with much more ease afterward instead of suffering from "the bends" or gasping for oxygen.

Circles

Circles are worked with the most by witches and as such they are the shape I focused on in *Psychic Witch*. Circles create a cycle and circuit of energy allowing for flow and movement. This movement creates an expansive endlessness, which makes it perfect for use in magickal ritual to partition oneself from time and space while simultaneously tapping into all of time and space. However, circles can also focus and concentrate energy as well. Think of a whirlpool or a tornado or even a camera lens zooming in and out and you'll begin to understand this side of its nature. We can place things within circles to keep their energy flowing and we can place things in a circle to home in on them. For example, many witches will place poppets in circles for both of these reasons. This is also why scrying crystals tend to be spheres and scrying mirrors are often recommended to be circles. Because there are no angles in a circle and each part of it is perfectly and equally distributed, it makes it the most protective of shapes since there's no weak spot to breach. Likewise, in her book *Weave the Liminal*, Laura Tempest Zakroff points out that within a circle energy flows in a perfect circuit since there are no angles for energy to get trapped in.[58]

---

58. Zakroff, *Weave the Liminal*.

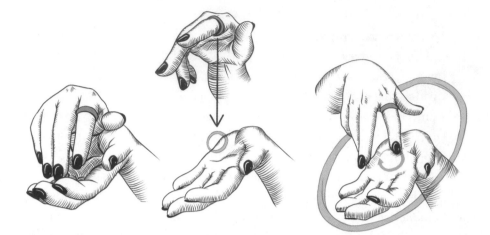

Exercise 36

~~~~

Jewelry Ring Circle Casting

Magickal timing: Any

Materia:

- A ring without a stone or any sort of setting on it

Purpose: This is one of my favorite tricks for a quick circle casting or a quick bubble of protection. The best part is that this casting is one of stealth, as it can be cast quickly and quietly without drawing attention. You will need a simple ring that fits on your pointer finger, since that finger is associated with Jupiter and therefore sovereignty, spiritual power, ceremony, and expansion. The one I use is a ring that's shaped like an ouroboros, the snake eating its own tail, which is perfect since that is a symbol of the magickal circle itself. When I'm not out and about I keep it on my altar to charge.

Directions: While wearing your ring, ground and center. Cup your hands as if you were holding something in them, with the hand with the ring (which should preferably be your dominant hand) on top of the other. Visualize blue electricity running through the ring, creating an energetic double of the ring. Feel the energetic ring double drop straight down through your finger between your hands and visualize the ring spinning clockwise. Slowly open your hands and as you do, feel this ring expand. With your dominant hand, draw a clockwise circle on the palm of your non-dominant hand. As you draw this, visualize the energetic ring expanding around you to the circumference you desire while either verbally stating or mentally declaring:

I cast this circle to create a space beyond space and a time beyond time.

Repeat this process again, dropping a second ring of energy into your hands and then expanding it through drawing on your non-dominant hand, this time saying or thinking:

I cast this circle to block out any energies and spirits that are not allies of mine.

Repeat this one more time and think or say:

I cast this circle so that all energies raised herein will be confined.

Visualize the three rings merging together into one giant ring and see it turn into a giant bubble surrounding you. Seal the circle by saying:

As above, so below! The circle is sealed!

Then snap your fingers on both hands in a statement of finalizing it.

To release the circle, hold out your dominant hand with your ring on it in front of you with your palm facing up. Envision the bubble forming back into a ring of electric blue energy and returning to your ring on your hand. As you do, feel all the energy of your magick rushing out into the universe to begin manifesting.

Exercise 37

❧

Healing Circle of Containment

Magickal timing: Anytime

Materia:
- the object you are containing (such as a poppet)
- if possible, a bell jar to fit the object, or a space for the object to be placed and remain where it won't be disturbed

Purpose: This is a technique in which you can cast a circle outside of yourself to keep the energy of the encircled object flowing, cycling, and moving. This is particularly useful when you're trying to keep a consistent flow of energy active on an object and be able to walk away from the object while keeping it in an energetic quarantine. I usually use this for healing purposes and have had great success with it. For this example, I'll be demonstrating how I use this for healing with a poppet, but use your imagination for ways you might apply this to other magickal workings as well.

Directions: Take the poppet and set it in a space where it won't be disturbed, such as a shelf or a counter. Just as you would cast a circle, take your hand and project energy out of it, drawing an energetic circle around the poppet three times, stating:

> *Three rings around you be*
> *I lock you now in quarantine*
> *A place for you to rest and to be blessed*
> *Where you can heal and grow as energy flows.*

I then draw, starting at the north of the object going clockwise, a spiral going inward and state:

> *Energy in and energy out.*

Then from the center of the object I reverse the spiral, tracing over the former spiral counterclockwise out to the edge until I'm back to the north of the object where I started and declare:

Energy flowing and growing round about.

I then draw a lemniscate (an "infinity" symbol) over the object stating:

The energy sealed as you begin to heal.

I then place a bell jar over the item. You can periodically keep sending energy healing to the item, including reiki or other healing works upon the item.

Exercise 38

Scrying with the Ancient Witch Eye

Magickal timing: Nighttime

Materia:
- a completely black bowl for scrying, preferably one made of stone
- water that you can pour into the bowl
- Moon and Moth Dust Scrying Sight Potion[59]
- incense (optional)
- instrumental music (optional)
- your journal (optional)

Purpose: Scrying is the act of gaining psychic information by clairvoyant means either internally or externally, or by both through gazing at an object, usually a reflective object. As mentioned earlier, most scrying techniques rely on the circle shape such as mirrors, bowls, and crystal balls due to the way the shape works energetically. When most people think of scrying, they tend to think of those methods of scrying, and while this is true, my favorite form tends to be water scrying. One of the reasons I like to teach this method

---

59. The recipe for this is listed right after this exercise.

before other methods of scrying is because you can quickly and easily "turn it off" and close it down when you are done. This is why most scrying mirrors and crystal balls used for scrying are traditionally covered up when not being used. With water scrying, you can quickly close that window you're gazing through by getting rid of the water. I like to keep my bowls upside down when I'm not using them. While you can use any type of water for this, it's traditional to use water from natural sources.[60] Most folks I know tend to use spring water. However, I have found that any water, including tap water, works perfectly fine.

In this scrying session you will be calling upon the spirits of the first seers that walked upon the earth to lend their assistance. The black bowl will be serving as their Witch Eye, which you will be gazing into. You will want low lighting for this, and candlelight is preferred. You want to ensure though that you can't directly see any light source reflected in the water itself. You can burn incense related to psychic ability or divination if you desire, as well as play any instrumental music that relaxes you or puts you in a mystical mood.

Directions: Ground, center, tune in, and enter alpha. I like to cast a circle and call on spirit allies I have a relationship with that are protective. If you do not yet have a relationship with protective spirits, you can simply verbally call out "I call upon my highest protective spirit guides to be here with me during the session to protect me." A sincere call will bring them forward, even if you don't perceive their presence.

Place the empty bowl upon the flat surface. Take your water and fill the bowl up. Call out to the first seers of humanity:

> *I call to the first seers,*
> *and those who divined,*
> *Those whose names have been lost in time.*
> *Those who could pierce and peek beyond the veil,*
> *Those who could see hidden truths clearly without fail.*

---

60. Eason, *Scrying the Secrets of the Future.*

Those who are willing to help and not harm,
Who desire to share their gifts and charms.
Into your Witch Eye, I ask to stare,
To be revealed these secret affairs:
(State your intent of what you wish to learn here, it doesn't need to rhyme)

Take your Moon and Moth Dust Scrying Potion and drop three full droppers worth of the potion into the very center of the water. Take your dropper and use it as a spoon, spinning the water counterclockwise. As you do, say out loud:

Witch Eye to Witch Eye
You and I
Let it be shown
What is unknown
Let that which is between
And beyond the veil be seen

Begin square breathing.[61] With a relaxed gaze like you would have when looking at auras, stare into the swirling water. It's important that you aren't trying too hard or forcing this process. Just relax into it.

Several things are likely to happen during your scrying session. You may begin seeing images in the swirling water, similar to seeing shapes in clouds. You may also find that your mind begins to wander; this is perfectly fine, allow it to, and pay attention to what image or thoughts your mind wanders to. Finally, you may begin to see images in the water itself. This usually begins as seeing a haze appear over the water, usually a white or greyish haze. Just allow this process to unfold. Eventually the haze will take on a color. After a while, this haze will begin to act rather like a video where you begin seeing clear images.

When you are finished, close down the scrying session by saying:

---

61. See Exercise 9 on page 32 of *Psychic Witch*.

Seers of old, I thank you for the assistance and give you my blessing.
Though your names may be lost to memory, your skills are not.
I bid you depart. May there always be peace between us.

Close your circle down and ground and center again. Dispose of the water. Dry your scrying bowl and store it upside down. Record your experiences in your journal.

Exercise 39

❧

Moon and Moth Dust Scrying Sight Potion

Magickal timing: Full moon

Materia:
- a tiny rainbow moonstone chip
- 15 mL (½ oz.) glass bottle with dropper top
- 2 tablespoons of copal resin (smaller is better, crushed is best)
- ground cinnamon
- ground ginger
- ¾ teaspoon white iridescent pigment powder
- a clear spirit such as vodka (high grade rubbing alcohol is an appropriate substitute)

Purpose: While people tend to think of potions as something you drink, in witchcraft a potion is often the term used for any magickal liquid regardless of how it's used.[62] When I worked at Enchanted in Salem, I was constantly asked by tourists and visitors if Laurie Cabot's potions were to be drunk. The answer was always no. She uses the term potion for her anointing oil blends.[63]

This potion isn't meant to be consumed or even to anoint anything. It's meant to be used in a scrying bowl filled with water such as in the scrying spell before this. It can also be used as a talisman as well, activating its assistance when shaken. Just make sure the cap is closed securely before you carry it with you or shake it.

---

62. Penczak, *The Plant Spirit Familiar*, 168–169.
63. L. Cabot, C. Penczak, *Laurie Cabot's Book of Spells & Enchantments*, 122–123.

In this spell we are calling upon the spirit of the moth to assist us with navigating through its lunar sight. We are using the pigment powder as moth wing dust through sympathetic magick. Sympathetic magick is when you ritually declare one object as another object through an association. The famous writings of Carlos Castaneda describe his experiences with the Yaqui sorcerer don Juan Matus. While it's commonly accepted that don Juan never existed and that Castaneda's writings are fictional, they still share profound spiritual truths within the novels. As such, they continue to inspire people of many diverse spiritual paths. In Castaneda's book *Tales of Power*, the sorcerer don Juan tells Castaneda that moths are the heralds and guardians of eternity and that the dust of their wings is knowledge itself.[64] As such, don Juan explains that they have been allies of sorcerers throughout time. While this idea may be entirely fictional, and we know today that moth dust is tiny scales on a moth's wings, I find inspiration in this poetic idea of moth dust being the knowledge of eternity linking the magickal practitioners through time. So, I have incorporated it into this working, as being symbolic of that. Since we don't want to harm any actual moths and to collect moth dust in such a quantity would be a massive undertaking, the iridescent pigment powder is symbolically used to invoke that imagery and its associations in this work.

Iridescent pigment powder can easily be found at most craft stores and online. Please use nontoxic biodegradable pigment powder for this, as you will be disposing of it outside when used for scrying. The iridescent form of pigment powder, particularly the one that shimmers blue is the one that I use because it looks like rainbow moonstone and that blue is the same color as the Witch Fire.

Directions: Begin by adding your rainbow moonstone chip in the empty bottle. Then add two tablespoons of copal resin, three pinches of ground cinnamon, and three pinches of ground ginger. Next add ¼ teaspoon scoop of the pigment into the bottle three times (adding up to ¾ teaspoon) to symbolize the triple moon goddesses. Fill the bottle up with your liquid spirit, being sure not to fill it too much as it will spill over when you place your dropper cap on it.

---

64. Casteneda, *Tales of Power*, 27–29.

Before placing your cap on it, hold your hands over it and visualize the spirit of a beautiful white moth lending its powers through your hands and into the bottle.

Say:

I call to the moth spirit of the night
To lend your powers of second sight.
Moth dust of white silver sliver
Mixed into this spirit's river,
Moonstone assist me in this spell
To show to me that which doesn't tell
With the visions beyond periphery
By the sight of psychic witchery
Do I therefore enchant this potion
To work when it is set in motion
Copal, ginger, and cinnamon,
As I will it, it is now done!

Close the bottle. Shake it well, knowing that the spirit of the moth has blessed it. As you shake, visualize a white fire with an electric blue shimmer flowing from your hands and charging the concoction even more. Shake well to activate it. Store it for one full moon cycle, shaking daily if possible and keeping out of direct light. After a moon cycle (about a month), the concoction is ready to use. Using it sooner won't yield the same results as the formula has to concoct with time. When it is ready to use, shake it before use and add a few drops using a pipette dropper into a black bowl of water and scry the images.

The Cross and the X

The next most common shape that you find that witches work with is the "crossroads" where one path of energy intersects with another path of energy. This is much more common to witches who work with more traditional forms of witchery, sometimes being cast within a circle and sometimes without being cast within a circle. A crossroads essentially is a nexus point of connection and unification. It can also serve to break and disconnect, sending outward to separate. Crossroads is the only one among the shapes being shared here that doesn't also serve as a container of energy raised by the witch themselves. While crossroads may not serve as a container, they are a common source of power. The crossroads creates an intersection of energy along its pathways, creating a liminal area energetically connecting one realm with another. The center of the crossroads is often used for summoning and the creation of it seems to attract the attention of various entities, because when this intersection is created it becomes visible on several planes of existence and realms at once.

Exercise 40

Conjuring the Crossroads

Magickal timing: Any

Materia:

- stang (optional but recommended)

Purpose: Calling the crossroads is a form of creating sacred space that is used in ritual work when the purpose is about connecting, uniting, and traveling through realms as opposed to partitioning yourself off or quarantining your energy. Usually the crossroads are worked with in a witchcraft context by using a stang, which is a staff with two prongs upon them representing the World Tree as well as the "Witch Father" in Traditional Witchcraft. The stang is an instrument representing the Axis Mundi, which is the cosmological axis the whole spiritual universe resides upon. It is also an instrument of the Anima/Animus Mundi, sometimes referred to as the "Star Goddess," which is the living spirit of the Axis Mundi, the spirit of the universe itself. Both the Axis Mundi and the Anima/Animus Mundi are connective in nature, serving as the force uniting and holding all things together, much like the purpose of the crossroads itself. So, you can see why it's the perfect tool to use in this casting. If you do not have a stang, it is completely acceptable to use a staff or simply your hand. This crossroads conjuration is a greatly simplified version I have created that is based upon the crossroads conjuration we do in the Sacred Fires Tradition of witchcraft.[65]

---

65. Hunter, *The Witch's Book of Spirits*, 141–143.

Directions: Face north and hold your stang between your hands in front of you, planted firmly in the ground.

Declare:

I stand in the center of the road of time.

Take your stang with your left hand and point it to your left, stating:

To my left stretches the path of the past.

Visualize a path to your left as you say this. Bring your stang back to center and hold it with both hands, firmly planted in the ground. Take your stang with your right hand and point it to your right, stating:

To my right stretches the path of the future.

Visualize the path to your right as you say this. Bring your stang back to the center, holding it with both hands, and visualize the path to your right and left simultaneously, with yourself in the middle, stating:

I stand where they merge as one.

Take a deep breath and declare:

I stand in the center of the road of form.

Take your stang in your right hand and point it before you, visualizing a path unfolding before you and state:

Before me stretches the path of matter.

Bring the stang back to center, holding it with both hands, just as before. Now with your left hand take your stang and point it behind you, stating:

Behind me stretches the path of energy.

Bring it back to center and hold on to it with both hands stating:

I stand where they merge as one.

Now bringing your visualization of yourself as the World Tree. Holding your stang with both hands, raise it toward the sky visualizing the branches of the World Tree reaching to the Upper World, stating:

With empyrean branches above me

Bring the stang back to center, then with both hands point it downward toward the earth, while visualizing yourself as the World Tree and your roots running deep through the Under World and state:

And chthonic roots below me

Bring your stang back to center, declaring:

The trunk within and around me
I stand planted firmly in the between.

Then perform whatever magickal working, spell, or ritual that you wish to engage with. When finished simply state: "To each time and each place, be as you were before I came" and simply walk away.

Exercise 41

The Cross of Absolution

Magickal timing: New moon or waning moon

Materia:
- a small piece of paper and a writing utensil
- the object you are deconstructing energetically
- space for the object to be placed and remain where it won't be disturbed
- a cauldron or a firesafe bowl

Purpose: This working is for "composting" the energy of objects that may have negative energy, or an item that has a lot of energy in it that you don't necessarily need anymore. It cleanses the energy as it breaks it down so that you can then use that energy for another magickal endeavor.

Another great use for this is on an item that has collected a lot of negative energy being thrown at you, such as curses, hexes, or general negativity. This can be an evil eye averting charm or something else that is apotropaic in nature. The spell breaks down the energy of the item to its barest energetic form. That raw energy is then used to empower your other spells and your other goals. Haters gonna hate. So why let the energy that other people are freely sending you to try to harm you or impede your goals go to waste? Why not take that energy, recycle it, and have your haters help you with your own goals?

Directions: On a small square piece of paper, write the word "deconstruction" from the top left-hand corner to the bottom right-hand corner. Now from the bottom left-hand corner toward the upper right-hand corner write the word "absolution." You should now have four triangles of space between the writing: one above, one below, one to the right, and one to the left. At the center where each of the triangles meet, draw two arrows from the center going outward at each direction framing the triangles. Between the arrows in the empty space draw an "X."

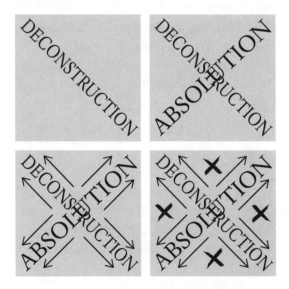

Absolution Paper

Place the piece of paper under the objects that you are working on. While directing energy just as you would when casting a circle, draw an energetic X above the object starting from the upper right-hand corner down to the lower left-hand corner and then again from the upper left corner down to the lower right-hand corner. Then say:

Just as earth decomposes and water dissolves
Just as fire does burn and the air then erodes
Your power and your memory,
Returns to purest energy.
Collecting there,
Within the square
I speak my fated witch's prayer:
Tabula rasa! Tabula rasa! Tabula rasa!

"Tabula Rasa" is Latin for "blank slate," "erased slate," or "scraped slate." Now leave to let the energy of the item break down on its own. You can periodically return over time and use a pendulum to see if the item has broken down by asking it. If it hasn't finished breaking down, you can draw the energetic X over it again and recite the words. If it has broken down successfully, you can then remove the object (and if it was an apotropaic charm, you can recharge it to its purpose). Take the piece of paper and cut it up along the words, creating four triangles. The next time you cast a spell, simply add the paper to your cauldron or a fire safe bowl and burn it alongside your spell while declaring:

This extra supply of energy
Enhances my spell successfully.

Triangles and Pyramids

Triangles serve to manifest and amplify. The energy of a triangle seems to rise within it, similar to the "cone of power" performed by many Wiccan traditions. The magickal geometry of this shape is that two points come together and manifest a third. Manifestation and creation are key themes with this shape. The mother and father come together to create the child. Mercury and

Sulfur come together to create Salt in alchemy. These three ingredients correspond loosely to the Three Souls in alchemy, with Sulfur being the Higher Self, Mercury being the Lower Self, and Salt being the Middle Self.[66] The Higher Self and Lower Self merge to create the personality of the Middle Self. Triangles also amplify energy due to this ability of manifesting and creating. This is the secret to the shape of the pyramid. It's also why the gesture called "the triangle of manifestation" is often used by witches to amplify the energy of an object.

On the other hand, triangles can mute and level energy as well. Furthermore, triangles can also trap energies or entities within them. This is also why triangles are used in grimoire magick to bring forth more dangerous entities outside of the magickal circle, which those using ceremonial grimoire magick refer to as the "triangle of manifestation"; this is the same term witches use for a different technique we will explore. Other sets of three are often assigned points in the triangle such as time, space, and energy, or mutable, fixed, and cardinal when working with astrological energies. The key is that the three things work in harmony with one another in a direct relationship.

G.O.D.	Generative	Organizing	Destructive
Triple Soul	Lower Self	Middle Self	Higher Self
Alchemical	Mercury	Salt	Sulfur
Astrological	Cardinal	Fixed	Mutable
Lunar	Waxing	Full	Waning
World	Under World	Middle World	Upper World
Cauldron	Warming	Movement	Wisdom
Manifestation	Energy	Space	Time
Fate	Lachesis	Clotho	Atropos

66. Hauck, *The Complete Idiot's Guide to Alchemy*, 100; Penczak, *The Three Rays*, 63.

Exercise 42

Triangle Of Manifestation

Purpose: This is a classic witchcraft / occult method of forming the hands in the shape of a triangle to direct, awaken, and amplify an energetic charge, or to bestow upon it a blessing. The three points in this triangle are symbolic of time, space, and energy.

The gesture and technique are named after a witchcraft teaching that indicates that for manifestation to occur those three components of time, space, and energy must be used. Simply put, if you tap into a time, create the space for it, and direct energy, you will manifest something.[67] While I believe this, I also find it to be a bit more basic and feel that there are more components involved with manifestation—or rather that these three things have aspects and steps within them, as I've discussed at length in *Psychic Witch*. The gesture is meant to invoke these three primary components symbolically.

The Triangle of Manifestation Gesture

Directions: Take your hands and hold them in from of you with palms facing outward. Touch your thumbs together and your index fingers together forming

---

67. Grimassi, *Spirit of the Witch*, 120–121.

a triangle of negative space between your thumbs and index fingers. Hold the triangle gesture close to your face with your eyes being within the triangle and the spot of your Witch Eye at your brow at the apex of the triangle. Gazing through the triangle, visualize your eyes and Witch Eye filling the space between your fingers, filling up with energy while looking at the object that you want to empower, for these purposes let's say a candle. Using your will power and intention push the energy into the candle while physically pushing your triangle gesture closer to the candle imbuing it with energy.

You can strengthen this technique by chanting something such as:

One in three, three in one.
Triangle of manifestation.

Exercise 43

❧

Pyramid of Amplification

Magickal timing: Any

Purpose: This is essentially a technique where you cast a triangle around you and then form it into a pyramid container for the purposes of amplifying your internal energies and clarity of inner guidance. In a sense, while the visualization is external, the focus of the energy work is internal, instead of external as in other castings such as a circle. This is a casting I like to do when I'm going to engage in deep meditation, trance work, psychic readings, or mediumship and I want to be fully immersed in the experience. For myself and others who've tried this, it often leads to profound experiences and messages from the world of spirit, while also keeping you protected.

Because this amplifies things so much, it's important that you ground before and after this working (and honestly you should before and after any energetic or magickal working or meditation). I've found that this exercise also greatly strengthens my energetic perception for the rest of the day, and it probably has long term effects of increasing sensitivity as well.

Directions: With your eyes closed and sitting down straight with your legs crossed, get into a meditative state of consciousness. Ground and center yourself. Visualize a triangle of white light around you on the ground with one point in front of you and one point on each side behind you. Now visualize that each point has a line drawing upward toward the apex, which rests right above your head. Visualize the empty spaces between the lines of energy filling in with white light forming "walls" and creating a pyramid around you.

Visualize a prismatic orb of opalescent white light directly above your head, hovering over the apex point of the pyramid. This is your Higher Self. Begin breathing deeply and slowly and see the Higher Self beaming down light into the pyramid, filling it with an opalescent white energy as if it were being filled with water. Feel this energy as it slowly surrounds you in the pyramid and fills your body. Feel it enhancing and adjusting your energetic body and strengthening your psychic perceptions.

Perform whichever meditations you wish at this point. They can be guided meditations, freeform journeying, or simply breathing and mindfulness exercises. I find this casting to be extremely powerful for meditation as well as psychic reading sessions and when I engage in mediumship. When finished, simply visualize all that liquid light returning back up to your Higher Self. See the pyramid around you fade away. Be sure to ground and center again when you are done.

Exercise 44

❧

The Triangle Charger

Magickal timing: Any

Materia:
- an item you want to cleanse and charge
- three sticks of selenite that can create a triangle
- wand (optional)

Purpose: Selenite is one of my favorite stones of all time. Not only is it an amazing stone ally for psychic enhancement and energetic cleansing, but it will also willingly assist in amplifying any energy that it comes across and will also synergistically blend different energies together.[68] When I was a professional psychic reader several years back in Salem, Massachusetts,

---

68. Simmons, Ahsian, and Raven, *The Book of Stones*.

a mentor of mine recommended that I grid my reading space with selenite to help keep a continual cleansing of the space and also to help keep my psychic energy amplified and flowing. He likened it to having energetic air fresheners in the room. I did as he suggested and noticed a huge difference. Since then, I've gained a whole new level of appreciation for this crystal ally. I find it very interesting that the stone is named after Selene, the Greek Titaness of the moon, and selenite seems to have all the main powers of the moon—removing, charging, and a strong emphasis on psychic ability. I also recommend placing three pieces of selenite at the three corners of the Pyramid of Amplification from the last exercise while holding on to one while meditating. You will notice an even greater enhancement of that exercise.

The Triangle Charger is a technique that I developed based on those experiences with gridding with selenite, just concentrated and miniaturized. I use this technique when I want to awaken, charge, and cleanse an object fairly quickly without much fuss. While its uses are limitless, let's use a piece of jewelry as an example for this exercise.

Directions: Take three sticks of unpolished selenite and lay them down so that they form the shape of a triangle. Now take your wand or your hand and direct energy out of it to trace over the triangle with energy starting at the top point down to the bottom right and then to the left and then back to the top point. Then place the necklace or whichever item you are cleansing or charging in the center of the triangle. Then call out the spirit of selenite, saying:

> *Just as the moon waxes and charges*
> *Just as the moon wanes and clears*
> *Spirit of selenite, do as your namesake*
> *For this treasure within your three spears.*

Then perform the Triangle of Manifestation over the object, having my hands frame the selenite borders. Voila! Cleansed and charged.

Exercise 45

Casting the Threefold Space

Magickal timing: Any

Materia:

- 3 tealight candles

Purpose: I have found that this sacred space casting is powerful when you want to empower a poppet or a sigil, or to assist a spirit in manifesting clearer. It calls on the three modalities and their phases of creation, existence, and destruction. Essentially this casting creates an energetic circuit where these three powers are summoned into one space, amplifying the energies of time and space in a manner that keeps increasing while within it. As such, it's perfect for "enlivening" thoughtforms as you desire. Try casting it within a magick circle, and try casting it outside of a magick circle. See what the differences are for you energetically. How you orient yourself within the triangle depends on what your intent is for your magickal working. If your working involves creation, you want to perform your work at the cardinal point of the triangle, if it's feeding or empowering, then you want to work at the fixed point of the triangle. If it's dismantling something you've enlivened you want to perform your working at the mutable point of the triangle.

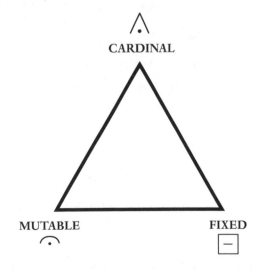

The Threefold Space

Directions: Set an unlit tealight candle at each point of your triangle. Like casting a circle, you're going to be "painting" with energetic light that you're projecting.[69] Starting at the cardinal point, light the tealight and say:

By the cardinal power of creation

Draw an energetic line to the fixed point from the cardinal point. Light the tealight candle and say:

By the fixed power of existence

Draw an energetic line from the fixed point to the mutable point. Light the tealight candle and say:

By the mutable power of destruction

Draw an energetic line from the mutable point back to the cardinal point and say:

I cast the threefold space

Repeat this process without lighting the already lit candles, while stating each line of the following in the same order of each point of the triangle:

A circuitry of energy
Where the three are one
And the one are three
I cast the threefold space

And then again one more time repeating the casting, saying:

Where the forces are distilled
Where all paradox is resolved

---

69. For a refresher on painting with light, see Exercise 62 on page 141 of *Psychic Witch*.

To serve as a crucible of my will
I cast the threefold space

To release this casting, simply walk the triangle blowing out each candle and stating:

This work done here is now complete.
The powers three now disembark
The threefold space is now released
As flames return into the dark.

Squares and Cubes

Squares stabilize, store, and hold energy. Inside a square, energy seems to settle and slow down, as opposed to other shapes where the energy seems to flow and amplify in different ways. The square is the Platonic solid related to the element of earth as a shape that stabilizes energy within nature into a seemingly stationary form. Interestingly enough, in magickal geometry the square is four lines creating balance and stability. Due to this, the square also has the ability to store and hold energy in the form of information. It's sort of like a data storage device in terms of being an energetic container. If all the other shapes (aside from the crossroads) function as containers of energy, the square operates the most as a container of energy, storing energetic information within it.

Exercise 46

Blocking a Harassing Spirit

Magickal timing: Saturday, hour of Saturn, dark moon, or new moon

Materia:
- black pen
- small square piece of paper
- black string
- large square ice mold (usually intended for whiskey)
- tin foil

Purpose: As a witch or even a psychic, it's highly likely that you will come across a spirit that has less than good motives when it comes to you, if you haven't already, or a bunch of times for that matter. If a spirit is harassing you or your loved ones (such as a child or even a pet), this spell works like a charm. This spell is like a block button for the spirit by putting their harassment into a block of ice.

Freezer spells have a long history throughout various magickal practices in Europe, the Americas, and Russia, and perhaps even other places. Usually, freezer spells are to bind someone who is causing you a lot of trouble, like a stalker or a harassing neighbor. The idea is that you are "freezing" their influence in a certain area if not them as a whole. One of the best uses I have found for freezer spells isn't even over people, but over spirits, entities, and thoughtforms that have an unhealthy obsession with you or are preying upon or attacking you. So, taking the traditional freezer spells as the base of my inspiration, this is how I've adapted it to successfully get malevolent spirits to leave me alone.

This spell specifies that it is only for a spirit that is harassing or intending you harm, so innocent spirits won't be affected by this. It also serves to weaken them after the spell is performed if they actively try to harass or come near you. Because of the magickal properties of squares as containers, I prefer to use large ice cube molds that are shaped in perfect squares. These tend to be sold fairly cheaply and are usually intended for whiskey glasses.

Directions: On a small square piece of paper, write down the phrase "the spirit that intends me harm" and while doing so, think of that spirit or what you know of it. Roll the square up into a small scroll and wrap black string around it to keep it scrolled shut. Place the scroll in your square ice cube mold and fill it with water. Hold your hands over the square ice cube mold and declare firmly:

Your power has no effect on me
O shade, O phantasm, O specter
Or whatever creature you may be
I restrain you from transgressing
I bind you from harassing
Your influence here I freeze
Unless you flee, you shall not be free.

Put it in your freezer and allow it to freeze. Once it has been frozen, take the ice cube out of the mold and then wrap it in tin foil. I find tin foil to be best for this sort of working because it reflects light yet you can't see your own reflection in it.

You aim for me, your sight is turned
Your shaking hand
Shall strike your foot
I bid you shade to now retire,
Your influence has now expired.

Place the tin foil wrapped ice cube in the back of your fridge. My rule of thumb for freezer spells is that once you feel you have been left alone, remove from your freezer three months afterward. I then go and bury it somewhere in the earth since it's just water, paper and string, all of which are biodegradable. (Recycle the tin foil.) I like to bury it away from my house, in case the spirit itself happens to be bound within it. Alternatively, you can always keep it in your freezer.

Exercise 47

Psychic Cube Embedding and Extraction

Magickal timing: Any

Purpose: This is a sacred space casting I do when I need to either store some psychic information into an object, or I need to extract psychic information from an object. It's incredibly simple and incredibly effective. For this exercise you don't need anything other than whatever object you're working with, and a place where you can meditate in peace without being disturbed. Let's start with imprinting information and then I'll show you how to extract information from an item.

Directions: Ground and center and enter into the alpha brainwave state. Hold the object that you're wanting to imprint with information softly between your hands. Visualize yourself inside of an energetic cube. Slowly begin to fill the cube with whatever information that you wish to imprint on the object.

Do this by conjuring up the emotions, the images, the sounds, the phrase, or whatever you are looking to put into it. For example, if I'm feeling extremely happy, I will conjure an energetic cube around myself and fill it with the happiness that is exuding outside of myself, and visualize that as a colored light filling the cube. This might be yellow or pink or another color that I associate with the feeling. Begin a slow steady breathing. With each exhale see the cube get smaller and smaller around you until eventually it's no longer around you and is only around your hands holding the object. As the square gets smaller, feel the imprint within the energetic container getting stronger and stronger. Eventually when the box is only barely big enough to surround the object itself, visualizing it breaking into thousands of tiny little energetic cubes and surrounding each molecule of the object you're holding.

When you are done, declare: "It is fixed!"

To extract information from an item, the item doesn't have to have gone through the process above of being imprinted. It most likely has an imprint of some sort, even if it's super old. I use this a lot when performing psychometry, which is receiving psychic information from an object, and I usually do it for the purposes of mediumship. Just like before, you want to ground, center, and enter into the alpha brainwave state while holding the item gently within your hand or hands. Visualize yourself inside of an energetic cube. Now envision the energy of the object within your hands. Visualize a small cube around it being filled with the energy of the object. Begin a slow steady breathing. With each exhale see the smaller cube get larger and larger until it fills the larger cube that you are within, having the whole space fill up with the energy of the item.

Once the cubes are united as one, sit patiently in meditative contemplation and be aware of anything you receive. What feelings do you feel? What images come to mind? Any names? Faces? Sounds? Temperatures? Tastes? Smells? Take note of anything that you feel. This process is sort of like a zipped file unzipping and unfolding the data. I often find that verbalizing what is coming to you helps the information flow stronger. When you are finished, simply imagine the united cube dissipating. Finish by grounding and centering yourself again.

Chapter 6

INNER AND
OUTER TOOLS

∽∾

T he four elements are extremely easy and extremely difficult to describe due to their abstract nature. That's because when describing the elements, we are using the language of metaphor, including the names we give them such as earth, air, fire, and water. The four elements are not their symbolic names. This is easier to understand when you realize that these are just poetic names for different energy types. For example, the element of fire is not literally a flame on a candle wick. Their namesakes are extremely ancient and extremely appropriate in an attempt to describe each of the elements. The elements are energetic building blocks, which we poetically describe as earth, air, fire, and water because the nature of how the element behaves and feels is reminiscent of those labels. We must again be clear to not mistake the symbol for what it's symbolizing. These four elements (along with the fifth element) compose what we call etheric energy. Etheric energy is the subtle energy closest to physical substance. It's more of a blueprint pattern or structure, which may or may not have a physical counterpart. The elements aren't just etheric energies, but also represent qualities within us and within all things. As the Law of Correspondence states, "As above, so below. As within, so without." As such, we see the elements expressed in different ways on different levels of being.

Witches work in the liminal, the space of paradox and union that is neither here nor there, but both and neither, where the boundaries blur and magick is afoot. When we can bridge that inner and outer world, the magick that we perform both internally and externally is enhanced and strengthened, as both are bridged. Occultists throughout time have emphasized the inner plane, the place where our inner faculties touch the astral realm. It is here that we can meet and work with spirits on a sort of middle ground and perform magick purely with our psyche. When we can bring a union between the inner and outer spaces, tools, allies, and materia, our magick truly becomes alive. The inner plane is accessed through various techniques such as guided meditation, focused visualization, trance induction, lucid dreaming, and astral projection.

One of the techniques that has been used by witches and many other magickal practitioners is the creation of an Inner Temple, a sacred space akin to a memory palace. The memory palace technique, also known as the Method of Loci, is credited to the Greek poet Simonides of Ceos. The legend goes that he attended a great banquet in a palace and stepped outside during the meal. Depending on which version of the story you read, the roof either collapsed on the banquet while he was outside, or a great fire occurred and burned the palace down. Since there were so many attendees, people were unsure of who had died within the palace as the bodies were so badly destroyed that most of them were unidentifiable. Simonides was able to remember who was there by mentally recreating in his mind's eye the memory of going through every room of the banquet to remember who had attended that was now dead. He later realized that by using this technique and taking inner mental imagery of a location and associating it with various information, the mind could store, retain, and remember information. This technique was shown in the BBC's *Sherlock*, where Sherlock had a mind palace in the form of a great library that he would use to access his memories of information that were too hard to consciously remember.

The concept of the Inner Temple is different in the sense that it isn't just a place of extracting conscious information like the memory palace, though it can do that as well. Instead, the Inner Temple is your magickal home base that you create on the inner planes. Everyone's Inner Temple is unique to them and based on their tastes, spiritual path, and psyche. Unlike the memory palace, the Inner Temple shifts through time accordingly on its own. Think of it as your inner TARDIS, from the longstanding series *Doctor Who*. The TARDIS (an acronym for Time And Relative Dimensions In Space) is the Doctor's vehicle, which takes the form of a small phonebooth but is massively "bigger on the inside." In it, the Doctor travels through time and space and it's where he has access to important resources. When the Doctor takes on a new form (played by a new actor or actress) the TARDIS completely changes inside, just as our Inner Temple changes as we change and grow. In our Inner Temple, we have direct access to the various planes of reality, deities, spirits, and all the magickal resources, tools, and information we may need. I would also say that it's the most important sacred space you will ever have, as it's a space that you will always have. You might think that the Inner Temple is simply just in your mind, and that's true. However, as the brilliant occultist Lon Milo DuQuette says, "It's all in your head…you just have no idea how big your head is."[70] Also remember that the *Kybalion* states that "The All is Mind; the Universe is Mental."

Exercise 48

Journey to Your Inner Temple for the First Time

Perform your journey to the World Tree. Call upon the Anima Mundi as you place your hand on the trunk of the tree. Ask to be taken to your Inner Temple, your personal sanctuary between the worlds. As you do, the bark beneath your hand begins to glow gold and vibrate. The golden glow begins spreading through the bark before you, outlining a door just large enough for your body. The golden bark disappears, creating a passage into the tree. Take a step inside the golden light of the passageway. Let the gold light completely fill your inner vision, just as the silver mist does when you journey to the World Tree.

As the golden light begins to fade, you realize that you're now inside your Inner Temple. What does it look like? Is it reminiscent of a certain time period or not? Is it cluttered or nice and organized? Is it spacious or small? Take a moment to look around, realizing that there's several doors throughout your Inner Temple to be explored later. As you are exploring your inner temple, take notice of a primary altar within it. There's nothing on the altar yet, just a flat surface. Take your time exploring and getting to know your Inner Temple, trying to take in the details. This is your safe haven, your

---

70. DuQuette, *Low Magick*.

place of power, and unique to you. When you are done exploring, visualize the golden light re-emerging from seemingly everywhere and nowhere until it fills your inner vision. When the golden light fades, you find yourself back in front of the World Tree. Thank the spirit of the Anima Mundi and once again turn away from it, finding the silver mist to return back to this reality. Finish by grounding and centering yourself again.

You can use this method to enter your Inner Temple at any time by venturing through the World Tree, and this method is ideal to get to know the spirit of the World Tree itself, particularly for future journey work. But also know that you can immediately enter your Inner Temple by just closing your eyes, willing yourself to be there, and visualizing it.

The Altar

The witch's primary altar is a work area that embodies their power and sovereignty in their magick. It's their workbench where they craft and cast spells, deepen their connection to universal powers, and commune with divinity within and outside of themselves. The primary altar serves as a bridge between the microcosm and macrocosm. In this sense, it's a macrocosm of the inner planes of reality within oneself and the microcosm of the outer, greater metaphysical planes of reality. At the witch's primary altar, the witch works as a deity themselves, wielding the forces within themselves to command and control the outer universal forces through connection and merging these inner and outer forces together. Traditionally, the altar holds the four elemental tools of the witch: the wand of fire, the athame of air, the chalice of water, and the pentacle or altar stone of earth. The bond between the witch and these four tools cannot be understated, as they serve as not just tools, but physical vehicles of aspects of the witch themselves and channels of energy of cosmic elemental forces external to the witch. In the traditions I've trained in, two more tools are added, the cauldron and the peyton, as the tools of spirit or quintessence, the fifth element.

Altars and shrines are sometimes two terms used interchangeably, but there's slight nuance in their differences in most witchcraft traditions. Altars tend to be flat surfaces where one works magick and connects with other spiritual energies and entities such as gods, ancestors, elemental forces, and so on. A shrine is similar, but tends to be more devotional, with only petitionary work occurring; it is mostly a place of reverence and a place to provide offerings for specific deities, spirits, or ancestors. Witches will often also have various altars and shrines. For example, I have my primary altar, as I'm describing here, as well as an altar to Hecate, a goddess I work with closely, which relates specifically to magickal workings related to calling upon her and the spirits under her command. I also have a separate shrine to Hecate, which is where I perform my devotions and give my offerings. I also have a healing altar where the deities it's dedicated to and the workings that occur there are specifically healing related. I have an ancestral shrine, and there are numerous different shrines to various deities in my household. How many altars or shrines you have is purely personal preference, but the main school of thought is that you shouldn't be creating shrines that get neglected. If you're going to erect a shrine for a spirit, you should be dedicated to regular devotional work and the upkeep and maintenance of that shrine.

Traditionally, the altar also has two items relating to the two polar aspects of the divine. These two aspects are the primary modes of how the singular universal spirit operates through polarity. The universal spirit, a non-binary, androgynous force (much like "the Force" in *Star Wars*) composes and runs through all reality. The two aspects of this singular force are opposite and complementary, creating a true polarity. One aspect is projective and electric in nature and associated with light and creation. The other aspect is receptive and magnetic in nature and associated with darkness and destruction. Historically in occultism, these two forces were referred to with outdated heteronormative language as the Great God and the Great Goddess, respectively.

In many Western esoteric practices, the Divine Androgyne divides into the gender-binary Divine Twins, and these two forces are symbolically brought together ritually, as well as internally, to create the divine child, referred to as androgynous and whole. This division and reunification process embodies the primary principles of the Baphomet, the symbolic representation of the forces of the androgynous universal divine force perpetually breaking apart and unifying, as written on Baphomet's arms *"solve et coagula."* The items upon the altar that represent these two forces tend to either be a black and a white candle, representing polar forces existent within the divine, or statues of polar deities that the practitioner holds in high regard.

Where items are placed on the altar holds symbolic significance as well. The black candle is traditionally placed on the left side of the altar, and all receptive tools are also placed on the left side of the altar, while the white candle is traditionally placed on the right side of the altar, and all projective tools are placed on the right side of the altar. The four elemental tools are placed in their traditional directions upon the altar. The pentacle or altar stone in the north, the athame in the east, the wand in the south, the chalice in the west, and the cauldron in the middle of the altar.

The power of the primary altar is based on the energy, connection, and symbolic meaning that you place upon it. That being said, there really are no hard and fast rules on how you put together your altar and many witches use all sorts of altars. This format just tends to be what has worked extremely successfully for me. The altar should reflect you and your connection to your magick.

Various schools of thought exist on the four elements, their tools, and their locations. The same goes for the orientation of which elements go in which direction. Some witches try to align their elements based on what is significant to their physical location. For example, if they live somewhere that has the ocean to the east and mountains to the south, they might place water in the east and earth in the south. I tend to stick to what I grew up with and am used to: earth at the north, air at the east, fire at the south, and water at the west, because for me the elements I'm tapping into are the "elements of the wise," the primordial forces that compose the universe, not their symbolic representations in the physical realm. Some schools of thought also switch the orientation of the elemental directions based on which level of reality they are working in. In the Temple of Witchcraft, Christopher Penczak teaches us these correspondences for the elemental directions based on which world we're operating in.[71]

71. Penczak, *Foundations of the Temple*.

	Earth	Air	Fire	Water
Upper World	East (*Taurus*)	North (*Aquarius*)	South (*Leo*)	West (*Scorpio*)
Middle World	North (*Winter and Midnight*)	East (*Spring and Sunrise*)	South (*Summer and Noon*)	West (*Autumn and Sunset*)
Under World	North (*Cold and Dry*)	South (*Warm and Dry*)	East (*Warm and Moist*)	West (*Cold and Moist*)

The logic behind this is that the Under World is elementally balanced, and so this positioning of the elements in their direction balances the elemental attributes with complementary and opposite elements across from each other, creating an alchemical synergy for creation with the moist and dry elements across from each other being the same. Earth, which is alchemically cold and dry (and the densest element), is opposite of air, which is warm and dry (and the least dense element). Fire, which is warm and moist, is opposite of water, which is cold and moist. The traditional attributes of the elemental directions are the placement of the Middle World and align with how we experience the cycles of life in relationship to the sun. The sun rises in the east and sets in the west; this orientation retains the traditional seasonal correspondences of the elements with spring and sunrise occurring in the east and air, to the setting of the sun and autumn being associated with the west and water, and earth being the barren liminal spot of winter and midnight. The logic behind the Upper World placement relates to the zodiac and their fixed elemental attributes with earth in the east with Taurus, air in the north with Aquarius, fire in the south with Leo, and water in the west with Scorpio. With this set of elemental orientations, we again have the Under World corresponding to the sub-lunar elemental energies, the Middle World corresponding to the solar energies, and the Upper World corresponding with celestial energies.

I recommend experimenting with these different placements depending on what the goal of your magickal working is. Are you doing magick related to the High Self or Upper World? Try the Upper World orientation of elemental placement. Are you doing magick related to your inner self, shadow work, Lower Self, or the Under World? Try the Under World orientation of elemental placement. For everything else, stick with the traditional Middle World elemental placement.

Honestly, it doesn't matter which directions you place with elements, as long as you have an understanding of why you are placing them where. The power lies in your personal connection and associations with the directions; in my magickal cosmology, I tend to stick to Christopher's orientations because it adds immense levels of symbolic meaning to the magick I work in relations to the Three Souls and the Three Worlds.

The Elemental Tools

The four primary elemental ritual tools of the magician come to us from the ceremonial magicians of the Hermetic Order of the Golden Dawn. Besides each tool being associated with an element, they can also be esoterically linked to Irish pagan mythology of the Four Hallows of the Tuatha Dé Danann. The association of the four elemental powers with the Four Hallows is thought to originate from visionary poet Fiona MacLeod (pen name of William Sharp), whose work influenced both the Golden Dawn and modern Wicca.[72] The Tuatha Dé Danann had Four Hallows, hallow meaning something sacred or holy. These elder gods are said to have brought these hallows from four mythical cities and a different deity possessed one of the three. These four hallows are the Cauldron of the Dagda from the mythical city of Murias, the Sword of Light of Núada from the mythical city of Finias, the Spear of Lugh from Gorias, and the Stone of Fal from Falias.

The Stone of Fal, also known as the Stone of Destiny, didn't belong to any particular deity but instead belonged to the land of Ireland and its people. According to legend, the Stone of Fal would make a roaring noise when the rightful king placed his feet upon it and allegedly would revitalize the king and bless him with a long reign. The Stone of Fal is symbolic of the tool of the element of earth and influenced the magician and witch's tool of the altar pentacle or altar stone. Núada's Sword of Light was said to be one which no one could escape once it was drawn. Núada's Sword is symbolic of the tool

72. Penczak, *The Temple of High Witchcraft*, 202.

of the element of air and influenced the magician and witch's tool of the athame. In witchcraft and ceremonial traditions, the athame and sword are often a more aggressive tool when working with spirits. It is used for banishing aggressive spirits, and in some traditions intimidating or threatening wild spirits to behave by its mere presence. While not all witches feel comfortable in dealing with spirits like this, there's a lot of symbolic meaning when we remember that this is a tool of air and thus mind and speech. Our words have power, as do our thoughts, and they allow us to not only formulate plans but express and execute them as well. If you've ever seen a sword fight, you also know that one must be quick-thinking when one is using a sword, as there's an almost martial dance that occurs when using it, having to block the opponent's sword while also trying to attack them with it.

The Spear of Lugh is said to have been one against which no battle was ever sustained, nor against the person who held it in his hand. Christopher Penczak notes that, "the translation of [Lugh's] name often is disputed, but he has been connected to solar, light, and lightning imagery, as well as 'flowing vigor,' which is perfect, as the fire element and his spear represent the power of drive."[73] We should also note that spears are weapons that we use by jabbing or charging forward. There's a thrusting motion to it that is more straightforward in movement than, say, the sword that is wielded and manipulated in battle with more complexity. Lugh's spear influenced the magician and witch's tool of the wand, which directs our willpower and energy.

The Cauldron of the Dagda (or "the Good God") would never empty, and all who partook from it were left satisfied and fulfilled. This was a tool of generosity and seems to be symbolic of emotional fulfillment and the generosity of the heart, properties of the element of water, and cauldrons hold liquids in them, whether they're soups, stews, brews, or potions. The Dagda's Cauldron is symbolic of the element of water and influenced the magician and witch's tool of the chalice. Irish Paganism and folklore scholar and author Morgan Daimler relates the four treasures to four values, the stone being sovereignty, the cauldron hospitality, the wand being defense, and the knife being offense.[74]

---

73. Penczak, *The Temple of High Witchcraft*, 294.
74. Daimler, *Pagan Portals—Fairy Witchcraft*.

Athame and Wand, Air or Fire?

Many witches are divided on whether the athame or wand represents air or fire. For some witches, the wand is air and the athame is fire. Some notable witchcraft teachers that embraced this included Raven Grimassi and his early student Scott Cunningham. For them, the logic is that wands come from trees that have branches that sway in the wind and reach up to the sky and athames are forged in fire and that the element shouldn't destroy the tool. This is perfectly fine, and again, as long as you have an understanding of the reasoning for associating an element with a tool, then go with it. When we assign a symbol with power and tap into that symbol over long periods of time it becomes deeply engrained in one's consciousness and this occurs much quicker when it's an actual physical tool used in ritual. For me, the tools are more about how they operate with the elements themselves. The wand is made of wood, which makes it the vehicle for carrying, directing, and fueling fire, just as the wand is an extension of our willpower and the tool to direct it. The athame, like a sword, cuts and parts the wind and often makes a sound while doing so, often described as singing. The English language is also full of terms and expressions that connect words and thoughts to the blade. When speaking of someone's intelligence we often say things like the person is "sharp" or "dull." When someone is long-winded, we ask them to "get to the point" or to "cut to the chase." There are countless other examples, but hopefully that illustrates the point, no pun intended.

The Wand of Fire

The wand is the tool of element of fire and perhaps the tool most closely associated with magick, from the wands and staffs of wizards and magicians throughout legend to Harry Potter, which helped the tool gain popularity again in the public eye. In traditional witchcraft lore, the wand should be the length of your elbow to the tip of your index finger. While this isn't a hard and fast rule, it gives us insight into the nature and use of the wand. Witches use their pointer finger to not just project their energy, but to focus and control it as well. The wand is an extension of the witch's will, power, drive, passion, and life force. It's reminiscent of the scepter or mace of a monarch, a symbol of power, might, and authority over the self, one's life, and one's magick.

The wand is typically made of wood, which echoes the World Tree and the Three Worlds. Just like Hermes' herald's wand, the caduceus, which gave him the authority to travel through the worlds freely. As such, it commands and symbolizes one's mastery over the different levels of reality and this is why I personally prefer to use the wand to cast a circle, as you are creating an energetic place outside of the physical world itself. Working with the wand strengthens your inherent energetic power and amplifies your will. One of the earliest depictions of the wand being used in magick is in the Greek story of Circe, who used it to channel her energy. We can also see parallels with the magick rods of Aaron and Moses, also symbols of their authority.

Exercise 49

Fire Journey

The World Tree stands in the center between the worlds. From this center, turn to face the south. Standing before you is a large golden gate, covered with climbing cactus with sharp needles and bold blooms. Upon this gate is etched the alchemical symbol for fire: an upward pointing triangle. Allow your gaze to become soft as you imagine gazing through this symbol. Breathe deeply and empty yourself of all thought and emotion. Nothing exists except yourself, this gate, and the symbol through which you now focus your attention.

Imagine stepping forward with every breath … every heartbeat. Getting closer to the gate it opens—as if by magic—and you see the blazing light of the summer sun. A warm breeze blows through the gate. Breathe deep … and as you reach the gate, mentally affirm your intention to journey to the realm of elemental fire. And with a breath of power, step through the threshold and into the light …

You stand in a desert temple courtyard, filled with soft sand, spotted with many little fires. Here it is eternally summer … and eternally noon. Before you, the stone wall cradles a large circular stained-glass window, set high above you, beautifully illuminated as the noonday light shines through. The blazing sunlight glares through the window and projects downward, illuminating an altar in the center of the courtyard.

Breathe deeply, and walk toward that altar, allowing yourself to become aware of any other details that may arise from this place. Use any and all of your senses to make this place feel more real to you. What do you see? Hear? Feel? Smell? Check in with your emotions. How do you feel about this place? Check in with your body. Notice any aches or pains. Notice your posture.

As you reach the altar, standing before it and the stained-glass window, mentally affirm your intention to call to the guardian of the element. Step into the light of the sun and imagine opening yourself more deeply to the elemental power. Upon the altar is a red candle. Calling upon your own inner light, use this now to light the candle and summon the guardian.

As the candle burns, the light of the sun seems to be getting brighter. With each breath this light shines more brightly from the heavens and through the stained glass, pouring down all around you and the altar in a circle of bright golds and deep reds. You feel a rumbling vibration in the ground and feel as if the very walls around you are shaking.

Before you, from just outside the circle of light, the guardian emerges, stepping into the circle, now fully illuminated by the sunlight. Notice how they come to you. What form (if any) do they take? How does their presence feel to you? Introduce yourself to them. Ask them for their name. Give yourself some time to receive this name. You may need to ask more than once. Take your time.

Once you have received a name, the guardian begins to radiate a bright crimson light. They step forward and hand to you a wand. As you take it, your hands touch, and you are enveloped in that crimson light, the essence of elemental fire … the light of the will. You feel this brightness enter your body, stirring your spirit, focusing your will.

Focus on this sensation as the sense of your own will grows larger and larger, completely enveloping you just as this crimson light does. Feel your determination, letting all of your thoughts, feelings, and attachments flow out into the crimson light, leaving you strong and fully present.

The guardian steps back and you hold the wand close. The light of the sun seems to project directly into the wand as you contemplate the lessons of elemental fire: It is hot and dry, it is active and projective, it is will. Feel how this wand embodies these qualities. Take a few moments to really feel this.

Now, ask the tool for its secret name. It may respond in some fashion, or the guardian may offer you an answer. Again, take your time. You may need to ask more than once.

Once you have received a name, know that you can use this name at any time to call the psychic essence of this tool into your work and that it will now appear on your own inner altar.

Take a moment to further commune with the guardian. Ask them if they have any message or teaching for you. When you are done, generate a sense of gratitude in your heart center and imagine sending that to the guardian, thanking them for their messages and for the gift. Bid them hail and farewell. Their light fades and they step backward and are gone.

Turn around and walk out of the circle of light, back the way you came, walking across the courtyard and back through the golden gate, returning to the center and facing the World Tree. Take a moment to allow all of your experiences to return with you. Take three deep breaths of power. It is done.

The Athame of Air

The athame, a ceremonial dagger, traditionally black-handled and double-edged, is the tool of the element of air. It is the symbolic power of our thoughts and our words, our inspiration, and our epiphanies. The athame is the most physically dangerous of all the altar tools and as such most of the ones you will find will be dull. This is also because in some traditions the athame is never meant to cut anything physical; in other traditions it's used in magick to physically cut things as well. Often another blade is used for physically cutting in magick, either the hand scythe (called a "boline") or just another, sharper blade. These blades traditionally are white-handled, while the athame is black-handled. Regardless of how sharp the blade is, you should always use the athame with caution to avoid injury to self or other. The athame can slice through illusions and planes of reality, particularly where thought and word are concerned. In larger group settings the athame is sometimes interchanged with the sword, which serves almost identical uses as the athame.

Exercise 50

Air Journey

The World Tree stands in the center between the worlds. From this center, turn to face the east. Standing before you is a large silver gate, covered with thin vines of delicate flowers. Upon this gate is etched the alchemical symbol for air: an upward pointing triangle, divided equally with a horizonal line. Allow your gaze to become soft as you imagine gazing through this symbol. Breathe deeply and empty yourself of all thought and emotion. Nothing exists except yourself, this gate, and the symbol through which you now focus your attention.

Imagine stepping forward with every breath…every heartbeat. Getting closer to the gate it opens—as if by magic—and you see the golden light of a new morning. A cool, refreshing breeze blows through the gate, invigorating you as you approach. Breathe deep…and as you reach the gate, mentally affirm your intention to journey to the realm of elemental air. And with a breath of power, step through the threshold and into the light…

You stand in a temple courtyard, filled with soft, green grass, spotted with many colored wildflowers. Here it is eternally springtime…and eternally dawn. Before you, the stone wall cradles a large circular stained-glass window, set high above you, beautifully illuminated as the morning light shines through. The morning sunlight gently cascades through the window and projects downward, illuminating an altar in the center of the courtyard.

Breathe deeply, and walk toward that altar, allowing yourself to become aware of any other details that may arise from this place. Use any and all of your senses to make this place feel more real to you. What do you see? Hear? Feel? Smell? Check in with your emotions. How do you feel about this place? Check in with your body. Notice any aches or pains. Notice your posture.

As you reach the altar, standing before it and the stained-glass window, mentally affirm your intention to call to the guardian of the element. Step into the light of the sun and imagine opening yourself more deeply to the elemental power. Upon the altar is a yellow candle. Calling upon your own inner light, use this now to light the candle and summon the guardian.

As the candle burns, the light of the sun seems to be getting brighter. With each breath this light shines more brightly from the heavens and through the stained glass, pouring down all around you and the altar in a circle of bright golds and soft greens. You feel a rumbling vibration in the ground and feel as if the very walls around you are shaking.

Before you, from just outside the circle of light, the guardian emerges, stepping into the circle, now fully illuminated by the sunlight. Notice how they come to you. What form (if any) do they take? How does their presence feel to you? Introduce yourself to them. Ask them for their name. Give yourself some time to receive this name. You may need to ask more than once. Take your time.

Once you have received a name, the guardian begins to radiate a bright golden light. They step forward and hand to you an athame. As you take it, your hands touch, and you are enveloped in that golden light, the essence of elemental air … the light of knowledge. You feel this brightness enter your lungs, clearing your mind and sharpening your attention. Focus on this sensation as the sense of knowledge grows larger and larger, completely enveloping you just as this golden light does. Feel the sharpness of your mind, letting all of your thoughts, feelings, and attachments flow out into the golden light, leaving you clear and fully present.

The guardian steps back and you hold the blade close. The light of the sun seems to project directly into the blade as you contemplate the lessons of elemental air: It is hot and wet, it is fresh and pure, it is knowledge. Feel how this blade embodies these qualities. Take a few moments to really feel this.

Now, ask the tool for its secret name. It may respond in some fashion, or the guardian may offer you an answer. Again, take your time. You may need to ask more than once.

Once you have received a name, know that you can use this name at any time to call the psychic essence of this tool into your work and that it will now appear on your own inner altar.

Take a moment to further commune with the guardian. Ask them if they have any message or teaching for you. When you are done, generate a sense of gratitude in your heart center and imagine sending that to the guardian, thanking them for their messages and for the gift. Bid them hail and farewell. Their light fades and they step backward and are gone.

Turn around and walk out of the circle of light, back the way you came, walking across the courtyard and back through the silver gate, returning to the center and facing the World Tree. Take a moment to allow all of your experiences to return with you. Take three deep breaths of power. It is done.

The Stone of Earth

Many traditions of witchcraft use the altar pentacle (also called a peyton) as the tool for elemental earth. Interestingly, none of the traditions of witchcraft I've personally trained in have embraced this line of thinking, though it's a common one, and not necessarily wrong. The tool that I use in my practice is an "altar stone." The altar stone is typically a crystal or stone of some sort used to anchor and ground elemental earth on the altar. Other traditions, such as Black Rose Witchcraft use a cube as the elemental tool. In tarot the suit of pentacles (usually made of wood or metal) is representative of the element of earth. The stone is symbolic of the providence of the witch that comes with right relationship with one's environment. The Lia Fáil, Ireland's fabled coronation stone, would only speak when the rightful ruler placed their feet upon it. In the Arthurian myth of the sword and the stone, the sword Excalibur could only be pulled out of the stone by the legitimate king. In Celtic myths and Arthurian legends, the king was married to the land, often personified as a goddess. As Celtic and Arthurian scholar Caitlin Matthews points out, "This idea has not been totally lost, as we can see if we look no further than the English coronation rite where the monarch is ceremonially wedded to the land with the wedding ring of England at the presentation of regalia."[75] The idea is that if the monarch is in right relationship with the land and its people then the land will be blessed with fertility, happiness, and safety. Stones have been around far longer than humans have been and will be around for much longer after we are gone. As such, they are also a symbol of the blessings of permanence, ancestry, and lineage.

Exercise 51

❦

Earth Journey

The World Tree stands in the center between the worlds. From this center, turn to face the north. Standing before you is a large stone gate, covered with thick tendrils of green ivy. Upon this gate is etched the alchemical symbol for earth: a downward pointing triangle, divided equally with a horizonal line. Allow your gaze to become soft as you imagine gazing through this symbol. Breathe deeply and empty yourself of all thought and emotion. Nothing exists except yourself, this gate, and the symbol through which you now focus your attention.

Imagine stepping forward with every breath … every heartbeat. Getting closer to the gate it opens—as if by magic—and you see nothing beyond but

---

75. J. Matthews, G. Knight, V. Chandler, *Arthurian Magic*, 125.

utter darkness. A cold, bitter wind blows through the gate, chilling you as you approach. Breathe deep…and as you reach the gate, mentally affirm your intention to journey to the realm of elemental earth. And with a breath of power, step through the threshold and into the darkness…

You stand in a large, stone room…an ancient temple of elemental earth. Here it is eternally winter…and eternally midnight. In the cold darkness your eyes take a moment to adjust, and you can now make out a dim light shining from high above and directly ahead: the North Star. You see it twinkling above you and slowly begin to notice that you are seeing this star through a large circular stained-glass window. This starlight gently cascades through the glass and projects downward, illuminating an altar in the center of the room.

Breathe deeply, and walk toward that altar, allowing yourself to become aware of any other details that may arise from this place. Use any and all of your senses to make this place feel more real to you. What do you see? Hear? Feel? Smell? Check in with your emotions. How do you feel about this place? Check in with your body. Notice any aches or pains. Notice your posture.

As you reach the altar, standing before it and the stained-glass window, mentally affirm your intention to call to the guardian of the element. Step into the light of the star and imagine opening yourself more deeply to the elemental power. Upon the altar is a green candle. Calling upon your own inner light, use this now to light the candle and summon the guardian.

As the candle burns, the light of the North Star seems to be getting brighter. With each breath this starlight shines more brightly from the heavens and through the stained glass, pouring down all around you and the altar in a circle of greens and browns. You feel a rumbling vibration in the stone floor and feel as if the very walls around you are shaking with anticipation.

Before you, from just outside the circle of light, the guardian emerges, stepping into the circle, now fully illuminated by the starlight. Notice how they come to you. What form (if any) do they take? How does their presence feel to you? Introduce yourself to them. Ask them for their name. Give yourself some time to receive this name. You may need to ask more than once. Take your time.

Once you have received a name, the guardian begins to radiate a deep green light. They step forward and hand to you a natural stone or crystal. As you take it, your hands touch, and you are enveloped in that green light, the essence of elemental earth…You feel the stillness and silence between each breath. Focus on this sensation as the stillness and silence grow larger and larger, completely enveloping you just as this green light does. Feel the stillness in your bones and delve even deeper down into the atoms and molecules and into the vast emptiness between them, and the silence that underlies it all. Let all of your thoughts, feelings, and attachments flow out into the green light, leaving you empty, still, and silent.

The guardian steps back and you hold the stone close. The light of the North Star seems to project directly into the stone as you contemplate elemental earth: It is cold and dry. It is still and silent. It is death. And yet it is also life. Feel how the earth beneath your feet is alive—even in the dead of winter!—life-force, slow and almost imperceptible, hidden in the land, in the roots, patiently waiting to arise in due time, and feel how this stone embodies all these qualities. Take a few moments to really feel this.

Now, ask the tool for its secret name. It may respond in some fashion, or the guardian may offer you an answer. Again, take your time. You may need to ask more than once.

Once you have received a name, know that you can use this name at any time to call the psychic essence of this tool into your work and that it will now appear on your own inner altar.

Take a moment to further commune with the guardian. Ask them if they have any message or teaching for you. When you are done, generate a sense of gratitude in your heart center and imagine sending that to the guardian, thanking them for their messages and for the gift. Bid them hail and farewell. Their light fades and they step backward, returning to the darkness.

Turn around and walk out of the circle of light, back the way you came, walking across the stone floor and back through the darkness and the stone gate, returning to the center and facing the World Tree. Take a moment to allow all of your experiences to return with you. Take three deep breaths of power. It is done.

The Chalice of Water

The chalice is the tool of the element of water. It is symbolic of our emotions, intuition, dreams, fluidity, receptivity, and adaptability. Water is also the element of love in all its forms, from divine love, to romantic love, to the love of family, friends, and strangers. Water, like emotions, can be extremely healing and nourishing or extremely destructive. The key to its energetic signature is that it flows and takes on the form of whatever contains it. The chalice is a vessel of containing that energy in a calm, centered, receptive, and steady state. The earliest form of the chalice was most likely the Dagda's cauldron of hospitality that never ran dry, and then Cerridwen's cauldron, in which she brewed her potion of divine inspiration called *greal*. Later it seems that the grail began taking its place in the form of the Holy Grail of Arthurian legend, a mix of Christianity and Celtic paganism. The Holy Grail was supposedly the cup that Jesus used at the Last Supper and also the vessel used to catch his blood on the cross, symbolic of the sacrifice of divine love. The legends of questing for the Holy Grail are often romance stories. Like the Dagda's cauldron, the chalice is a tool that represents communion and sharing with others, whether it's other coven mates or the spirits and gods themselves. Through the chalice we receive energies and blessings from our deities and spirit allies and integrate them into our physical and energetic bodies through drinking them in.

Exercise 52

∞

Water Journey

The World Tree stands in the center between the worlds. From this center, turn to face the west. Standing before you is a large silver gate, covered in algae and seaweed. Upon this gate is etched the alchemical symbol for water: a downward pointing triangle. Allow your gaze to become soft as you imagine gazing through this symbol. Breathe deeply and empty yourself of all thought and emotion. Nothing exists except yourself, this gate, and the symbol through which you now focus your attention.

Imagine stepping forward with every breath … every heartbeat. Getting closer to the gate it opens—as if by magic—and you see the soft light of the setting sun. A cool breeze blows through the gate, carrying the scent of the salty sea. Breathe deep … and as you reach the gate, mentally affirm your intention to journey to the realm of elemental water. And with a breath of power, step through the threshold and into the light …

You stand in an open temple on a beach. A large stone archway stands erect in the west, open to the vast ocean, and cradling a large circular stained-glass window, set high above you. Here it is eternally autumn…and the sun is eternally setting beneath the watery horizon. The evening sunlight shines through the window and projects downward, illuminating an altar set in the sand.

Breathe deeply, and walk toward that altar, allowing yourself to become aware of any other details that may arise from this place. Use any and all of your senses to make this place feel more real to you. What do you see? Hear? Feel? Smell? Check in with your emotions. How do you feel about this place? Check in with your body. Notice any aches or pains. Notice your posture.

As you reach the altar, standing before it and the stained-glass window, mentally affirm your intention to call to the guardian of the element. Step into the light of the sun and imagine opening yourself more deeply to the elemental power. Upon the altar is a blue candle. Calling upon your own inner light, use this now to light the candle and summon the guardian.

As the candle burns, the light of the setting sun seems to softly intensify. With each breath this light shines more brightly from the heavens, across the waters, and through the stained glass, pouring down all around you and the altar in a circle of soft blues and grays. You feel a rumbling vibration in the ground.

Before you, from just outside the circle of colored light, the guardian emerges, stepping into the circle, now fully illuminated by the sunlight. Notice how they come to you. What form (if any) do they take? How does their presence feel to you? Introduce yourself to them. Ask them for their name. Give yourself some time to receive this name. You may need to ask more than once. Take your time.

Once you have received a name, the guardian begins to radiate a bright sapphire light. They step forward and hand to you a chalice. As you take it, your hands touch, and you are enveloped in that blue light, the essence of elemental water… the light of daring. You feel this brightness enter your body, stirring your emotions, opening your heart.

Focus on this sensation as the sense of your own feelings grows larger and larger, completely enveloping you just as this sapphire light does. Feel your feelings, thoughts, and attachments flow out into the blue light, leaving you feeling open-hearted and daringly bold.

The guardian steps back and you hold the chalice close. The light of the sun seems to project directly into the chalice as you contemplate the lessons of elemental water: It is cold and wet; it is passive and receptive. It is depth … the unconscious … emotions … dreams. Feel how this chalice embodies these qualities. Take a few moments to really feel this.

Now, ask the tool for its secret name. It may respond in some fashion, or the guardian may offer you an answer. Again, take your time. You may need to ask more than once.

Once you have received a name, know that you can use this name at any time to call the psychic essence of this tool into your work and that it will now appear on your own inner altar.

Take a moment to further commune with the guardian. Ask them if they have any message or teaching for you. When you are done, generate a sense of gratitude in your heart center and imagine sending that to the guardian, thanking them for their messages and for the gift. Bid them hail and farewell. Their light fades and they step backward and are gone.

Turn around and walk out of the circle of light, back the way you came, walking across the beach and back through the silver gate, returning to the center and facing the World Tree. Take a moment to allow all of your experiences to return with you. Take three deep breaths of power. It is done.

The Fifth Element(s)

The fifth element is even more difficult to discuss and describe, because it's many things but also one thing. I really love Ivo Dominguez Jr.'s take on the fifth element as the "fifth elements." He defines and divides them in a brilliant way that makes perfect sense to me and fits perfectly into my cosmological framework of magick. He divides the fifth element into three parts, using terms that historically have been used interchangeably with one another: ether, spirit, and quintessence. Here is how he differentiates them, along with my own understanding and epiphanies about this three-division model.

Ether in this sense is divinity as immanent. Immanence refers to the idea of divinity existing within and being fully integrated within all things in the physical universe. Ether is divinity as the "generative" force in our G.O.D. acronym. It's the force of "Coagula" in alchemy, the force that brings together, binds, forms, and unites as it arises. It's the force that the sixteen sub-elements (as combinations) emerge from to form the four primary elements. I associate etheric energy with the Lower Self, the Under World, the Cauldron of Warming, and being of a cardinal nature. In the Sacred Fires Tradition of witchcraft we refer to this force as Z-Energy.[76] Z-Energy is what comprises all of reality and the force of creation itself. To avoid confusion with other uses of the term "etheric" I will refer to this concept as Z-Energy moving forward.

The element of spirit, on the other hand, is divinity as transcendent. Transcendence refers to the idea of divinity existing outside of the confines of our physical reality and universe. Spirit is divinity as the "destructive" force in our G.O.D. acronym, or rather, it's the dissolving aspect, like a drop of water merging with the ocean. As such, it's the force of "Solve" in alchemy, the force that breaks apart as it descends. I suppose it really depends on your vantage point, though. As ether ascends toward spirit, it builds and unifies aspects of energy. As spirit descends toward ether, it breaks apart and divides aspects of energy. I associate spirit with the Higher Self, the Upper World, the Cauldron of Wisdom, and being of a mutable nature.

Where Z-Energy and spirit meet is quintessence. Quintessence in this sense is a bit of a paradox. It is the membrane, the liminal space, the container, and the core divinity within something. If spirit is breaking down as it descends, it's quintessence that is increasing. If Z-Energy is solidifying as it ascends, it's quintessence that is decreasing. Z-Energy is what gives intrinsic and central constituent identity to something, whether physical or nonphysical. Just as the Middle Self gives the sense of personality and individuality from things outside of self, so does quintessence give the core defining energy of something through what it is containing, like the use of the word quintessential. For example, in our view of the seven-layer body of the individual, each defining boundary and the liminal spot of overlap where it is paradoxically both things and neither thing is quintessence.

The Peyton and the Cauldron

The two primary tools I use on my altar for the fifth elements are the peyton[77] and the cauldron. The peyton is a physical pentacle, often a disc made

---

76. Hunter, *The Witch's Book of Mysteries*, 39–40.
77. Also known as a paten; the Cabot Tradition uses the spelling of peyton.

of wood or metal. It is a tool of balance, connection, blessing, protection, and the elements in harmony. As an amulet, the peyton can be thought of as a spiritual shield, neutralizing unbalanced energies that come your way. This is also why many witches wear pentacle amulets. It's not just a symbol of their path but also spiritually shields them from unbalanced energies. It also serves to bless by balancing one's energies. As a tool of blessing and manifestation, petitions and spells can be placed to speed and amplify the realization of the spell's goal, and it can also be used to charge and activate the potency of materia placed upon it.

In the Cabot Tradition of witchcraft, we use the peyton to call and dismiss elemental energies, particularly when calling the four elements and their guardians into the magick circle. The peyton is held up in the moon hand, the receptive hand, when calling in elemental energies and the sun hand, the projective hand, when dismissing them. When a peyton isn't available the hands themselves are used in the same way with the five fingers spread out symbolizing the five elements. You can see an example of the peyton being used this way in the music video for "Voodoo" by Godsmack, which features Laurie Cabot and Cabot initiates throughout it, as lead singer Sully Erna is a Cabot initiate himself.

The other tool is the cauldron, which has been briefly touched on already when discussing the element of water. The cauldron is the epitome of Coagula and Solve, creation and destruction, combining and separating. It is a tool of rebirth and regeneration. As a vessel that can hold all four of the elements it is incredibly versatile in its uses. It can serve as a physical focal point for the three spiritual cauldrons within ourselves and the personal changes we would like to make to ourselves, our lives, and our world.

On my personal primary altar, I place the peyton in the center and the cauldron on top of it when working with the cauldron and likewise place the peyton over the cauldron when working with the peyton. The center of the altar and one's sacred space is the direction often assigned to the fifth element(s), which is also why the witch or magician conducts most of their work within the circle surrounded by the four elements in their designated spot around the magick circle.

Exercise 53

⧼∾⧽

Spirit Journey

Enter your Inner Temple. Notice a door within the temple. This is the entrance to your spirit temple.

Imagine stepping forward with every breath … every heartbeat. Getting closer to the gate it opens—as if by magic—and you that the temple walls seem to be composed of the void of space itself and a billion tiny stars throughout it, illuminating the temple. It's as if the Under World and the Upper World are one and the same here. High up in the room you notice the four stained glass windows of the previous elemental temples; the water bearer of Aquarius to the north, the bull of Taurus to the east, the lion of Leo to the south, and the eagle of Scorpio to the west.

Breathe deeply, and walk toward that center of the temple, allowing yourself to become aware of any other details that may arise from this place. Use any and all of your senses to make this place feel more real to you. What do you see? Hear? Feel? Smell? Check in with your emotions. How do you feel about this place? Check in with your body. Notice any aches or pains. Notice your posture.

Reaching from a place of your own inner divinity, you call out to the Great God and the Great Goddess, glowing like the sun and the moon respectively. Take a moment to feel their presence, two complementary but dual forces. What do they look like to you? Are they familiar or unfamiliar? Are they what you expected, or do they differ? Can you see them clearly or are they veiled somehow, preventing you from directly seeing them at this time?

You hold out your left hand and the Goddess places the cauldron on it. Take a moment to reflect on its mysteries: of birth and rebirth, of creation and destruction, of life and death, of tomb and womb. From the Great Cauldron all things emerge and unto the Great Cauldron all things return.

Now, ask the cauldron you received for its secret name. It may respond in some fashion, or the Goddess may offer you an answer. Again, take your time. You may need to ask more than once.

Once you have received a name, know that you can use this name at any time to call the psychic essence of this tool into your work and that it will now appear on your own inner altar.

You hold out your right hand and the God places the peyton on it. Take a moment to reflect on its mysteries; everything is intricately connected, because all things are aspects of spirit: all the elemental forces, all matter, all energy, all thought, and all emotions. Everything contains within it everything else. Everything is alive and enspirited and conscious on some level. Every cause has an effect and every effect had a cause.

Now, ask the peyton you received for its secret name. It may respond in some fashion, or the God may offer you an answer. Again, take your time. You may need to ask more than once.

Once you have received a name, know that you can use this name at any time to call the psychic essence of this tool into your work and that it will now appear on your own inner altar.

Take a moment to further commune with the God and the Goddess. Ask them if they have any message or teaching for you. When you are done, generate a sense of gratitude in your heart center and imagine sending that to them, thanking them for their messages and for the gift. Bid them hail and farewell. Their lights merge together as one and slowly seemingly dissipate into everything and nothing.

Turn around and find the door you came in from; open it, and return to your Inner Temple. Take a moment to allow all of your experiences to return with you. On your inner altar are all six tools. Whenever you need to perform magick, you can do so here. You have all the tools, materia, and resources available to you in your Inner Temple. When you are finished, take three deep steady breaths and return to waking consciousness.

Rite of Soul Inspiration Layout

Exercise 54

The Rite of Soul Inspiration

Magickal timing: Any

Materia:
- frankincense
- a cauldron or container of water
- 10 tealight candles

Purpose: This ritual calls upon Mnemosyne (Nem-oh-zeen-ee) and the nine Muses to bless you with inspiration. Mnemosyne is the Greek Titaness of memory. Working with Mnemosyne I have found her to be not just memory itself, but the goddess governing mental faculties, including visualization, the bridge between Middle Self and Higher Self, which is where psychic ability occurs. This is my own personal gnosis, and the closest I've come to verifying it is one line from the *Orphic Hymn* to her, which states: "vigorous to excite the mental eye from dark oblivion's night."[78] As such, I have found her to be

---

78. Orpheus, *The Hymns of Orpheus*, 93–94.

an excellent help in activating the psychic powers of the mind, particularly clairvoyance, as well as assisting in discovering one's True Will. The Muses are the goddesses of inspiration, creativity, and innovation. By working with the Muses, you will gain greater creativity in your life, including in spellcrafting and ritual. Working with the Muses and their mother can also gain soul-level wisdom and innovation to your spiritual path, including witchcraft.

Mnemosyne resides over a pool in the Under World with her namesake. The pool is a counterbalance to the river Lethe in the Under World, from which souls would drink, forget their mortal lives, and reincarnate. In Orphism, initiates were instructed to not drink from Lethe but rather to wait and drink from the pool of Mnemosyne so that they would remember their past lives, end the cycle of rebirth, and dwell among Orpheus and other heroic and legendary souls in the afterlife. So, for me, Mnemosyne isn't just the goddess of memory itself, but the memory of the Higher Self, the immortal soul.

In Greek mythology, she slept with Zeus nine consecutive nights, giving birth to the nine Muses. As the mother of the Muses, I connect her further with the Higher Self since true inspiration was said to come via the daemon in ancient Greek culture (called the genius in ancient Roman culture). Plato viewed the daemon as a personal spiritual being that watched over a person, which modern occultists correlate to the concept of the Holy Guardian Angel or Higher Self. So, for me, she is the goddess of the inspiration of the Higher Self's True Will. The *Orphic Hymn* states that Mnemosyne is "by whom the soul and intellect is join'd," which relates to Plato's views of memory (as a cosmic force) being the power of uniting the intellect (the mind, or Middle Self) with soul (or the Higher Self).[79]

Instructions: Begin by burning frankincense as an offering, as it's sacred to the Muses and Mnemosyne.[80] Place a cauldron or another vessel filled with water in the center of your altar. Place a tealight candle within it. It should float on top. Then take nine more tealights and place them in a triangle in groups of three around the cauldron. Light the candle in the cauldron and say:

---

79. Orpheus, *The Hymns of Orpheus*, 72.
80. Orpheus, *The Hymns of Orpheus*.

I call to the mother of Muses, Mnemosyne
I call to the Titan goddess of memory
Revealer of the soul's true light
Bestower of the inner sight
By flame of light within this water
I open the way for your daughters!

Pause for a moment and focus on Mnemosyne's presence. Then say:

Spirits sired by Zeus most high
Sisters nine, now come, draw nigh.
Three by three are your holy flames
One by one I call your sacred names.

Now light each candle starting from one to nine. As you light the candle, say the Muses' name and spend a moment focusing on their presence.

1. Calliope (Kuh-lye-uh-pee)

2. Clio (Clee-oh)

3. Erato (Arrow-toe)

4. Euterpe (You-terp-y)

5. Melpomene (Mel-paw-men-y)

6. Polyhymnia (Poly-him-nee-uh)

7. Terpsichore (Terp-sick-ery)

8. Thalia (Thaw-lee-uh)

9. Urania (Yur-awn-ee-uh)

When all the candles are lit, focus on your Cauldron of Wisdom, which is the energetic anchor point of the Higher Self, located on the crown of your head. See the cauldron in your mind's eye above your head. Visualize the Muses, pouring inspiration into the cauldron as if it were liquid light. See the liquid light begin to overflow and pour all around your energetic body, filling your aura. As you do, say:

I ask that you fill my cauldron of wisdom
With the sparks of your inspiration.
Through my holy daemon's will divine
Illuminate creativity within my mind.
And by my words and by my hands
I will give it form within this land.

You can now spend time in meditation and communion with the Muses if you desire. Let the tealights burn entirely out. When they have finished, take out the tealight from inside the cauldron and pour the water into a cup. Add the water to a bath or, if you don't have a bathtub, pour it over your head at the end of a shower. After you have done so, thank the Muses for their gifts of inspiration. I recommend burning more frankincense as an offering of gratitude.

The Psychic Pentacle

The Elements, the Senses, and the Clairs

I was taught that each element is associated with a primary sense and its psychic clair counterpart. Earth governs our sense of touch and physical interactions and clairtangency, the ability to psychically feel information through touch or bodily sensations. Air is associated with smells carried in the air and its psychic counterpart is clairalience, the psychic phenomenon of smelling.

Likewise, water's physical sense is taste due to the saliva of the tongue and mouth and its psychic counterpart is clairgustance, gaining psychic information from phantom tastes occurring in the mouth. Fire is associated with sight, mostly due to vision relying on light being picked up by the eyes, and clairvoyance is naturally the clair associated with it. The element of spirit is associated with hearing and clairaudience, psychic hearing. Clairaudience tends to be the closest psychic sense associated with mediumship and spirit communication. As such, I have found that calling upon your elemental ally (that you met in the journeys) can help to strengthen those areas when you're working on developing them and strengthening them. All you need to do is mentally or verbally call out to the spirit for its assistance with the name that it provided you.

Chapter 7

SYNCHING WITH THE SUN, MOON, AND SEASONS

M agickal timing has its origins in astrology. Astrology is a study of the movement of celestial bodies and how it affects people's lives on Earth. Many different cultures have used astrology throughout history, and although it's been practiced for thousands of years, its exact origins are unknown. Astrology's historically recorded roots go back to ancient Egypt and Mesopotamia, where our earliest cultures and civilizations used the stars to understand the world around them. Ancient people saw patterns with celestial movements, both in nature and among themselves. This observational science of the heavens above later turned into a practice of making predictions through its use. It wasn't long until they realized that people could use astrological timing in magick for more efficacy.

While magickal timing isn't necessary for the casting of spells or practicing magick, it's a powerful component that is easily overlooked. Witches view the universe as a vast space of energies interacting with each other through cause and effect and influence, and astrology is what allows us to track and understand these energetic influences at a macrocosmic level.

The easiest way to think about magickal timing is to think of your spell as if it were bowling. The pins at the end of the bowling alley are the goal you're aiming for, and your bowling ball is the spell. Ideally, you would like to get a strike, knocking all the bowling pins down with one hit; you don't

183

want your bowling ball to fall into the gutter and not hit any of the pins at all. When we incorporate astrological magickal timing into our spells, it's like putting a bumper in the bowling alley. The more magickal timing that is incorporated into the spell, the more "bumpers" you are placing in the alley to help you achieve your goal and hopefully get that strike.

While, of course, it would be ideal to have all astrological correspondences be perfect for our magickal timing in regard to spellcasting, you could be waiting years or decades for the right conditions to line up. Due to this, we try to focus on the astrological influences that have the strongest impact upon our magick: the Moon and the Sun. This is especially true since they are the ones that complete a full cycle the fastest. This means that there are more opportunities to align your magick with this timing for success than waiting thirty years for the perfect conditions to cast the perfect spell. None of us have time for that.

The Sun

Witchcraft historically tends to be associated mostly with the moon and night, with witches performing their magick under the darkened veil of secrecy. While this isn't untrue, it's not the whole story. Witches work with the sun just as much as they do with the moon, and working with the sun is of great benefit to any witch, especially since most of us, with the exception of those who work night shifts, are awake and living our lives during daylight. To the witch, the sun is pure active life force, which is why its rising, setting, and disappearance is often seen as a life cycle in relation to death and rebirth by many ancient people. Sunlight nourishes life. It assists in the growth of flora on our planet, which is the main link on the food chain of all our ecosystems. These plants dependent upon our sun also create and regulate oxygen levels, which creates the perfect condition for animals including ourselves to live and breathe. The sun also brings warmth and comfort. The sun's relationship to our planet determines how warm an area is, such as the equator, which is directly aligned with the sun; or how cold an area is, such as our North and South Poles.

Spring

From the spring equinox to the summer solstice is springtime. Springtime is when the energy for magickal manifestation starts to build and increase, as well as psychic ability related to external events and people in your life. This is a time to set magick into motion for larger manifestations related to major changes you'd like to see come to fruition throughout the year. In other words, this is the perfect time to begin casting magick to manifest your larger goals for your life. Contact with spirit guides and familiar spirits tends to come more readily to folks around this time, as well as an increase in the powers of psychic empathy and emotional energies. Dreams around this time tend to be more prophetic in nature.

Summer

From the summer solstice to the autumn equinox is summertime. During summer, the wave of magickal energy tends to be heightened, and casting magick for quicker manifestation for things that are already in effect tends to be more successful around this time. What I mean by this is that whereas spring would be a great time for casting magick for a new career, summer is a great time for casting magick for a career that you already have. This is a time when you can use magick to fine-tune and adjust things in your life, instead of manifesting something completely new into your life. Summer is a time that is traditionally more difficult for psychic work such as mediumship, but is a great time for using your psychic ability to look at the structure of your life as well as how the past is currently influencing the present and future. Upper World journeying is easiest during this season.

Autumn

From the autumn equinox to the winter solstice is autumn. Magickally, autumn is a fantastic time to do magick to increase your harvests in life, whatever that may be to you. During autumn you may notice a drastic increase in psychic ability, particularly related to mediumship and intense clarity with divination that pertains to the future. Mediumship is so strong during this time that it can occur almost effortlessly or accidentally, and it's not uncommon to have spirits visit you in your dreams more often during this season than any other. This is also the ideal time to evaluate the aspects of your life that aren't serving you, divine how your life would be without those things, and cast magick to shed those people, places, events, attitudes, situations and habits from your life that are hindering you. During autumn, astral projection starts to become easier, as does lucid dreaming, and any sort of dream magick.

Winter

From the winter solstice to spring equinox is wintertime. Winter tends to be when the current of magickal energy is at its weakest. Energies are more focused inward than outward. This makes for intense astral projection, and very vivid and lucid dreams. This is the period where self-care is the most crucial, not just due to the biological/psychological effects that the lack of sunlight has, but because this is the period to truly rest and recharge yourself magickally for the next season as the wheel restarts its cycle. Magick related to changing psychological and emotional aspects of the self is heightened as well as healing related to these areas of yourself.

This is a time of deep contemplation, meditation, and gratitude for the blessings in your life (which is a key element in a life of manifestation). This is an ideal time for cleansing, purification, and banishing. Spirit activity is still heightened during this time period as well, though trying to communicate with them through mediumship may be a bit more difficult than other times. Under World journeying is the easiest during this season.

Times of the Day

When it comes to times of the day related to the sun and magickal timing, we tend to divide the day and night into four main periods: dawn to noon, noon to sunset, sunset to midnight, midnight to dawn.

Dawn

From dawn (sunrise) to noon is when magick related to attracting and manifesting new things into your life or just setting the tone of the day tends to be performed. Dawn is one of the strongest times for this magick, and taps into the powers of increase.

Noon

From noon, when the sun is at its highest peak during the day, to sunset, magick related to increase, as well as growth, strength, stability, and abundance is most beneficial. Noon is the most beneficial time for these types of workings.

Sunset

From sunset to midnight magick related to resolutions, banishing, bindings, cleansing, endings, and severing ties tend to be preferred, with sunset being the peak time.

Midnight

From midnight to dawn has all the same attributes as sunset to midnight, as it's still a period of darkness. However, this period of time tends toward magick that is ideal for necromancy, spirit contact, and astral projection, and dream magick tends to be immensely increased; we'll explore some theories about why in a moment. The peak time for magick at this time is tradition-ally midnight.

Exercise 55

A Spell to Open Your Third Eye
By Melanie Barnum

Magickal timing: Sunset

Materia:
- jar of bio-degradable glitter (preferably multi-colored)

Purpose: This spell is intended to help you open your third eye, the space in the center of your forehead, slightly above your eyebrows. Your third eye is the seat of your clairvoyance or your clear psychic sight. This spell will enhance your current psychic or intuitive abilities and help to clear out any debris that may be blocking your gifts from blossoming and coming through.

Directions: This is a simple spell, but you need to perform it with clear intention of opening your clairvoyance. You'll want to be outdoors, under the sky, at dusk, preferably somewhere in grass and with a bit of privacy so you won't be disturbed. It is critical, as well, to have a dry evening. Any type of precipitation, such as rain or snow, will be counterproductive.

Bring your jar of glitter outside with you. Before you begin your spell, take a deep breath in and then exhale. Breathe deeply again and say the words:

> *My intention is to open my third eye to help*
> *me tune in to my natural psychic abilities.*

Now, with your jar open and ready in your right hand, look to the north and recite these words out loud:

> *The colors of the world abound*
> *And are freely available to see*
> *From the sky to the ground*
> *For all who believe and wish it to be.*

Then, still facing north, with your right hand, throw a bit of the glitter into the air. As it comes down, catch some with your left hand. Then, rub a bit with that same hand on your third eye.

Now, turn your body to the south, and with your face to the sky say:

> *My psychic sight is clear*
> *My intention is true*
> *Images will begin to appear*
> *As the sky turns dark from blue.*

With your glitter in your right hand, throw a bit up toward the sky, again catching some with your left hand and rub it in a circle over your third eye.

Next, turn eastward. With your soul open and ready state aloud:

> *Enhancing my intuitive gifts*
> *By opening my third eye*
> *Will lead to a complete shift*
> *And allow my vision to fly.*

Repeat your glitter ritual, finishing with placing the glitter on your clair-voyant seat on your forehead. Then, turn toward the west. Say the following:

> *I declare with complete intent*
> *That I'm now able to comprehend*
> *The sights and visions that present*
> *My clairvoyant abilities have no end.*

For the last time, throw glitter into the air in front of you, catching a small amount with your left hand. This time, rub the glitter into your third eye area and then hold the jar of remaining glitter to your forehead, giving thanks that you're now able to open your clairvoyant gift.

Finally, slowly spin and throw up the remaining glitter as you turn in a complete circle, repeating all the phrases aloud as you do. Allow the colors of the glitter to blend with all of the colors of the universe, opening your clair-voyance to all of the colorful messages you will receive.

Psychic Ability, Spirit Manifestation, Periods of Light and Dark

The sun appears to have a direct effect on not only our psychic ability but also the manifestation and activity of certain types of spirits. First, the sun is directly tied to our circadian rhythms. Circadian rhythm is the body's inter-nal clock that regulates our cycles of sleep and wakefulness by altering our brainwave cycles via melatonin. In my previous book, *Psychic Witch*, I discussed the connection between the pineal gland, circadian rhythms, light, melatonin output, brainwave states, and psychic ability. I also discuss why this makes dark lighting and working at night the more preferred time to cast magick.

What is particularly interesting about this is that the melatonin output via the circadian system peaks two times during the day for the average adult. In doing so it alters our brainwave states to be more firmly in alpha slipping to theta (which is when psychic ability occurs). The first is 1–3 a.m. and the other is 2–4 p.m. This would suggest that these are the periods when psychic abilities are naturally heightened in the average person on a regular sleep cycle. What I find particularly fascinating about this is that 1–3 a.m. is smack dab in the middle of the Witching Hour, where spirit activity and perception of it tends to be increased.

The other fascinating aspect in relationship to the sun and spirits is the correlation between spirit manifestation and sunlight. There seems to be a range of spirits that manifest much stronger in darkness. Not only are tales of spirits appearing at night almost a universal norm taken for granted by most, but the interesting thing is that these types of spirits tend to also manifest and interact with our plane of reality regardless of time if it's a place devoid of any light, especially sunlight. Think about how many times people report spirits in attics and basements completely secure from any light, especially sunlight. This is not only a common experience, but it has become a trope in our culture's media and stories.

So, before we begin, I want to make it completely clear again that higher vibrational and lower vibrational are not markers of morality or of being a "good" or "bad" spirit. Unlike certain religions or mainstream media's presentation on the subject, residing on a certain vibrational plane doesn't make a spirit inherently good or bad. This is like saying animals who live on the ground are inherently evil and animals who live in the trees are inherently morally superior. Not only is this a broad statement of ignorance ignoring any form of nuance, but it's also a strong prejudice many carry with them.

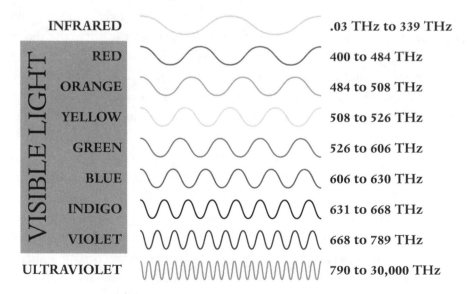

INFRARED		.03 THz to 339 THz
RED		400 to 484 THz
ORANGE		484 to 508 THz
YELLOW		508 to 526 THz
GREEN		526 to 606 THz
BLUE		606 to 630 THz
INDIGO		631 to 668 THz
VIOLET		668 to 789 THz
ULTRAVIOLET		790 to 30,000 THz

VISIBLE LIGHT

Spectrum of Light

In regard to frequency, let's look at the spectrum of light. The spectrum of light that humans can see physically with their eyes ranges between 430 terahertz (THz) and 750 terahertz. The red light spectrum exists at 400 to 484 terahertz and is the slowest light wavelength we can visibly see. From 399 terahertz to .03 terahertz has such a low wavelength vibration that it's invisible to the naked eye and falls in what we call infrared light. The violet spectrum occurs at 668 terahertz to 789 terahertz and is the fastest light wavelength we can visibly see. From 790 terahertz to 30,000 terahertz vibrates at wavelengths too fast for the eye to see and is referred to as ultraviolet. The sun is the primary source of ultraviolet light.

Returning back to our discussion of light and spirits, it's interesting to note the long history and lore of certain spirits, particularly ghosts and demons, being more active at night or in darkness, when there's no visible light, especially sunlight. I believe this is because those spirits are residing in a lower vibrational frequency that is compatible with the slower and lower light frequencies beyond human perception somewhere in the infrared spectrum. Interestingly in classical mediumship and seances, mediums would use red lights when calling upon spirits believing through their experiences that it made it more conductive for spirit manifestation of the deceased as well as the creation of the phenomenon of ectoplasm. They're creating ideal conditions for spirits in that frequency of reality to interact with ours, creating a bridge of overlap.

Since the slower the light wavelength, the less energy exerted, it would seem that the slower vibrational wavelength of light makes it easier for them to manifest and interact with our level of reality, which again is all coinciding in the same multidimensional space as ours. From my experience, beings of a higher vibration don't have difficulty interacting with us or manifesting whenever they want to. Since they're already vibrating at a faster rate and exerting more energy than our visible light spectrum, they would simply just need to lower their speed of vibration to do so.

On the other hand, it would also appear that higher frequencies of light, especially ultraviolet light produced by the sun, makes it much harder for a lower vibrational being to manifest and interact directly on our plane. I even know of one witchcraft elder who brings ultraviolet lights into particularly nasty hauntings. It may seem unconventional by witchcraft standards, but it's an effective way of ending those malicious hauntings. Sometimes it's permanent, but often it's temporary, and more banishing and exorcism is then performed. I feel those practices should be reserved for the most extreme cases of the nastier spirit beings. Connecting with and figuring out what the spirit wants or needs is a much more helpful and long-lasting approach that benefits everyone, physical and non-physical folks alike. Some spirits are completely harmless and would rather not be bothered or bother you. Some are in search of assistance and don't know how to get our attention without doing things that might scare us.

While it's absolutely possible to contact, communicate, or work with any spirit at any time of the day, there are definitely conditions that make it much easier to do so. Between the internal conditions of the mind's brainwave cycles due to our circadian rhythm at 1–3 a.m. and the lack of light that occurs at midnight, there's definitely something to the concept of the Witching Hour as a time when spirit contact, communication, and apparition are the most ideal.

Exercise 56

≈

Solar Adorations

Magickal timing: Throughout the day as specified

Purpose: Solar adorations are a regular practice within Thelema wherein one greets the sun throughout various times of the day. The practice is often referred to as "performing Resh," as the practice was given in Aleister Crowley's *Liber Resh vel Helios*.[81] "Liber" means book, "Resh" is a Hebrew letter that in Qabalah is associated with the sun, solar deities, and the Sun tarot card. Helios is the solar Titan of ancient Greek religion. Crowley was partially inspired by the Islamic practice of praying five times a day during different timings: sunrise, noon, afternoon, sunset, and night.[82] In Crowley's version the magician addresses various Egyptian solar deities associated with

---

81. Crowley, Waddle, and Desti, *Magick: Liber Aba.*
82. DuQuette, et al., *Llewellyn's Complete Book of Ceremonial Magick*, 343.

four times of the day while facing different cardinal directions. During these times of day, the sun is at "stations" within the sky.

There are several purposes to this practice. It connects one to solar energy and vitalizes one's energetic bodies and magickal power. It also helps to sync one with the rhythms of nature, since it is cycling in a much quicker way than the seasons or even the moon due to the fact that the sun rises and sets daily. Most of all, it's meant to be a focal point of meditative reflection wherein the practitioner views the sun as a symbol of their Higher Self, the part of them that is divine. The significance of this is that from our point of living life in a physical body here on the planet Earth, it appears that the sun rises and sets, but that is an illusion. In many ancient cultures, they believed that the sun was born each day and died each night or that it was journeying through the Upper World during the day and then the Under World in the night in a daily cycle. But it isn't the sun that is moving. The sun is eternal and stationary; instead, it's us moving in our relation to perceiving the sun as our planet rotates.

So, if we think of the sun as a symbol of our Higher Self and us here on Earth as our current incarnation, we can see that we are indeed eternal and that our existence does not rely upon our physical incarnation, nor does it end upon death. Therefore, it also reminds us of the Great Work of the occultist, which the French occultist Éliphas Lévi defines as being "above all things the creation of man by himself. That is to say, the full and entire conquest of his faculties and his future, it is especially the perfect emancipation of his will, assuring full power over the Universal Magical Agent. This Agent, disguised by the ancient philosophers under the name of the First Matter, determines the forms of modifiable substance, and we can really arrive by means of it at metallic transmutation and the Universal Medicine."[83] In other words, the Great Work is to transform the self on an inner level to unlock our full potential as humans to be once again in alignment with our true divine nature, as symbolized by the alchemist's quest to turn lead into gold.

So, in a nutshell, the practice of the solar adorations strengthens our magick and energetic bodies; it syncs us to the rhythms of nature; it puts us in alignment with our Higher Self; it reminds us of our eternal nature; and

---

83. Lévi, *Transcendental Magic*, 104.

it reminds us of the Great Work. Here I've provided my version of it, which removes specific deity names as well as gender and re-emphasizes the main points of it. I've also integrated the Witch's Pyramid, which is a blueprint for the Great Work of the witch's path. While some Thelemites might take offense to any of Crowley's rituals being changed, Crowley himself wrote that his rituals "need not be slavishly imitated; on the contrary the student should do nothing the object of which he does not understand; also, if he have any capacity whatever, he will find his own crude rituals more effective than the highly polished ones of other people."[84]

Directions: Upon awakening (but preferably at sunrise) face the east and raise your arms with palms facing outward in salutation to the sun. Close your eyes and say:

> *Hail unto the Solar Sovereign of Light*
> *As you appear to rise in the world of form*
> *Ever steadfast on your throne*
> *I call to you as a companion*
> *Soul to Soul and Sol to Sol*
> *That you may teach me To Know*
> *In alignment with the Great Work*
> *So that I too, may know myself in all parts.*

At noon when the sun is at its apex, face the south and raise your arms with palms facing outward in salutation to the sun. Close your eyes and say:

> *Hail unto the Solar Sovereign of Light*
> *As you appear to reign in the world of form*
> *Ever steadfast on your throne*
> *I call to you as a companion*
> *Soul to Soul and Sol to Sol*
> *That you may teach me To Will*
> *In alignment with the Great Work*
> *So that I too, may know myself in all parts.*

---

84. Crowley, *The Equinox.*

At sunset face the west and raise your arms with palms facing outward in salutation to the sun. Close your eyes and say:

Hail unto the Solar Sovereign of Light
As you appear to descend in the world of form
Ever steadfast on your throne
I call to you as a companion
Soul to Soul and Sol to Sol
That you may teach me To Dare
In service of the Great Work
So that I too, may know myself in all parts.

Sometime during the night (though preferably at midnight) face the north with palms facing outward in salutation to the sun, even though you cannot visibly see it. Close your eyes and say:

Hail unto the Solar Sovereign of Light
As you appear to be cloaked in the world of form
Ever steadfast on your throne
I call to you as a companion
Soul to Soul and Sol to Sol
That you may teach me To Be Silent
In service of the Great Work
So that I too, may know myself in all parts.

The Moon

The heavenly body most associated with witches and witchcraft is the moon. The image of a coven of witches gathering together at night under the full moon is one that is pretty hardwired into our cultural ideals of what witches do, and it's not that far off from the truth. The moon is tied into witchcraft culturally in several different ways. Most obviously, the moon is a source of light in the night sky, and it's hard to get away from the fact that many of the symbols associated with witchcraft are derived from ancient times when the moon was the only source of light people had at night.

The moon also represents the mystery of the unknown and the unconscious realms. The connection between witches and the moon is also likely rooted in ancient myths, legends, and religions. Goddesses in Greco-Roman mythology explicitly associated with witchcraft and magick were also lunar goddesses, such as Hecate, Diana, and Selene. Likewise, many of the famous witches and sorceresses of Greco-Roman mythology, such as Circe and Medea, were either described as being children or priestesses of Hecate.

The moon is also the perfect physical representation of psychism and magickal ability, which are two sides of the same coin and just a matter of whether we're receiving and perceiving energy or whether we're wielding it and sending it out into the universe. The moon receives the sun's light and then reflects it to Earth. The moon is also a shapeshifter, changing form throughout the month, balancing itself in both darkness and light, just like the spiritual path of the witch. The moon also rules these magickal and psychic tides of energies, just like it has tides of light and darkness via its phases and the way the moon's gravity affects both the Earth's ocean and molten tides. In witchcraft, the moon affects the flow of psychic and astral energy in tides through its phases.

New Moon / Dark Moon

The new moon and the dark moon are often used interchangeably by some, and their difference is argued by others on what differentiates the two. Different traditions and schools of thought will define the two a little differently. For me, the dark moon is part of the new moon. The dark moon is when the moon phase is exactly 0 percent illuminated and is completely invisible to the naked eye. The period right after that when the moon is beginning to crescent is how I define the new moon. Astronomically, the new moon is the period of time when the moon is between the sun and the Earth, so very little is reflected during this time.

This is a period of time that I do little to no spellwork involving external manifestation. Instead, this is a time period for me to focus on going inward and resting. Shadow work, inner journeys, self-improvement, meditation, and contemplation are extremely empowered during this time. Likewise, it's an excellent time to start planning and preparing for magickal work. I often use this time to focus on determining what my will for a spell is and deciding what I want to manifest with my magick. I suggest taking this time to become as crystal clear with your will and its end result as possible and then start formulating a plan of how you want to go about casting your spell.

Full Moon

The full moon is when the moon phase is exactly 100 percent illuminated. Astronomically, the full moon is the period of time when the moon is on the complete opposite side of the Earth from the sun, and the sun is fully reflected from it. The full moon is historically the phase of the moon that has been the most associated with witches throughout history, and for good reason. Magickally, when the moon is full, it is at the height of its power, but also in a liminal state between fully waning and fully waxing. Many witches consider the day before and day after a full moon to be a full moon for all magickal intents and purposes. This is a good time to do pretty much anything magickally, and the efficacy of any spellcasting is greatly increased. This is a preferred time to cleanse and charge magickal items (again, being at that perfect liminal spot between the waxing and waning).

Waxing and Waning

The phasing between full moon and new moon and back is where we get the second main division of the moon's phases, which are waxing and waning. These are the main tides of movement for the moon's energy. Simply put, when the moon is waxing, its light is increasing and headed toward being a full moon. When the moon is waning, its light is decreasing and it's headed toward being a new moon. A great way to think of the waxing and waning moon in terms of magickal ability is to think of it this way; when the moon is waxing, it's increasing its reflection of light outward and is a great time for sending out magickal goals that relate to manifesting changes in your life and in the physical world. When the moon is waning, it's reducing its light reflection, which makes it a great time to for magick related to banishing things from your life and the physical world and for drawing in those changes you've sent out. Think of your magick like a boomerang that you sent out into the universe while the moon was waxing; its results start coming in stronger during the waning moon as the metaphorical boomerang returns to you.

A simple way to look at the moon and determine if it's waxing or waning is to shape your hand like a crescent moon and look at which hand it matches. If it looks like the crescent of your right hand (being the more common projective hand of energetic anatomy), the moon is waxing. Likewise, if the moon looks like the crescent of your left hand (being the more common receptive hand of energetic anatomy), the moon is waning. Another great memory device for determining which moon the phase is in is to think of the Roman goddesses Diana and Hecate. When the moon is curved like the D in Diana, it's waxing and increasing in its energy. When the moon is curved like the C in Hecate, it's waning and decreasing in its energy. The last method to easily discern if the moon is waxing or waning is related to what we learn as children in school; it's to think of the mathematical symbols for lesser than and greater than. When the moon looks more like the greater sign (>) it is waxing. When the moon looks like the lesser sign (<) it is waning.

Moon Quarters

The next division of the moon is referred to as quarters, and as the name implies there are four of them. The quarter system includes the new moon and full moon, but also the midway points between them, which is roughly seven days afterward. Just like the moon affects the currents of magickal energy, it also affects the waves of psychic energy.

First Quarter

The first quarter is the period from the new moon to the halfway point of reaching the waxing full moon. The moon is halfway shaded in, looking like the capital letter D. This is a great time to be using your magick to shape and build energies and set them into motion to begin manifesting your will. Magick related to motivation is also particularly powerful at this time. The first quarter of the moon tends to be the time when psychic perception naturally begins increasing. This is a great time to do psychic readings or divination related to things that are just beginning or coming into being. You will most likely feel more tuned in to divination practices, and you will feel like you can understand what your readings are saying with much more clarity than normal. You may notice that your spirit allies begin relaying messages to you. During this phase of the moon people tend to be a bit more empathic and sensitive to the emotional energies of others. I personally find this to be a time when my dreams are much more vivid than usual and I'm more likely to lucid dream or astral project.

Second Quarter

The second quarter is the period from that halfway point to the full moon itself. This is a great time for focusing on the fine detail aspects of your magickal castings, increasing things, speeding things up, and enhancing them. This is a great time for magick that is related to expansion and bringing harmony and balance into your life. The second quarter of the moon is when psychic perception tends to be the strongest for people. Everything from emotions, to dreams, to spiritual guidance from allies feels like the volume has been turned up to max. This is a great time to work on psychic development, and divination tends to be about the clearest it will get in regard to the moon's influence. This is an ideal time for mediumship development and practices, and you're most likely to recognize your intuition feeling like it's in full swing. This is a period of time when dreams tend to be the most prophetic, and the closer to the full moon you are the more ideal it is to do oneiromancy, which is the practice of receiving answers from your dreams. This is also the time when you are more likely to get a response to an inquiry from a spirit, deity, or your guides.

Third Quarter

The third quarter is the period from the full moon to halfway between full moon and new moon. This is a great time for magick to complete a goal, and to reap its results. It's a great time to banish things from your life and to integrate the results you've reaped from your manifestations into your life. It's a great time for magick related to warding, protection, self-defense, and banishing things. The third quarter of the moon is when psychic perception tends to start withdrawing a bit and going inward. You may notice external spirits become a bit more noticeable, particularly land spirits and the spirits of the deceased. You'll find meditation and visualization ability may be heightened around this time while divination and psychic readings feel like they're starting to lose some of their clarity or understanding of what you're perceiving.

Last Quarter

The last quarter is the halfway point between a full moon waning into a new moon to the new moon itself. The moon is half-shaded in, looking like the capital letter D in reverse. This is a period that is traditionally used for destructive magick, malefic magick, endings, separations, limitations, bindings, and reversal work. It's also a great period for resting and recovering. The fourth quarter of the moon is when spirit activity is the most heightened in my own experience. Divination and psychic ability tend to be much more difficult to decipher during this quarter when trying to perceive things outside of yourself. This is the ideal time to meditate and to do inner work, shadow work, and unlock and uncover aspects of yourself and your inner wisdom. This would be an ideal time to rest your psychic and divinatory attempts and give them a break, especially as you are closer to the new moon.

Moon Void of Course

The moon void of course is when the moon is moving out of its current sign but not quite in the next one yet. This period is generally considered to be a time of instability. It's considered "void" in the sense that it does not create an aspect, a term in astrology meaning the specific angle in relationship to any of the other planets, until it enters the next zodiac sign; it's also "void" because we are not receiving any energetic information from the moon in a stable, usable manner. Due to this, it's often considered magickally null. I have always been taught that the moon's void of course is an inauspicious time to cast spells, but some people disagree. The truth, in my experience, is that spells cast during the period when the moon is void of course tend to be weaker than spells cast during other times—and that's the best-case scenario. Usually, in my experience, the spells tend to only partially manifest or don't manifest how I intend them to at all. In worst-case scenarios, they backfire. In astrology, it's advised not to start anything new or sign any new contracts during this time, or else it's considered a bad omen. I firmly recommend not casting magick during this time, which shouldn't be that huge of a deal since they don't last long—usually only a few hours to about a day at the most. You can find out if the moon is void of course by looking at an astrological ephemeris or magick-oriented annuals such as *Llewellyn's Witches' Spell-A-Day Almanac*. The moon's void of course is usually annotated as "v/c" in almanacs and astrological resources.

Exercise 57

Luminary Waters

Magickal timing: Any, depending on your intention with your correspondence

Materia:
- a clear jar or glass bottle with a lid
- water that is drinkable
- something to label it

Purpose: Luminary water (also sometimes called sun water or moon water) is one of the easiest practices to engage in and is extremely versatile. Essentially, these waters capture sunlight or moonlight and energetically infuse them with their power. Water is energetically and literally both receptive and a solvent. Think of water as sort of an energetic sponge. If you are making lunar water, take a mental note of the moon phase and the sign the moon is in, as it will have those inherent properties. Likewise, the same is true with solar water and whatever zodiac sign the sun is in. Regardless of what phase or signs they're in, they'll have the energy of the moon or sun and sometimes that might be enough.

You can drink the water to take those energies into yourself; you can add some of it to ritual baths, clean magickal tools, clean and bless your home, or use as a spray. Essentially, you can use it for anything you would normally use water for, and as such it is a fantastic way to integrate magick into the seemingly mundane. Be sure to use a clear jar or bottle, as colored glass prevents certain light from coming in, which is why pill bottles and essential oil bottles are never clear.

Directions: Fill the bottle with water and set it outside or on your windowsill with the lid on. The key is not to just set out a bottle under the moonlight or sunlight. If you can get it in direct light that is definitely preferred, but not always possible due to weather and other factors; don't worry, it will still work, just not as powerfully. Be sure that there is a lid on it as you don't want dust or who knows what getting in the water as you set it out. The key to luminary waters, like any magick, revolves intention and will. Simply setting water out thoughtlessly isn't going to do a whole lot. I like to connect with the water itself and let it know what I'm asking of it. I'll tune in, holding the water and recite the following.

For lunar water I say:

> *Spirit of water remember and know*
> *The power of tonight's lunar glow*
> *Remember its sign, remember its phase*
> *So that I may use it in magickal ways.*

For solar water I say:

> *Spirit of water remember and know*
> *The power of mighty solar glow.*
> *Remember its sign upon this day*
> *So that I may use it in magickal ways.*

That's it! Now just leave it out and let it soak up the energy. Lunar water is usually left out at night and removed from the moonlight outside before the sun rises. Likewise, solar water is usually left out during the day and removed from the sunlight outside before the sun sets. If you miss these timings, don't worry. They aren't suddenly magickally null, especially since you specified which energy you want it to absorb and remember. Be sure to label your waters so you know what the water is.

Exercise 58

Full Moon Third Eye Oil
By Kate Freuler

Magickal timing: Any full moon

Materia:
- a small photo or drawing of an eye in the design of your choice. Simply drawing the outline of an eye invokes power because of its ancient symbolism.
- 1 small amethyst crystal
- 1 teaspoon dried mugwort
- 1 teaspoon dried lavender
- 1 fresh flower in full bloom with the stem removed. Any kind of flower is fine.
- a jar with a tight-fitting lid
- ½ cup carrier oil such as jojoba or olive oil

Purpose: The symbol of the eye is seen all over the world and throughout history, representing knowledge, enlightenment and heightened spiritual wisdom. This oil is meant to help open the third eye, located in the center of the forehead. Opening the third eye enhances perception, intuition, and psychic abilities. Corresponding to our third eye is the pineal gland, a tiny gland located in the center of our brain that is shaped in spiral formations like a pinecone. The spiral is an important part of the sacred geometry that makes up the natural world. Flower petals also grow in this pattern. Therefore, the fully bloomed, open flower in this oil reflects the opening of the third eye.

Directions: On the night of the full moon, gather your ingredients on your altar or on a work surface outdoors. Feel the energy of the full moon illuminating your space (even if you can't physically see the moon, you will be able to feel its energy). Spend a moment focusing on the picture of the eye, visualizing it bathed in the energy and light of the full, bright moon. The eye and the moon are now connected in your mind.

Place the amethyst, herbs, and flower on the eye picture. Imagine them soaked in the full moon energy from above, and the mystical eye symbolism from the picture underneath them. Spend a few moments seeing the ingredients bathed in this shared power. This can look like purple and white light spiraling around them, or a bubble of energy surrounding them.

Place all the ingredients in the jar, cover with the oil, and close the lid. Hold the jar to your forehead. Say:

> *My third eye opens like a flower in full bloom.*
> *My third eye reveals the unseen like the moon.*

Place the jar on the eye picture for three nights while it soaks up the essence of the herbs and flower.

Strain and store the oil in a dark dry place.

When you want to do any kind of psychic work, anoint your forehead with a small amount of this oil and repeat the above chant, while imagining your third eye blossoming open like a flower. You can also anoint your forehead prior to sleep for prophetic dreams, before doing a reading with your oracle of choice, during divination, or while meditating.

Chapter 8

THE PLANETARY ENERGIES

I n Mesopotamia, the cradle of civilization, ancient astrologers named the seven visible classical planets after their gods. The Hellenic Greeks, who were influenced by Babylonian astrology, also associated the planets with their own deities that seemed to correspond the most to the Babylonian and Sumerian deities. The Romans adopted this tradition and assigned each day of the week to one of the planets. Our planets are still named after the Roman deities in Romance languages, and we see this tradition maintained with our namesake of the days of the week assigned to deities; however, in English we see many Roman deities replaced with Nordic deities that share an archetypal function to the planet's power. This is not at all saying they are equivalent or the same deities, but that their roles share a similar archetype of areas that they govern in life.

In our English calendars, Tuesday (Tiw's day) is named after the Norse god Tyr (and his Old English name of Tiw) who is the Norse god of war, a role shared by the Roman god Mars. Wednesday (Woden's day) is named after Woden, who is the Norse god of learning, of poetry, and of magic which are traits that the Roman god Mercury possesses. Thursday (Thor's Day) is named after the Norse god Thor, and the connection with the Roman god Jupiter seems the flimsiest, but both are gods of thunder and lightning, and both are children of the king of the gods of their respective pantheons (with Jupiter usurping that position from his father Saturn), though the comparison seems to end there. Friday (Frigga's day) is named after the Norse goddess Frigga, who like the Roman Venus was a goddess of love, beauty, and fertility. Saturday (Saturn's day) maintains its Roman namesake and Sunday (Sun's day) and Monday (Moon's day) keep their planetary association pretty clear. While the Sun and Moon aren't planets by modern astronomical definitions, they are by ancient astrological definitions, referring to the objects that wandered the night sky.

Looking at Planetary Powers Through the Lens of Psychism and Magick

Now that we have an understanding of which planets rule which days of the week, let's take a deeper dive into what those planets govern and what their energetic function is to get a better understanding of what these forces are in relation to magick and psychic ability. When folks think of planetary powers, they tend to think of them in terms of what areas they govern and use them solely for that, without looking at why they do that. Each planet has an archetypal energetic effect upon energy. To put it into a very simple metaphor, think of each planet as a filter on an image. One filter will turn a photo black and white, one will make it sepia, one will invert the colors, one will sharpen the detail, another will blur the image, and so on. You can apply any of the filters to a photo, but some will work better for your purposes and what you're trying to express with the photo than others. You can also use a combination of different filters to create a synthesis of effects to convey a certain feel to the image. Likewise, each planet alters energy in different ways. You can apply any planetary energy to any magickal goal and you'll get different outcomes, some more pleasing to what you desire and some straight up ruining what you were planning to achieve.

I bring this up, because understanding this will help you to understand how each planetary energy can be applied to psychism, as well as any other area of life. For example, most folks will work with Jupiter and only Jupiter when it comes to money magick. I don't. Jupiter's effect on energy is expansion, but you need something to expand to begin with. So I use Venus (which is most often used solely for love magick) to draw money to me first, then use Jupiter to expand it, because Venus has a magnetizing and drawing effect upon energy. So instead of discussing the areas each planet governs as I did in *Psychic Witch*, we're going to look at the core energetic function of each planet as well.

The seven planets function energetically in opposing but complementary pairs of forces: the Sun and the Moon, Jupiter and Saturn, Mars and Venus. Mercury doesn't have a complementary opposite planetary energy to be paired with, as it is considered a planet of union and synthesis of opposite energies in itself. Mythologically, Mercury is a psychopomp and liminal deity, one of the few beings who could travel freely in any realm, betwixt and between all places and things.

Sun

While not considered a planet by modern astronomical definitions, the Sun was considered one of the primary seven ancient planets by ancient astrologers, though of course it's actually a star. The Sun's main energetic function is creating and sustaining. We can easily understand this by looking at the life-giving properties of the sun itself in relationship to our planet. The sun grows plants from the ground via photosynthesis, which is crucial to the creation and sustaining of the whole food chain and ecosystems. From this humankind was able to farm and eventually create civilizations and empires. Due to these abilities, as well as giving light and warmth and a sense of safety and survival, it's easy to understand why many ancient cultures associated the sun with creator deities.

Seeing that the sun is often linked with divinity, it also then becomes symbolic for many of the personal divine aspects of our soul. We also know that everything in our solar system, including our own planet, revolves around the sun, which symbolically makes it the most important planet in our solar system. It is from the sun that each planetary body in our solar system was literally created. It is from the solar nebula that the sun became the center of and everything else formed around it. The sun is also the only body in our solar system that can generate its own light. Due to these energetic functions, the Sun (astrologically speaking) governs aspects of ourselves and our lives that we want to create, grow, shine, heal, vitalize, or empower.

> **Solar energetic effects:** Creation and restoration. Manifesting externally and illuminating.

> **Ways to use Solar energy:** You can tap into Solar energy to gain clarity on any of the areas of magickal endeavors that the Sun rules. You can also tap into solar energy to reveal information that is hidden, to perform psychic health scans, to connect with higher forces and higher vibrational entities, to connect with one's Higher Self, and to receive divine guidance.

Moon

Like the Sun, the Moon is no longer considered a planet by modern astronomical definitions of the word, but it was in ancient astrology. We know now that the moon is a satellite. The Moon's main energetic function is that of rhythm and transmutation. When I say rhythm, I mean the Hermetic Principle of Rhythm as outlined in the *Kybalion*, which states that "Everything flows out and in; everything has its tides; all things rise and fall; the pendulum-swing manifests in everything; the measure of the swing to the right, is the measure of the swing to the left; rhythm compensates."[85] The implication of this principle is that a person can transmute anything in varying degrees of a scale into its opposite from one pole or another.

---

85. Anonymous, *The Kybalion*.

The moon perfectly exemplifies this with its phasing and its effects upon the tides of the earth and the growing of crops.

The Moon is the most versatile of the planetary energies and runs the gamut of energies. At times it's projective, at times it's receptive, at times it's illuminating, at times it's dark—ever waxing and waning in the night sky. This range and versatility have made it a favorite energy to work with among witches, particularly since a lot of our magick is about transformation, whether it be ourselves or our lives. The Moon projects light only to seemingly create the illusion of bringing that light inward in receptivity, making it powerful for internal work such as psychic ability, dream work, and astral projection on one hand, and the external work of magickal manifestation in our lives on the other. I would also argue that to some degree it exemplifies all the energetic effects of each planet, depending on which lunar phase it's in. When it comes to energy it can manifest and banish, it can project and receive, it can expand and contrast, and so on.

> **Lunar energetic effects:** Cycles and transformation. Going inward and reflection. Lunar energy can transmute anything to its polar opposite; it can also keep things flowing and circulating.

> **Ways to use Lunar energy:** The Moon is sort of the standard energy to tap into for anything related to psychism, but especially to gain clarity on any of the areas of magickal endeavors that the Moon rules. Lunar energy is particularly powerful for psychism because it can help you to see the cycles and patterns of things, assisting you in seeing where things are headed.

Mercury

Mercury's main energetic function is that of exchange and movement. Mercury is the fastest moving planet in our solar system, which reflects its ability to stir things up and get them moving about. Mercury tends to be associated with communication, which is exchanging thoughts from one person to another, whether that's speaking, writing, text messages, social media posts, emails, or sign language. Other ways that Mercury's energetic function of movement is exemplified include anything dealing with travel, which is moving from one place to another, whether that's by plane, train, car, boat, or even walking.

Among its other domains are other areas related to exchange and movement, such as business transactions, electronics, machinery, or anything else
that involves functioning on the transferring of energy, whether that's cur-
rency, electricity, data, and so on. Just like electronics, which are based on the
movement of information within them, things pertaining to the mind such
as thoughts are related to Mercury, as the brain moves electrical information
in the brain to think.

Mercury's influence is subtle but persuasive, unlike Mars, which is forceful and direct. While Venus is traditionally viewed as receptive and feminine
and Mars is viewed as forceful and masculine, Mercury is considered the
union of these two as an androgynous middle-ground. Mercury links projection with reception to creation connection.

> **Mercurial energetic effects:** Movement and connection. Mercu-
> rial energy can speed anything up and connect different things
> together as well as synthesize them. It can also subtly affect situa-
> tions in manners that are more covert and not obvious.

> **Ways to use Mercurial energy:** You can tap into Mercurial energy to
> gain clarity on any of the areas of magickal endeavors that Mer-
> cury rules. Mercury is ideal for any sort of psychic communica-
> tion, whether it's telepathy, mediumship, or channeling.

Venus

The main energetic function of Venus is that of drawing and reception.
A magickal force that attracts—and in this sense, Venus is magnetic, ever pulling toward itself, receiving. Venusian energy can be pleasurable, and often car-
ries the visual aesthetics of beauty and all the things that make us feel good.
This planetary force could be best summed up in the old adage "it's easier to
catch flies with honey than with vinegar." Energetically, Venus can be thought
of as a pied piper, calling, and waiting. Letting things come, rather than going
to them. And the things that do come? They come to venerate—the very word
flowing from Venus herself—that receptive force that pulls, creates, gives.

Regardless of the one-sided reputation that Venus tends to have—that
stereotypical feminine beauty, wrapped in romance and love—that energy is
all about how it's used, not what it is. Venusian energy can be used for good

or ill. Sirens singing songs of such beauty that it drives sailors to jump off their ship only to be drowned; the anglerfish, drawing their mate to them, only to slowly dissolve them into their own body; the praying mantis, biting the head off its mate. Not everything enticing and seductive is beneficial, and Venus can teach us this lesson. Venus can seduce for love, for creation, for union—or for its own agenda. With a heavy glamoury to it, in both the positive and negative connotations of the word, Venus reminds us that these energies always create—but they can destroy. It's just a matter of what that union looks like, and it could very well be a union within one's digestion. Never forget that the carnivorous Venus flytrap is well named.

> **Venusian energetic effects:** Magnetism and receptivity, drawing and luring anything toward it like a magnet.

> **Ways to use Venusian energy:** You can tap into Venusian energy to gain clarity on any of the areas of magickal endeavors that Venus rules. You can also tap into Venus to enhance your receptivity of the psychic senses or to draw specific psychic information to you.

Mars

Mars' main energetic function is that of projection and direction of force—the kind of forceful energy backed by pure willpower, very nearly the opposite of Venus. Proactive, perhaps sometimes to its detriment, Mars rushes in head first. Pure drive and willpower and initiative; desire in every sense of the word; driven by want, in whatever form it might take. The embodiment of yearning for personal ambition, Mars sees what it wants—and goes after it. A fiery erupting volcano with persistent lava flowing forth, Mars will keep marching forward, destroying anything in its path, never stopping until victory is achieved or they themselves are destroyed. Whereas Venus lures, Mars shows up at the door. Dynamic, impulsive, and active—Mars is an energy of asserting and dominance, of invigoration, of fearlessness.

For these reasons Mars is often called upon in conflict to either provide defense and protection, or to act as an energetic offense. That conflict, however, is not without its counter. It is often forgotten that Mars is a god of gardens, of growth—and that the ever-persistent drive to push forward is needed to grow. Much like Venus, Mars acts as a polarity, driving production, manifestation, ideas, and the kind of destruction necessary for healing and change.

> **Martial energetic effects:** Dynamisms and force, propelling, project-
> ing forward like an arrow to a target.

> **Ways to use Martial energy:** You can tap into Martial energy to gain
> clarity on any of the areas of magickal endeavors that Mars rules.
> Mars can also be used to break through psychic blockages and to
> obtain the hard-to-access information you might seek.

Jupiter

Jupiter's main energetic function is that of expansion and elevation and increase. Jupiter as an archetype has the most elevated position a being could have as not only a sovereign or a god, but a ruler of the gods themselves. The energy of Jupiter is that of elevation of anything, not just one's status. Whether it's raising one's emotions to being "jovial" or mythically appointing sovereigns or deifying them. Jupiterian energy is focused on elevating the human spirit and mind, and as such rules over religion, spirituality, and philosophy. Just as kings desire to expand their kingdoms, Jupiterian energy is always seeking to expand and looks at the big picture without getting lost on the details.

Jupiterian energy is that of increase and abundance, whether that's good fortune in the sense of both good luck and money, or any other sphere of life. That abundance energy can also be negative. Abundance just means a lot of something (which is why it's ill advised to cast or manifest "abundance" with-out clarifying abundance of what exactly). Anything positive Jupiterian energy can increase, it can also increase the opposite. Jupiterian energy seeks to break through confines and barriers. However, without being tempered correctly Jupiterian energy can be over-extending and over-exhausting. Jupiterian energy being of an expansive nature can cause something to become spread too thin.

> **Jupiterian energetic effects:** Elevation and increase. Jupiterian energy
> is that of magnification and amplification.

> **Ways to use Jupiterian energy:** You can tap into Jupiterian energy to
> gain clarity on any of the areas of magickal endeavors that Jupi-
> ter rules. Jupiter can assist you in seeing the bigger picture when

it comes to psychism and can assist in amplifying your psychic perception.

Saturn

Saturn's main energetic archetype is that of restriction and structuring and decrease. Whereas Jupiter is the energy of expansion, elevation, and the broader picture, Saturn has the energy of constriction, decline, and details. Saturn sees the forests for the trees, so to speak. It is the first step on the ladder of the Great Work, and in alchemy, Saturn is symbolized by the metal of gross lead and the calcination and incineration processes. The word calcination comes from the medieval Latin word *calcināre*, which means "to reduce to calx."[86] Calx is the powdery oxide residue left over from incinerating a metal thoroughly with fire. The spiritual process of calcination is what we might refer to as ego death; it's burning away that which is considered impure, our overidentification with our personal egos that distracts from our true pure spiritual natures and our True Will. In other words, it's about recognizing what is restricting us from spiritual realization and that's often false beliefs, ideas, and perceptions that we have built in response to life and society. We metaphorically burn away these self-created limitations by tapping into the inner spiritual fires of transformation. It is the process of the phoenix dying and burning to ash before it can be reborn. This is often a very humbling process and has us confront often harsh truths. This is the process of what Jung referred to as shadow work. Shadow work takes a lot of discipline, and discipline is the restriction of our personal desires in favor of willpower. Shadow work also takes a lot of honest evaluation of ourselves, and not just what we want to see or believe about ourselves.

Saturnine energetic effects: Restriction and structuring. Saturnine energy is that of fine-tuning and decrease.

Ways to use Saturnine energy: You can tap into Saturnine energy to gain clarity on any of the areas of magickal endeavors that Saturn rules. Psychically Saturn can assist you in destroying illusions and glamouries to reveal truths. Saturn can also be invoked for

---

86. https://www.etymonline.com/word/calcify#etymonline_v_27603.

anything dealing with the realm of death, such as necromancy, mediumship, or ancestral work. Magickally, Saturn rules restrictions in the sense of creating hurdles and barriers for ourselves or others. These barriers can be in the form of psychic or magickal protection, or it may be about creating those for others in the form of malefic magick, curses, and hexes. Saturn helps us to see what is limiting us and teaches us lessons that we may not necessarily want to learn but need to learn to progress spiritually in life. You can employ Saturn to increase your discipline, which is the first step in mastering your own life, as well as to learn. You can also employ Saturn when trying to look at details and specifics. All learning has to deal with confronting problems or lessons, whether that's spiritually or in the mundane. Saturn is used to restructure things in our life, and all structures need rules, plans, discipline, and boundaries.

Planetary Hours

Another form of magickal timing is the planetary hours. It has been a very old magickal belief that each hour of the day is governed by one of the seven classical planets. What this means is that each hour of the day holds a specific energy that is in residence with a planetary power. That means that these hours are more flavored with that planet's energy, which can then be tapped into to boost spells that relate to that planet's area of rulership. The use of magickal planetary hours goes as far back as ancient Greece. It most likely has roots in ancient Egypt where each of the twenty-four hours of the day was governed by a different deity.[87]

In the Renaissance, when clocks began phasing out sundials, it became a popular trend for magicians to base their planetary hours on the sixty-minute increments and divisions of the clock for planetary hour assignment.[88] Ceremonial magician Arthur Waite, most popularly known for his Rider-Waite-Smith tarot deck, even favored that method, preferring the human defined sixty-minute hour increments as opposed to the older traditional

---

87. DuQuette, et al. *Llewellyn's Complete Book of Ceremonial Magick.*
88. Pepper, *Witches All*, 26–27.

methods such as the Key of Solomon and older grimoires that calculated planetary powers from sunrise to sunset.[89] I disagree with Waite's method, as I feel the astrology of the calculation in its relation to sunrise to sunset is much more powerful and much more precise. One of the main misunderstandings that Waite seemed to have is that "hours" in the ancient world weren't perfect sixty-minute increments, but rather astrologically defined by sunrise to sunset divided by twelve, whereas the sundial calculated time based on sunrise and sunset by the shadow that it cast. While Waite's method is simpler, as witches we are trying to sync with the forces and cycles of nature. Plus, as we know from the Wheel of the Year, the length of daylight varies throughout the year and when you throw in other humanmade concepts like Daylight Saving Time, time zones, and location, using the midnight-to-midnight method of magickal timing based on a clock seems to fall apart as inaccurate and flimsy.

---

89. Waite, *The Book of Black Magic.*

Planetary Day Hours

Hour	Sunday	Monday	Tuesday	Wednesday	Thursday	Friday	Saturday
1	☉	☽	♂	☿	♃	♀	♄
2	♀	♄	☉	☽	♂	☿	♃
3	☿	♃	♀	♄	☉	☽	♂
4	☽	♂	☿	♃	♀	♄	☉
5	♄	☉	☽	♂	☿	♃	♀
6	♃	♀	♄	☉	☽	♂	☿
7	♂	☿	♃	♀	♄	☉	☽
8	☉	☽	♂	☿	♃	♀	♄
9	♀	♄	☉	☽	♂	☿	♃
10	☿	♃	♀	♄	☉	☽	♂
11	☽	♂	☿	♃	♀	♄	☉
12	♄	☉	☽	♂	☿	♃	♀

Planetary Night Hours

Hour	Sunday	Monday	Tuesday	Wednesday	Thursday	Friday	Saturday
1	♃	♀	♄	☉	☽	♂	☿
2	♂	☿	♃	♀	♄	☉	☽
3	☉	☽	♂	☿	♃	♀	♄
4	♀	♄	☉	☽	♂	☿	♃
5	☿	♃	♀	♄	☉	☽	♂
6	☽	♂	☿	♃	♀	♄	☉
7	♄	☉	☽	♂	☿	♃	♀
8	♃	♀	♄	☉	☽	♂	☿
9	♂	☿	♃	♀	♄	☉	☽
10	☉	☽	♂	☿	♃	♀	♄
11	♀	♄	☉	☽	♂	☿	♃
12	☿	♃	♀	♄	☉	☽	♂

Essentially, to calculate planetary hours you find the time of sunrise and sunset for where you live (most newspapers or weather websites have this information) and divide that by twelve to create the hours. The hours go in order of the Chaldean planetary order, starting with the planet that rules the day. However, there are many apps available today that use GPS to pinpoint your location and take that data to pull the sunrise and sunset information of where you live and then automatically calculate the planetary hours throughout the day. Most witches I know use these apps today as it saves a lot of time and math.

PLANETARY DAYS

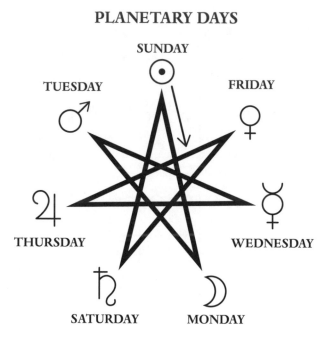

Planetary Days

A simple method to remember the order of planetary hours is to draw a septagram, a seven-pointed star. At the top of the septagram, start with the first day of the week, Sunday and its ruler, the Sun. Tracing the septagram starting from the top down to the right, place all the days of the week in order with their planetary power. Once completed, the order of planetary hours for the day starts with the Sun (on Sunday) and goes around each point of the septagram clockwise. Since there are twelve hours and only seven points, the circle will continue from the seventh hour of Mars back to the Sun as the eighth hour and continue until you reach Saturn as the twelfth planetary hour of the day. The planetary hours of the night continue there, moving to Jupiter after Saturn as the first hour of the night on Sundays and circling around until it hits Mercury as the twelfth hour. Once the twelfth hour of the night ends, the circle restarts and resets at sunrise for the first planetary hour of the next day (e.g. the Moon on Monday).

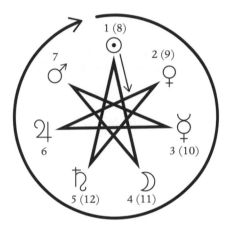

PLANETARY DAY HOURS

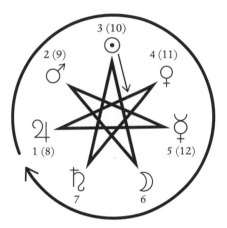

PLANETARY NIGHT HOURS

Planetary Day Hours and Planetary Night Hours

Exercise 59

❦

Working with Pisces to Receive Psychic Guidance and Vision
By Durgadas Allon Duriel

Magickal timing: For optimal effect, perform this spell at night when the Moon is in Pisces, Scorpio, or Cancer, on a Monday ("Moon day"), or during another time when watery energy is amplified in the astrology (e.g. Moon conjunct Jupiter, which is Pisces' traditional ruling planet)

Materia:
- a blank sheet of paper
- an indigo or dark purple marker
- a white, indigo, or purple candle (perform this by candlelight)

Purpose: This spell involves the invoking pentagram of Pisces. In its higher frequencies, Pisces is associated with psychic vision, spirituality, and other planes of consciousness. Consciously attuning ourselves to the frequency of Pisces can help us open our psychic senses and receive guidance and vision from our Higher Self or the other benefic higher plane entities of our understanding that we seek to work with. Sometimes a vision or message is available to us and we just need an extra boost of energy to open the passageway for it to reach us, or to get ourselves in a state to receive it, or to build up our ability to open ourselves psychically at will. This spell aids with that process.

Directions: *Note:* drawing the sigil in this spell eventually becomes optional. At first, it is drawn to aid in developing the thoughtform of it in our minds that is harnessed in the spell. Once that thoughtform is clearly accessible to you, you needn't redraw the sigil (and you can also reuse the sigil paper until then, which will accumulate power on its own).

First, engage in whatever form of grounding, centering, banishing, and warding you use. It's important to not only clear the psychic space, but to also banish any influences that might seek to confuse or cloud your vision.

Next, sit in a chair at a table and draw the invoking pentagram of Pisces (pictured) in indigo. Indigo is a color some associate with the third eye, and the frequency of indigo is said, therefore, to facilitate opening or activating the third eye.

After drawing this symbol, write a question you have prepared on a piece of paper and place that under the symbol. Try to phrase it as concisely and precisely as you can. If it is more of a request for general information or a vision, indicate what topic you seek information about as specifically as you can.

Next, enter a semi-trance state and gaze at the symbol for at least thirty seconds. Strive to feel the energy coming from it. Close your eyes and visualize the symbol at the point between your eyebrows (the location of the third eye), with the invoking pentagram of Pisces in an orb of warm, golden light. As you visualize this, recite the following incantation three times, allowing your voice to fade in volume such that by the end, it is almost inaudible, while visualizing the symbol glowing brighter and brighter within you.

Sign of vision,
Sign of sight,
Grant me guidance,
On this night.

After this, allow the visualization to fade and wait in a comfortable meditative posture for a response to come. Do your best to put no pressure on yourself for that response to take a particular form. Simply let your mind go blank, remain in the semi-trance state, and allow images to appear. If you feel like you're struggling with this, you can request that an image come in a form that is familiar to you, like a tarot card. (I once did that in a guided meditation for vision and a card appeared. Later that day, I drew the same card on the physical plane in a one card reading!)

Once you've received what feels like a complete flow of images (and the vividness of the images is less relevant than their content) open your eyes and write down what you saw. Don't judge or interpret it, simply write it all down. After capturing this, begin the process of reflecting on its meaning. Then do what you typically do to cleanse a space after spellwork and return to a more everyday mental state.

Zodiacal Energy and the Three Modalities

There are twelve zodiac signs, and each one is associated with one of the four elements being expressed in a different way, or modality. The three modalities are cardinal, mutable, and fixed. Each show how the four elements are expressed in different manners. There's the fire signs of Aries, Leo, and Sagittarius. For water we have Cancer, Scorpio, and Pisces. Next, we have the air signs of Libra, Aquarius, and Gemini. Finally, we have Capricorn, Taurus, and Virgo for earth signs. Each of the element groups represents one of the three modalities of cardinal, fixed, or mutable in that respective order. The cardinal signs consist of Aries (fire), Cancer (water), Libra (air), and Capricorn (earth). The fixed signs are Taurus (earth), Leo (fire), Scorpio (water), and Aquarius (air). This means that Gemini (air), Virgo (earth), Sagittarius (fire), and Pisces (water) are the mutable signs.

From sign to sign the zodiac alternates through the four elements in the order of fire, earth, air, and water. Likewise, from sign to sign the zodiac alternates through the three modalities. Therefore, Aries, which starts the wheel of the zodiac, is a fire sign and cardinal. After Aries is Taurus, which is an earth sign and fixed. Then comes Gemini, which is an air sign and mutable. Following Gemini is Cancer, which is a water sign and restarts the pattern of three modalities, being cardinal. The pattern keeps repeating until all twelve zodiac signs are expressed as three modalities of the four elements.

Many witches work with a concept called the Wheel of the Year, which marks the eight sabbats. Sabbats are days of magickal celebration honoring the cycles of the earth and the sun. The four Lesser Sabbats are marked by the two equinoxes and two solstices, which occur at the start of the cardinal zodiac signs. The four Greater Sabbats are astrologically marked by calculating the exact midpoint between each sabbat, and these occur during fixed signs.

Cardinal Energy

The word cardinal comes from a Latin root meaning a "hinge."[90] Like a hinge on a door that allows it to open, the four cardinal signs open the metaphorical door that ushers in the beginning of seasons, as we explored in the Wheel of the Year, with the Lesser Sabbats of the solstices and equinoxes. It's at these

---

90. https://www.etymonline.com/word/cardinal#etymonline_v_33702.

points where the Wheel of the Year truly turns from season to season. We can think of cardinal energy similarly to how we would a waxing moon, in the sense that it's a flow of energy coming into being. We can also compare it to the Greek Fate Clotho, the spinner in the sense of her spinning the thread of life into being. The glyph for cardinal is the dot of spirit inside a triangle without a base line. The symbol represents spirit building and focusing. Cardinal energy can correspond to the Lower Self.

Fixed Energy

Next comes the four fixed signs, which mark the middle and height of a season. The fixed signs are marked by the Greater Sabbats. Fixed signs are steady and stabilized in their energy and elemental influence, being at their zenith of power. This is quite possibly why Doreen Valiente referred to them as the Greater Sabbats, not to mean they're better or more important than the Lesser Sabbats but rather in reference to the height of astrological and elemental energy coming through the zodiac. We can think of fixed energy similarly to how we would a full moon, in the sense that it's when the moon's power is at its height and stabilized, neither waxing nor waning.

We can also compare it to the Greek Fate Lachesis, the allotter in the sense of her holding the fullness of the thread of life stable and steady. The glyph for fixed is a line inside of a square. As discussed earlier, the square is a symbol of balance and stability, where the energy is contained in an equal but still manner. The line represents equilibrium, emphasizing again that the energy is distributed in an equal, balanced, and stable manner. Fixed energy can correspond to the Middle Self.

Mutable Energy

Lastly, we have the four mutable signs, which aren't a part of the Wheel of the Year. Mutable means to be changeable and marks the ending of a season about to transition into the next one.

The signs are liminal in nature, being in the process of transformation from one thing to the next. We can think of mutable energy similarly to how we would a waning moon, in the sense that it's the fullness of power decreasing to be transformed into the new moon and starting a new moon cycle. We can also compare it to the Greek Fate Atropos, the Fate who cuts the thread of life, ending it. But death isn't the end, it's the transition from one state of being to another. The glyph for mutable energy is the dot of spirit under a half circle of soul. Instead of being dynamic and focused outward like the cardinal glyph, the crescent half circle illustrates a focusing inward as well as a softness of flexibility. Mutable energy can represent the Higher Self.

Cardinal: Creation, action, growth

Fixed: Stability, equilibrium, apex

Mutable: Adaptability, transformation, completion

Each zodiac sign has a planetary ruler. In classical astrology and magick it only employs the first seven known planets and luminaries in our solar system. Later, as Uranus, Neptune, and Pluto were discovered they took over a few of the zodiac signs as rulers. Those three newer outer planets are considered higher octaves of the planets whose rulership they took over. Neptune is a higher octave of Jupiter, Uranus is a higher octave of Saturn, and Pluto is a higher octave of Mars. With the original rulership, each planet ruled over two signs while the Sun and the Moon ruled over one sign each. With modern astrology each planet rules over one zodiac sign except for Mars, Venus, and Mercury, which still rule over two. Personally, when it comes to performing magick I prefer sticking to the traditional classical seven planets. I definitely encourage you to investigate the three outer planets, get familiar with their energy and experiment with it in your magick and then decide which system you prefer. The reason I prefer the seven-planet system for my magick (though not in terms of astrology itself, where I acknowledge the outer planets) is not just because I feel there's more symmetry and balance to this distribution but because cosmologically it makes sense for my paradigm.

As I discussed in *Psychic Witch*, the seven planetary powers relate to astral energy, while the elements refer to etheric energy, which is how the forces of the building block energy of the universe structures and expresses itself allowing things to take form, visible and invisible. Therefore, the twelve signs of the zodiac are the four elements and the seven planets united. I like to think of the zodiac signs as the primary seven currents of astral energy (as the planets) as they are expressed through the four channels of elemental energy, thereby creating energetic structures of influence and potential that allow situations to take form and manifest on the physical. I view a planet's rulership as the astral energy that is held within the etheric pattern of the element. The modalities express the functions of those planetary and elemental rulerships, showing if the function is of an energetic waxing, waning, or full energy expression.

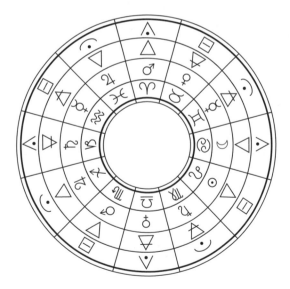

Energy Wheel

When it comes to the topic of astrology, the zodiac is probably the subject discussed the most. It's almost effortless to find information in books or online about what areas of life each sign governs, and there's tons of lists with keywords. For psychic ability and magick, I recommend meditation on a sign by contemplating its element, planetary ruler, and its modality, and how those three combined express a certain flavor of energy to work with. You can implement zodiacal energy regardless of what sign any planet is currently in, just by tapping into its power, glyph, and energy. However, by observing which planets are currently in which sign, you can see the potential energy channels of influence available to tap into to amplify and speed your spell along.

Exercise 60

Buttercup Sock Talisman for Second Sight
By "Dr. Buck" Jake Richards

Magickal timing: Best performed when the Moon is in Aries

Materia:
- The heel of your left worn sock, cut out in a circle
- buttercup flowers, one each for the age of the person
- New salt
- Tobacco purchased with silver coins
- Needle and red thread

Purpose: In Appalachia and the greater American South, there are whispers of a continued belief in the ability of folks born a certain way, whether with a veil over their eyes, "born blue," at midnight, or even on special days such as Halloween and Christmas. These particular people, it is said, have a gift given by God and the spirits for seeing and speaking with things beyond the veil. Many times, these types of events at birth used to be life threatening and the parents were made aware. Because they had gone through the "jaws of death" and the "jaws of life" in order to be born, they walk between the veils that hang as a curtain between worlds, like walking down the center of a clothesline full of bed sheets and dresses that part here and there giving glimpses to either side. However, because this is a gift from birth and not something to be trained, it has been said to show up spontaneously either early in childhood or later in life. Because of its tendency to just show up, it has had the power to run people mad. Literally crazy.

Now I'm not saying mental illnesses rightfully diagnosed may simply be outward appearances of the Sight; however, because medical technology has advanced, these conditions at birth aren't heeded as much nor are the parents made aware by the doctor. So there's many people walking around who were born with a caul, born blue, born breach, or sunny-side-up that have no idea of their potential to have the Sight. The beginning signs of the Sight include random visions of events regarding people or places you may or may not be familiar with; dreaming of events before they happen; or seeing people and animals that are deceased but you're not aware until they disappear into a wall or simply vanish. The most common sign in the beginning though is seeing shadows flit around in your peripheral vision, much like fast glimpses between the bed sheets. Having the Sight is like having extra eyes that need glasses. No one can teach you to see, but this charm can act as glasses for it, to see at your own pace.

Directions: Cut the heel from your left worn sock that hasn't been washed. In the center of this place the buttercup flowers, new salt bought specifically for this, and tobacco that has been purchased only with silver coins such as quarters and dimes. Fold the fabric away from you once, giving an oblong, eye shape to the package. Sew the openings shut with the red thread while praying for the Sight to be eased and then stitch a red cross on the front, in the center. Make a loop at one corner of the eye package with the thread and tie it so a string can be brought through to make it into a necklace. Wear it close to your skin and never let anyone touch it; never let it hit the ground either. Powder it with baby powder and anoint it with whiskey once a week and every time the Moon is in Aries.

Tying It All Together

Sometimes magick can't wait. While planning spells ahead and performing magick regularly helps you to avoid the need to cast magick as an emergency, sometimes life just happens and it's unavoidable. The methods of magickal timing aren't provided here to obsess over or make you think that you can't cast magick if the timing isn't right. Magick operations rarely employ every form of magickal timing.

Instead, think of magickal timing as your options of currents to tap into to assist your spell. This allows you to still plug in at least one energy booster to your spellcraft. Let's say that nothing is in alignment with your spell's intention, which is to bring in some much-needed money. It's the wrong day of the week, you missed the planetary hour, the Moon is in the wrong phase, and nothing in the zodiac is in alignment. However, it's springtime and the morning. Perfect. There's your timing correspondence.

While preplanning and scheduling to perform your spells makes your spell stronger, your magickal timing doesn't need to be perfect. It's better to cast a spell during the "wrong time" than to not cast a spell at all for the same reason. The thing is, you can tap into any magickal timing, it's just a matter of how precise or broad of timing you choose to tap into. You can tap into magickal timing by simply declaring it in your spells. Here's an example using all the different types of magickal timing, and I usually make statements like this right before I perform the actual spell once my sacred space is in place:

Upon this day of Jupiter, on Jupiter's holy hour, during the waxing Moon of Taurus, in the season of spring, while the sun is rising in the sky, do I perform this working.

Now obviously every spell won't call upon every aspect of magickal timing, only those that align with my goal. So even if the only timing in alignment is the position of the sun, I would say:

While the sun is at its peak of power during high noon…

The Wisdom of Laurie Cabot and Sybil Leek

Laurie Cabot used to correspond with the famous British witch Sybil Leek after meeting her via letters. Through these letters Sybil would also mentor her and give her advice on being a public witch, something that was not nearly as common as it is today. One of the pieces of advice she gave Laurie was to write on the back of petition spells the words, "In no way will this spell reverse or place upon me any curse."[91] Way before I met Laurie, when I was learning magick from Silver RavenWolf's books she would pair this as a statement at the end of spells as "May this spell not reverse or place upon me any curse. May all astrological correspondences be correct for this working."[92] The last line about astrological correspondences, Silver credits to Laurie Cabot after acknowledging the first line is from Sybil Leek. In the Cabot tradition of witchcraft, the terms "correct" and "incorrect" have special meaning.[93]

Essentially anything correct refers to forces and energies that are beneficial, while anything incorrect refers to forces and energies that are harmful or unbeneficial. This is to avoid the use of the word "positive" and "negative" energy with any sort of moralistic projection upon those words, as they're seen energetically as just opposite and complementary aspects of the energetic polarity, not necessarily "good" or "bad." What this statement about astrological correspondences being correct is in reference to is avoiding detrimental and invoking beneficial astrological forces. It's essentially a statement neutralizing anything astrologically that would conflict and hinder the magick being cast. I've used Silver's statement most of my life with great success at the end of spells but over time changed it so that it rhymes:

May this spell not reverse
Or place upon me any curse.
May all astrological correspondences be correct
For this spell I now project.

---

91. L. Cabot, P. Cabot, C. Penczak, *Laurie Cabot's Book of Shadows.*
92. RavenWolf, *To Ride a Silver Broomstick.*
93. L. Cabot, P. Cabot, C. Penczak, *Laurie Cabot's Book of Shadows.*

CONCLUSION

I opened this book by sharing one of my most personal and private stories not to invoke sympathy or sadness. I don't see this story as being sad. On the contrary, I see it as one of the most triumphant moments in my life. Witchcraft gave me hope. It allowed me to change my life drastically at one of the darkest times of my life when I had absolutely no influence or personal power, and it still does to this day. That wasn't the first tragic experience nor the last. But with magick I have developed the tools to not only cope with life but also to change my circumstances. I want that for you as well.

Regardless of who you are, you can use magick to change your life. We all have our own stories, our trials, and our tribulations. You also don't need to have gone through trauma or abuse to gain access to magick. Magick is within and around us at all times; all it takes is the ability to acknowledge and connect with it. Every single human has the capacity for magickal and psychic abilities. I am not a special case. It doesn't matter if this is the first book you've ever picked up on witchcraft or if you've been practicing for fifty years. Witchcraft can empower you to change your situation for the better. More importantly, it can change *you* for the better, and that transformation assists in changing the world at large through a ripple effect of influence. We all have our own stories, and magick can help us to write where that story goes from here.

I strongly encourage you to experiment with the ideas and techniques in this book and as always, to rework them so that they are personal to you and reflect your own personal spiritual path. I also strongly encourage you to try performing spells in this book within your Inner Temple. By working regularly in the inner and outer world your magick will greatly increase. I also suggest re-reading this book when you have a chance. Things might click a bit differently on a second or third read. Remember that this is your journey. Be sure to take care of yourself as well. I have added three final recipes from some of my friends as a parting gift on our journey together for the duration of this book. These three recipes—a bath, a tea, and incense for dreaming—will also assist you in relaxing, unwinding, and most importantly assist you as a form of self-care.

Exercise 61

∞

Psychic Journey Ritual Bath
By Juliet Diaz

Magickal timing: Any new moon, preferably in the evening

Materia:
- 4 sprigs rosemary
- 1 tablespoon spirulina
- ½ cup activated charcoal
- 1 cup Epsom salts
- 1 whole sliced pomegranate
- 1 whole sliced blood orange
- handful white rose petals
- white candle (optional)

Purpose: Indulge in this activating bath that will not only cleanse your energy but send a remembrance of wisdom through your entire being. I perform this ritual at least once every three months, especially during times of uncertainty. This psychic journey bath is meant to connect you to a higher power within, one that will unveil the truth to answers you seek. With time, you will learn to trust the journey and become more rooted as Spirit travels with you into the depths of sight.

Directions: Start by setting your bath; warm to hot water works best. Before placing any materia in, stand or kneel beside the tub, thank the water spirit for being present. Give yourself a moment to connect to the running water sound and allow it to fill you with its waving energy. When ready, mindfully start to place each materia in the bath while thanking those spirits as well.

I prefer to have a white candle lit to include the fire spirit, which helps me dive into sight better, but it is optional.

Step into the bath and sink below water and back up again; alternatively, you can use a cup to pour the bathwater over your head. Close your eyes, take three deep breaths, and then start to visualize the water glowing a brilliant light blue that embraces every inch of your body. Take another three deep breaths, and with each inhale, allow that glow to enter your body, filling you from feet to head.

Start to whisper the words "unveil what's hidden, sinking deeper into sight, into truth" seven times while envisioning a golden light right above your brows in the center of your forehead beaming inward and filling your brain.

When you feel vibrations or tingles, it is time to ask your question or express your concerns. Ask in your mind, and be still. Relax into the water and keep your eyes closed. Allow the journey to unravel. Make sure not to let the materia go down the drain. You can dispose of them however you like.

Exercise 62
Psychic Tea Time Potion
By Madame Pamita

Magickal timing: Can be performed at any time, but it is especially powerful when the Moon is in Pisces or Cancer

Materia:
- water
- tea kettle
- tea pot (optional)
- tea cup
- infuser or tea strainer
- any combination of the following for the tea:
    * roasted dandelion root (*Taraxacum officinale* or *Taraxacum erythrospermum*)
    * anise seed (*Pimpinella anisum*)

           * althea root (*Althaea officinalis*)
           * Chinese star anise (*Illicium verum*)
      • honey (optional)

Purpose: Even the most adept psychic witch can feel like their intuitive pipeline gets clogged from time to time. When that happens, some meditation, a walk out in nature, or even a nap can hit the reset button, but we can also call on our herbal allies to help us to receive clear messages and strengthen our intuition.

I love brewing this psychic tea for so many reasons. First, the act of brewing a tea itself is a ritual that can bring comfort, calm, and focus—all things that assist with opening up your psychic channel. Teas are also quite magickal in that when we ingest a blessed tea, we are actually taking that blessing into the cellular structure of our bodies. And third, teas are potions! What could be more witchy than that? (If you want to say, "Bubble, bubble, toil and trouble" over your cup, I won't stop you!)

Each of the herbs in this tea brings its own unique magical imprint. Dandelion root is especially good for opening up clairvoyance and psychic dreams. Anise assists with clairaudience and makes divine messages come through crystal clear. Althea root amplifies clairsentience, gives you more confidence in your gut feelings, and also is exceptionally helpful for mediumship or spirit work. Chinese star anise activates the third eye and brings clarity, focus, and awareness of spiritual truths to your psychic work. (Make sure you have Chinese star anise [*Illicium verum*], as Japanese star anise [*Illicium anisatum*] is toxic.)

Purchasing these herbs from reliable sources, such as grocery stores or health food stores, will ensure that you're getting good quality, food-grade product. In other words, I don't recommend pulling up dandelions from the side of the highway where they may have been sprayed with toxic chemicals. And while all of these herbs are considered safe to ingest, if you have any medical conditions, it's smart to do some research to see if there are any contraindications to you using them before you drink them.

If you are just beginning to develop your psychic gifts, you can try a blend of all of these herbs together to kick your abilities up a notch. If you have been doing psychic work for a while, you can drink just the herbs that will address the problem that you are having. You can also try experimenting by drinking the herbs one by one and see the effect that each has on your psychic faculties.

Lastly, one of my favorite things to do with this tea is to serve it during divination get-togethers. Try making a pot for your next tarot reading party or Ouija board seance and see if it doesn't bring in more psychic breakthroughs and intuitive "ah-ha" moments.

Directions: Put fresh spring water into a tea kettle (spring water from a bottle is fine). Put your herbs in the tea pot or infuser. Pour the boiling water into the teapot or the cup, over the loose herbs or the infuser. As you pour, ask the herbs to do their work and say these words with loving conviction.

You can use your own words or say this simple incantation:

> *Dandelion, let me see true*
> *Anise, let me hear true*
> *Althea, let me feel true*
> *Star anise, let me know true*

Close your eyes and hold your hands in the steam over the cup or teapot and focus your intention on your spell. After the tea has brewed for several minutes, your potion is ready. Pour and strain the tea from your pot into your cup or pull the infuser out of your cup. As you let the infusion cool a little before drinking, you can talk with the herbs, having a little mental (or verbal) conversation about what the brew will do for you. For example:

> *Althea, you know I have been having troubles trusting*
> *my gut. I'd like for you to strengthen my intuition and*
> *help me to follow my feelings when I know they're right.*

Let this monologue go on for several minutes, telling the herbs all the ways that you want them to help you. When you've finished the conversation, the tea will have cooled to the point that you can drink it. It has been imbued with all your words of intention, all your thoughts, and all your will. This is truly a magic potion. If you like a sweeter brew, add a little honey to your cup. Then close your eyes and, sip by sip, drink it all in. Feel the power of the magic permeating your body, mind, and spirit. Thank the spirit of the herbs for their assistance and then begin your divination practice, go to sleep for dream work, meditate, or do whatever psychic practice you are working on.

Exercise 63

⚖⚖

Eleven-Ingredient Dream Incense
By Judika Illes

Magickal timing: Any

Materia:
- anise (*Pimpinella anisum*)
- bay leaves (*Laurus nobilis*)
- cardamom (*Elettaria cardamomum*)
- cinnamon (*Cinnamomum zeylanicum*)
- copal (*Protium copal*)
- peppermint (*Mentha piperita*) (other mints such as spearmint may be substituted.)
- mugwort (*Artemisia vulgaris*)
- myrrh (*Commiphora myrrha*)
- rose petals, dried (*Rosa spp.*)
- sandalwood (*Santalum album*)
- wisteria (*Wisteria spp.*)

Purpose: Dreams can stimulate visionary experiences, deliver prophetic and revelatory information, and increase and enhance psychic abilities. One can essentially receive a psychic upgrade as you dream. This may sound daunting and, of course, as with everything else—dancing, singing, playing the piano, math—some possess more of an aptitude for the art of dreaming than others. However, magical dreaming is an art that virtually anyone can learn with practice and persistence. In other words, if it doesn't work the first time, keep trying; eventually it will. Various aids make it easier, ranging from amulets and charms to dream pillows and, not least, incense.

This incense recipe does not derive from any one tradition. It's my own personal blend concocted from tried-and-true dream enhancers. This combination of botanicals simultaneously enhances psychic vision and provides spiritual protection, so that you can dream intrepidly.

Do *not* burn the incense while sleeping. Always be aware of fire safety. Instead, prepare your bed chamber, as if preparing for a ritual. Arrange bedding so that you will be comfortable. Burn the incense just *before* sleeping in proximity to where you will sleep so that the scent lingers. Some ingredients are easily obtained from a garden or supermarket, while others such as copal or ethically sourced sandalwood may be more challenging to find. I have not included measurements, as it's crucial that this blend suits *your* personal olfactory tastes. If you hate the scent of cinnamon, for example, then use only a sprinkle.

Directions: Combine the ingredients listed above. There are eleven, as the shape of the number eleven is reminiscent of a pair of pillars or pylons—they remind me of passing through the gates of Dreamland, something you can visualize as you prepare to dream. Grind them together with a mortar and pestle if you wish, but it's not required. Burn your incense blend in an incense burner.

Store extra botanical material together in a box or bag, so that if you wake in the middle of a dream or have trouble remembering it, you can quickly open the container and inhale the scent deeply. This should help revive either dreams or memory. This incense may also be supplemented by other magical dream enhancers. For example, place living gardenia plants near where you sleep, as their scent stimulates visionary dreams, or call in your personal guardian spirits to guide and direct you.

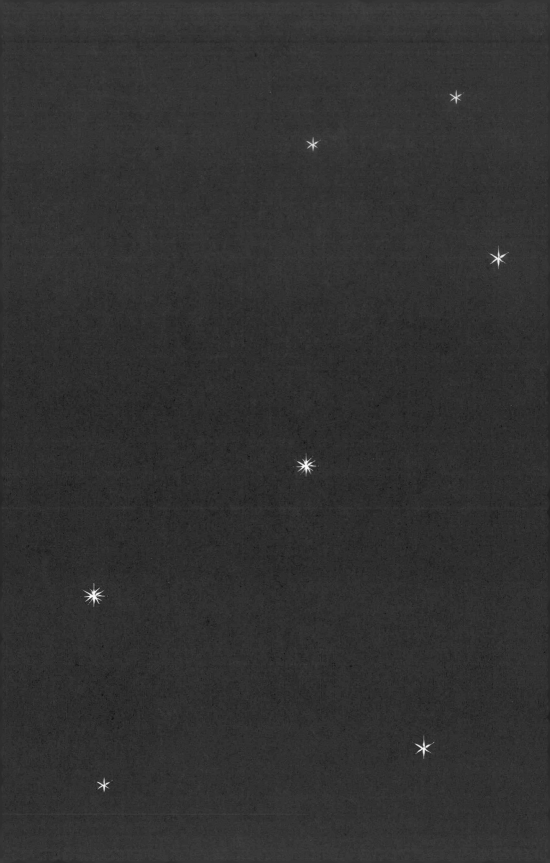

ABOUT THE CONTRIBUTERS

JUDIKA ILLES

A lifelong student, lover, and practitioner of the magical arts, Judika Illes is the author of numerous books devoted to spells, spirits, and witchcraft, including the bestselling *Encyclopedia of 5000 Spells* and *Encyclopedia of Spirits*, *Daily Magic: Spells and Rituals for Making the Whole Year Magical, Pure Magic: A Complete Course in Spellcasting*, as well as *Encyclopedia of Witchcraft, Encyclopedia of Mystics, Saints, and Sages, Magic When You Need It*, and *The Weiser Field Guide to Witches*. Judika is the editor and curator of two books of mystical fiction, *The Weiser Book of the Fantastic and Forgotten* and *The Weiser Book of Occult Detectives*. A certified aromatherapist, she has been a professional tarot card reader for over three decades. A native New Yorker, Judika teaches in the US and internationally, live and virtually. Follow her on Instagram @judikailles.

BENEBELL WEN

Benebell Wen is the author of *Holistic Tarot* and *The Tao of Craft: Casting Fu Talismans in the Eastern Esoteric Traditions*.

ASTREA TAYLOR

Astrea Taylor is the author of *Intuitive Witchcraft: How to Use Intuition to Elevate Your Craft, Air Magic: Elements of Witchcraft Book II*, and *Modern Witchcraft with the Greek Gods: History, Insights, & Magickal Practice*. She's an eclectic pagan witch whose life goals include empowering other magical practitioners and encouraging them to use intuition in their craft. She mentors magical people to help them find their truest paths. In her books and classes, Astrea shares her love of science, magic, history, mental health, energy awareness, and self-love. She has contributed passages to several books and periodicals, including *Witchology*, *Green Egg*, *Llewellyn's Spell-A-Day*, *We'Moon*, *The Magical Almanac*, *The Witch's Book of Spellcraft*, *The Witches' Companion*, and *The Witch's Altar*. Learn more at AstreaTaylor.com.

LILITH DORSEY

Lilith Dorsey, MA, hails from many magickal traditions, including Afro-Caribbean, Celtic, and Indigenous American spirituality. Their traditional education focused on Plant Science, Anthropology, and Film at the University of Rhode Island, New York University, and the University of London, and their magickal training includes numerous initiations in Santeria/Lucumi, Haitian Vodoun, and New Orleans Voodoo. Lilith Dorsey is also a Voodoo Priestess and has been doing successful magick since 1991 for patrons, is the filmmaker of the documentary *Bodies of Water: Voodoo Identity and Tranceformation*, and is the choreographer/performer for jazz legend Dr. John's "Night Tripper" Voodoo Show. They have long been committed to providing accurate and respectful information about the African Traditional Religions and are proud to be a published Black author of *Voodoo and African Traditional Religion*, *55 Ways to Connect to Goddess*, *The African-American Ritual Cookbook*, *Love Magic*, the bestselling *Orishas, Goddesses and Voodoo Queens*, and *Water Magic*.

JULIET DIAZ

Juliet Diaz is a Bruja, Seer, and Spiritual activist. She's an Indigenous Taino Cubana from a long line of curanderos and Brujas. She believes Magic lives within us. She feels passionate about inspiring others to step into their truth, wake to their remembrance, and liberate themselves from the oppressor within. Juliet is a multiple bestseller author; her works include *Witchery: Embrace the Witch Within* (sold to over nine countries), *Plant Witchery*, *The Altar Within*, and decks. Juliet is also the cofounder of Spirit Bound Press and Literary Craft Society. She has been featured in major publications like *Oprah Magazine*, *The Atlantic*, *Wired*, *People Español*, *Mind Body Green*, and *Refinery*, to name a few.

ADAM SARTWELL

Adam Sartwell (New Hampshire) works as a certified Consulting Hypnotist with the National guild of Hypnotists and ICBCH and as a professional Tarot reader. He is a cofounder of the Temple of Witchcraft, a religious non-profit. Award-winning author of *Twenty-One Days of Reiki* and *The Blessing Cord*. He has been published in anthologies such as *Green Lovers*, *Ancestors of the Craft*, and *Foundations of the Temple*. For more information on his work as a hypnotist and online courses, go to www.hypnointuitive.com. To see more about his work as an author, psychic reader, and teacher, go to his website www.adamsartwell.com.

THERESA REED

Theresa Reed, also known as The Tarot Lady, is a professional tarot reader and astrologer. She is the author of many books, including *Tarot for Kids*, *Tarot: No Questions Asked—Mastering the Art of Intuitive Reading*, and *Twist Your Fate: Manifest Success with Astrology and Tarot*. Theresa is also the host of two podcasts: *Tarot Bytes* and *Astrology Bytes*. When she's not reading the cards or writing books, you can find her hanging in the kitchen, cooking up a storm with a cat nearby. Learn more about her at: www.thetarotlady.com.

MADAME PAMITA

Madame Pamita is a Ukrainian diaspora witch, teacher, author, candlemaker, spellcaster, and tarot reader. She has a popular YouTube Channel for teaching witchcraft, she hosts the *Magic and the Law of Attraction* and *Baba Yaga's Magic* podcasts, and she is the author of *Baba Yaga's Book of Witchcraft*, *The Book of Candle Magic*, and *Madame Pamita's Magical Tarot*. She is also the proprietress of the online spiritual apothecary, the Parlour of Wonders, and lives in Santa Monica, California. You can find her at www.parlourofwonders.com.

STORM FAERYWOLF

Storm Faerywolf is a published author, experienced teacher, visionary poet, and professional warlock. Drawn to the occult at an early age, he went on to be trained and initiated into various streams of witchcraft, most notably the Faery tradition, where he holds the Black Wand of a Master. He is the chancellor of Modern Witch University, an online school offering spiritual and magical instruction, and a founding teacher of Black Rose, a course in practical folkloric witchcraft. He is also the founder of BlueRose, a lineage of the Faery tradition, as well as BlueLotus, his school of Reiki. His books include *Betwixt & Between, Forbidden Mysteries of Faery Witchcraft, The Witch's Name,* and *The Satyr's Kiss.* He makes his home in the San Francisco Bay area with his loving partners and a menagerie of animals and plants. For more about his work, or to book a private session, visit www.faerywolf.com.

LAURA TEMPEST ZAKROFF

Laura Tempest Zakroff is a professional artist, author, performer, and Modern Traditional Witch based in New England. She holds a BFA from the Rhode Island School of Design, and her artwork has received awards and honors worldwide. Her work embodies myth and the esoteric through her drawings and paintings, jewelry, talismans, and other designs. Laura is the author of the bestselling Llewellyn books *Weave the Liminal, Sigil Witchery,* and *Anatomy of a Witch,* as well as the *Liminal Spirits Oracle* (artist/author), *The Witch's Cauldron,* and *The Witch's Altar* (coauthor with Jason Mankey). Laura edited *The New Aradia: A Witch's Handbook to Magical Resistance* (Revelore Press). She is the creative force behind several community events and teaches workshops online and worldwide. Visit her at www.LauraTempestZakroff.com.

MELANIE BARNUM

Melanie Barnum (Connecticut) is a psychic, medium, international author, intuitive counselor, life coach, and hypnotist who has been practicing profes-sionally for over twenty years. Melanie's low-key and down-to-earth man-ner plus amazing psychic insight make her readings unique and powerful for assisting you with questions related to relationships, family, career opportuni-ties, and education, as well as communicating with guides and deceased loved ones. In addition, she offers psychic guidance and support for those looking to expand their own intuitive abilities and/or fulfill their soul's mission. Mel-anie enjoys helping others connect through private sessions, workshops, and mentoring. Her multiple books have been translated into many languages and include her latest, *Intuition @ Work,* through Llewellyn Publications. Also available is Melanie's card deck, *Psychic Symbols Oracle Cards.* She has been featured in various magazines, podcasts, radio shows, and books and can be reached at www.MelanieBarnum.com.

CHRISTOPHER PENCZAK

Christopher Penczak is a modern Witch working in the Temple of Witch-craft tradition and community he helped cofound. His practice focuses on the intersection of Love, Will, and Wisdom as an ethos for today's Witch and upon relationships with the plant realm, the patterns of astrology, and the use of trance in the Craft. He is the author of many books, including the Temple of Witchcraft series and *The Mighty Dead*. His vision is of an evolving Witchcraft culture making magick accessible to all, yet preserving the heart of the mystery. For more information, visit www.christopherpenczak .com and www.templeofwitchcraft.org.

DURGADAS ALLON DURIEL

Durgadas Allon Duriel (San Francisco, CA) is a licensed clinical social worker and a certified holistic health practitioner working in private practice. He is also an astrologer, yogi, and magic worker, having practiced magic since childhood and eventually discovering modern paganism and Wicca in high school and later initiating into a Hermetic order in 2005. He trained there intensively for two and a half years, focusing on astrology, Kabbalah, Yoga, tarot, and ritual, which he continues to study and practice. He holds a master's degree in social welfare from UCLA.

KATE FREULER

Kate Freuler lives in Ontario, Canada, and is the author of *Of Blood and Bones: Working with Shadow Magick and the Dark Moon*. She owns and operates White Moon Witchcraft, an online witchcraft boutique. When she isn't crafting spells and amulets for clients or herself, she loves to write, paint, read, draw, and create. Visit her at www.katefreuler.com.

DEVIN HUNTER

Devin Hunter (San Francisco, CA) is the bestselling author of the Witch Power series as well as the critically acclaimed pictorial formulary *Modern Witch: Spells, Recipes, and Workings* (Llewellyn, 2020). Initiated into multiple occult orders himself, Devin is the founder of the Sacred Fires Tradition of Witchcraft as well as cofounder of the Black Rose Tradition of Witchcraft. In addition to his *AV Club*– and *Glamour Magazine*–favorited podcast *Modern Witch*, Devin has been seen on television shows like ABC's *To Tell the Truth* and is expecting the release of his fifth book, *Crystal Magic for the Modern Witch*, in the summer of 2022 from Llewellyn Worldwide.

JAKE RICHARDS ("DR. BUCK")

Jake Richards, a Melungeon, holds his Appalachian-Melungeon heritage close in his blood and bones. His family has lived in southwest Virginia, east Tennessee, and the western Carolinas for a good four hundred years. He spent most of his childhood at his great-grandmother's house on Big Ridge in North Carolina, wadding the Watauga River by his ancestral home on the ridge and traipsing the mountains. Jake has practiced Appalachian folk magic for over a decade. Aside from being an author, Jake is a member of the Melungeon Heritage Association, holds a seat on the board of WAM: We Are Melungeons, and is the creator of HOM: House of Malungia, Melungeon cultural society. Follow him on Instagram at @jake_richards13.

SKYE ALEXANDER

Skye Alexander is the author of more than forty fiction and nonfiction books, including *The Modern Guide to Witchcraft*, *The Modern Witchcraft Book of Tarot*, *The Modern Witchcraft Spell Book*, and *Magickal Astrology*. She also writes the Lizzie Crane mystery series. Her stories have been published in anthologies internationally, and her work has been translated into more than a dozen languages. The Discovery Channel featured her performing a ritual at Stonehenge for the TV special *Secret Stonehenge*. After living in Massachusetts for more than thirty years, she now makes her home in Texas. Visit her website www.skyealexander.com.

BIBLIOGRAPHY

Anonymous. *The Kybalion: Centenary Edition.* Penguin Publishing Group, 2018.

Auryn, Mat. *Psychic Witch: A Metaphysical Guide to Meditation, Magick, and Manifestation.* Llewellyn Worldwide, Ltd., 2020.

Barton, Tamysn. *Ancient Astrology.* Taylor & Francis, 2002.

Betz, Hans Dieter (translator). *The Greek Magical Papyri in Translation, Including the Demotic Spells, Volume 1.* University of Chicago Press, 1996.

Blackthorn, Amy. *Blackthorn's Botanical Magic: The Green Witch's Guide to Essential Oils for Spellcraft, Ritual and Healing.* Weiser Books, 2018.

Bogan, Chas. *The Secret Keys of Conjure: Unlocking the Mysteries of American Folk Magic.* Llewellyn Worldwide, Ltd., 2018.

Bowman, Sarah Lynne, and Kjell Hedgard Hugaas. "Magic is Real: How Role-playing Can Transform Our Identities, Our Communities, and Our Lives." In *Knutepunkt Book Project 2021.* Oslo, Norway, 2021.

Buckland, Raymond. *Buckland's Book of Spirit Communications.* Llewellyn Worldwide, Ltd., 2004.

Cabot, Laurie, Penny Cabot, and Christopher Penczak. *Laurie Cabot's Book of Shadows.* Copper Cauldron, 2014.

Cabot, Laurie, and Christopher Penczak. *Laurie Cabot's Book of Spells and Enchantments.* Copper Cauldron Publishing, 2014.

Cabot, Laurie, and Tom Cowan. *Power of the Witch: The Earth, the Moon, and the Magical Path to Enlightenment*. Random House Publishing Group, 2013.

Case, Paul Foster. *An Introduction to the Study of the Tarot*. Azoth Publishing Company, 1920.

Castaneda, Carlos. *Tales of Power*. Atria Books, 2013.

Crowley, Aleister. *The Equinox: Keep Silence Edition, Vol. 1, No. 2*. Scott Wilde, 2018.

Crowley, Aleister. *Liber II: The Message of the Master Therion*. Pangenetor Lodge Publications/The O.T.O., 1994.

Crowley, Aleister. *Magick Without Tears*. New Falcon Publications, 1991.

Crowley, Aleister, Leila Waddell, and Mary Desti. *Magick: Liber Aba: Book 4*. Red Wheel/Weiser, 1997.

Crowley, Aleister, and Rose Edith Crowley. *The Book of the Law, Liber al vel legis, with a facsimile of the manuscript as received by Aleister and Rose Edith Crowley on April 8,9,10, 1904* e.v. Weiser Books, 2004.

Crowther, Patricia. *Lid Off the Cauldron: A Handbook for Witches*. Muller, 1981.

Cunningham, Scott. *Wicca: A Guide for the Solitary Practitioner*. Llewellyn Worldwide, Ltd., 2010.

Daimler, Morgan. *Pagan Portals—Fairy Witchcraft: A Neopagan's Guide to the Celtic Fairy Faith*. John Hunt Publishing, 2014.

Dispenza, Joe. *Becoming Supernatural: How Common People Are Doing the Uncommon*. Hay House, Inc., 2019.

Dionne, Danielle. *Magickal Mediumship: Partnering with the Ancestors for Healing and Spiritual Development*. Llewellyn Worldwide, Ltd., 2020.

Dominguez Jr., Ivo. *Casting Sacred Space: The Core of All Magickal Work*. Red Wheel/Weiser, 2012.

Dominguez Jr., Ivo. *The Four Elements of the Wise: Working with the Magickal Powers of Earth, Air, Water, Fire*. Red Wheel/Weiser, 2021.

Dominguez Jr., Ivo. *Keys to Perception: A Practical Guide to Psychic Development*. Red Wheel/Weiser, 2017.

Dominguez Jr., Ivo. *Practical Astrology for Witches and Pagans: Using the Planets and the Stars for Effective Spellwork, Rituals, and Magickal Work*. Red Wheel/Weiser, 2016.

Dominguez Jr., Ivo. *Spirit Speak: Knowing and Understanding Spirit Guides, Ancestors, Ghosts, Angels, and the Divine*. Red Wheel/Weiser, 2008.

DuQuette, Lon Milo; et al. *Llewellyn's Complete Book of Ceremonial Magick (Llewellyn's Complete Book Series)*. Llewellyn Worldwide, Ltd., 2020.

DuQuette, Lon Milo. *Low Magick: It's All in Your Head … You Just Have No Idea How Big Your Head Is*. Llewellyn Worldwide, Ltd., 2011.

Eason, Cassandra. *Scrying the Secrets of the Future: How to Use Crystal Ball, Fire, Wax, Mirrors, Shadows, and Spirit Guides to Reveal Your Destiny*. Red Wheel/Weiser, 2006.

Elliott, John H. *Beware the Evil Eye (Volume 2): The Evil Eye in the Bible and the Ancient World: Greece and Rome*. Lutterworth Press, 2016.

Fay, Elizabeth A. *Romantic Egypt: Abyssal Ground of British Romanticism*. Lexington Books, 2021.

Faerywolf, Storm. *Betwixt and Between: Exploring the Faery Tradition of Witchcraft*. Llewellyn Worldwide, Ltd., 2017.

Fortune, Dion. *Applied Magic*. Red Wheel/Weiser, 2000.

Foxwood, Orion. *Mountain Conjure and Southern Rootwork*. Red Wheel/Weiser, 2021.

Freuler, Kate. *Of Blood and Bones: Working with Shadow Magick and the Dark Moon*. Llewellyn Worldwide, Ltd., 2020.

Gardner, Gerald B. *The Meaning of Witchcraft*. Red Wheel/Weiser, 2004.

Grayle, Jack. *The Hekatæon*. Ixaxaar Occult Literature, 2020.

Grimassi, Raven. *Encyclopedia of Wicca and Witchcraft*. Llewellyn Publications, 2000.

Grimassi, Raven. *Spirit of the Witch: Religion and Spirituality in Contemporary Witchcraft*. Llewellyn Publications, 2003.

Hauck, Dennis William. *The Complete Idiot's Guide to Alchemy*. Alpha Books, 2008.

Herbert, Frank. *Dune, 40th Anniversary Edition (Dune Chronicles, Book 1)*. Ace Books, 2005.

Holden, James H. *A History of Horoscopic Astrology*. American Federation of Astrologers, 2006.

Horowitz, Mitch. *Initiates, Three. The Kybalion Study Guide: The Universe Is Mental*. Ascent Audio, 2020.

Howard, Michael. *Educating the Will*. Waldorf Publications, 2015.

Hunter, Devin. *Modern Witch: Spells, Recipes and Workings*. Llewellyn Worldwide, Ltd., 2020.

Hunter, Devin. *The Witch's Book of Mysteries*. Llewellyn Worldwide, Ltd., 2019.

Hunter, Devin. *The Witch's Book of Power*. Llewellyn Worldwide, Ltd., 2016.

Hunter, Devin. *The Witch's Book of Spirits*. Llewellyn Worldwide, Ltd., 2017.

Huson, Paul. *Mastering Witchcraft: A Practical Guide for Witches, Warlocks, and Covens*. iUniverse, 2006.

Jenkins, Greg. *The Theban Oracle: Discover the Magic of the Ancient Alphabet That Changes Lives*. Red Wheel/Weiser, 2014.

Kynes, Sandra. *Crystal Magic: Mineral Wisdom for Pagans and Wiccans*. Llewellyn Worldwide, Ltd., 2017.

Lévi, Éliphas. *Transcendental Magic*. Red Wheel/Weiser, 1968.

Magdalene, Misha. *Outside the Charmed Circle: Exploring Gender and Sexuality in Magical Practice*. Llewellyn Worldwide, Ltd., 2020.

Mankey, Jason. *Transformative Witchcraft: The Greater Mysteries*. Llewellyn Worldwide, Ltd., 2019.

Mankey, Jason. *Witch's Wheel of the Year: Rituals for Circles, Solitaries and Covens*. Llewellyn Worldwide, Ltd., 2019.

Mathiesen, Robert, and Theitic. *Rede of the Wiccae*. Witches Almanac Ltd., 2006.

Matthews, Caitlin, John Matthews, Gareth Knight, and Virginia Chandler. *Arthurian Magic: A Practical Guide to the Wisdom of Camelot*. Llewellyn Worldwide, Ltd., 2017.

Miller, Jason. *The Elements of Spellcrafting: 21 Keys to Successful Sorcery*. United States: Red Wheel/Weiser, 2018.

Miller, Jason. *The Sorcerer's Secrets: Strategies in Practical Magick*. United States: Red Wheel/Weiser, 2009.

Mooney, Thorn. *The Witch's Path: Advancing Your Craft at Every Level*. Llewellyn Worldwide, Ltd., 2021.

Morrison, Dorothy. *Everyday Moon Magic: Spells and Rituals for Abundant Living*. Llewellyn Worldwide, 2003.

Morrison, Dorothy. *Everyday Sun Magic: Spells and Rituals for Radiant Living*. Llewellyn Worldwide, 2005.

Morrison, Dorothy. *Utterly Wicked: Hexes, Curses, and Other Unsavory Notions*. Red Wheel/Weiser, 2020.

Murphy-Hiscock, Arin. *Spellcrafting: Strengthen the Power of Your Craft by Creating and Casting Your Own Unique Spells*. Adams Media, 2020.

Orapello, Christopher, and Tara-Love Maguire. *Besom, Stang and Sword: A Guide to Traditional Witchcraft, the Six-Fold Path and the Hidden Landscape*. Red Wheel/Weiser, 2018.

Orpheus. *The Hymns of Orpheus: With the Life and Poetic Theology of Orpheus*. Pantianos Classics, 2020.

Pamita, Madame. *The Book of Candle Magic: Candle Spell Secrets to Change Your Life*. Llewellyn Worldwide, Ltd., 2020.

Pearson, Nicholas. *Flower Essences from the Witch's Garden: Plant Spirits in Magickal Herbalism*. Inner Traditions/Bear, 2022.

Pearson, Nicholas. *Stones of the Goddess: Crystals for the Divine Feminine*. Inner Traditions/Bear, 2019.

Penczak, Christopher. *Foundations of the Temple: A Witchcraft Tradition of Love, Will and Wisdom.* Copper Cauldron Publishing, 2014.

Penczak, Christopher. *Magick of Reiki: Focused Energy for Healing, Ritual, and Spiritual Development.* Llewellyn Publications, 2004.

Penczak, Christopher. *The Outer Temple of Witchcraft: Circles, Spells and Rituals.* Llewellyn Worldwide, 2004.

Penczak, Christopher. *The Plant Spirit Familiar.* Copper Cauldron Publishing, 2011.

Penczak, Christopher. *The Temple of High Witchcraft: Ceremonies, Spheres, and the Witches' Qabalah.* Llewellyn Publications, 2007.

Penczak, Christopher. *The Three Rays of Witchcraft: Power, Love and Wisdom in the Garden of the Gods.* Copper Cauldron Publishing, 2010.

Pepper, Elizabeth. *Witches All: A Treasury from Past Editions of the Witches' Almanac.* Witches' Almanac, 2003.

RavenWolf, Silver. *HexCraft: Dutch Country Magick.* Llewellyn Publications, 1995.

RavenWolf, Silver. *Solitary Witch: The Ultimate Book of Shadows for the New Generation.* Llewellyn Worldwide, 2003.

RavenWolf, Silver. *Teen Witch: Wicca for a New Generation.* Llewellyn Publications, 1998.

RavenWolf, Silver. *To Light a Sacred Flame: Practical Witchcraft for the Millennium.* Llewellyn Publications, 1999.

RavenWolf, Silver. *To Ride a Silver Broomstick: New Generation Witchcraft.* Llewellyn, 1993.

RavenWolf, Silver. *To Stir a Magick Cauldron: A Witch's Guide to Casting and Conjuring.* Llewellyn Worldwide, Ltd., 2013.

RavenWolf, Silver. *The Witching Hour: Spells, Powders, Formulas, and Witchy Techniques that Work.* Llewellyn Worldwide, Ltd., 2017.

Regardie, Israel, and John Michael Greer. *The Golden Dawn: The Original Account of the Teachings, Rites, and Ceremonies of the Hermetic Order.* Llewellyn Publications, 2015.

Reed, Theresa. *Astrology for Real Life: A Workbook for Beginners (a No B. S. Guide for the Astro-Curious)*. Red Wheel/Weiser, 2019.

Sebastiani, Althaea. *By Rust of Nail & Prick of Thorn: The Theory & Practice of Effective Home Warding*. N.p.: Althaea Sebastiani, 2017.

Simmons, Robert, Naisha Ahsian, and Hazel Raven. *The Book of Stones: Who They Are and What They Teach*. Inner Traditions/Bear, 2015.

Steiner, Rudolf. *Knowledge of the Higher Worlds and Its Attainment*. Read Books Ltd., 2013.

Valiente, Doreen. *Natural Magic*. Crowood Press, 1999.

Valiente, Doreen. *Witchcraft for Tomorrow*. Crowood Press, 2018.

Wachter, Aidan. *Changeling: A Book Of Qualities*. Red Temple Press, 2021.

Wachter, Aidan. *Six Ways: Approaches and Entries for Practical Magic*. Red Temple Press, 2018.

Wachter, Aidan. *Weaving Fate: Hypersigils, Changing the Past, and Telling True Lies*. Red Temple Press, 2020.

Waite, Arthur Edward. *The Book of Black Magic*. Red Wheel/Weiser, 1972.

Weschcke, Carl Llewellyn, and Joe H. Slate. *The New Science of the Paranormal: From the Research Lab to Real Life*. Llewellyn Worldwide, Ltd., 2016.

Whiteley, C. M. K. "Aphantasia, imagination and dreaming." *Philos Stud* 178, 2111–2132 (2021). https://doi.org/10.1007/s11098-020-01526-8

Zakroff, Laura Tempest. *Anatomy of a Witch: A Map to the Magical Body*. Llewellyn Worldwide, Ltd., 2021.

Zakroff, Laura Tempest. *Weave the Liminal: Living Modern Traditional Witchcraft*. Llewellyn Worldwide, Ltd., 2019.

INDEX

To Write to the Author

If you wish to contact the author or would like more information about this book, please write to the author in care of Llewellyn Worldwide Ltd. and we will forward your request. Both the author and the publisher appreciate hearing from you and learning of your enjoyment of this book and how it has helped you. Llewellyn Worldwide Ltd. cannot guarantee that every letter written to the author can be answered, but all will be forwarded. Please write to:

Mat Auryn
℅ Llewellyn Worldwide
2143 Wooddale Drive
Woodbury, MN 55125-2989
Please enclose a self-addressed stamped envelope for reply,
or $1.00 to cover costs. If outside the U.S.A., enclose
an international postal reply coupon.

Many of Llewellyn's authors have websites with additional information and resources. For more information, please visit our website at http://www.llewellyn.com.